DESPERATE HIGHWAY

The True Story of A Criminal

Memoirs from the life of Jeff Andrews
by Jesse Stretch

ISBN no. 1-4392-2394-7

Executive Editor, Cheryl Cooper

Book & Cover Design, Steve O'Brien

Dedicated To...
The Lord Jesus Christ,
My Wife, Friends and Family,
and Eloise Christine.

"Time is Short"

PROLOGUE

1980

PEOPLE SAY THAT THE DAY YOU DIE IS BETTER THAN THE DAY YOU'RE born. No armed fugitive would believe a saying like that. A guy like me, a guy on the run, has to take things as they come. I had narrowed my philosophy down to this: some days are shit and some days are roses, and this one wasn't shaping up to be roses. I dragged on my cigarette and tried not to think about it.

I had been on the run for 22 hours in a stolen Mercedes when night fell for a second time. From Denver to Seattle should have taken no more than a full day, but I was hardly halfway there because of the blizzard.

Montana: A desolate stretch of highway just north of Billings; a wild and unknown territory where not even a plow driver dared to brave the ice. I tossed the cigarette from the car, closed the window, and held tight to the steering wheel. High winds tailed the storm and the empty canyon bridges rippled like flying carpets.

It was at that very moment, several hours beyond the blinding snow-storm, when I felt the first inkling that something had gone hideously wrong with my plan.

I could tell by the temperature in the cabin that I was no longer trav-eling alone. There was a rustle, the burping noise of bare flesh sliding across new leather, and from the back seat I could hear the gasp of insid-ious lungs.

My MAC-10 machine pistol, a beast of a weapon, was lodged beneath the passenger seat. Behind the MAC was about 10 grand cash and a kilo of cocaine, all of it stolen.

Out of nowhere a smell overtook me and I came dangerously close to hurling onto the instrument panel. I let down the window and reached for my gat. Someone had snuck into the back seat of my car. I raised the gun but stopped myself. I had come dangerously close to firing 30 rounds into my own back seat.

A hot palm wrapped my neck. Whoever was back there had to make sure that I remained facing forward. I heard the unmistakable sound of a double-action revolver being cocked. I was pretty sure that the barrel wasn't being aimed at the road sign:

CAUTION
STEEP CLIFFS AHEAD
55 MPH

Ten years on the run and this is how it's going to end? I sure as hell hope not.

"Who's back there?" I checked the mirrors. Nothing. "WHO'S BACK THERE?"

The Benz, which I had stolen using my notoriously effective bank draft scam, increased speed and began to howl around even the slightest corners. I was outrunning my headlights at 90 mph or more, no way to stop the car within a reasonable distance, especially with ice sporadically ruining the grip.

The smell became worse. It tormented me into severe nausea. I couldn't be sure what it was. Maybe rotten meat? A dead body? It had to be one of the two.

"Who's back there? If you're a Fed you better just speak up or I'm gonna let loose with this thing." I tapped the MAC, which I had placed in my lap. No... it wasn't a Fed. A Fed would have shot me when my hand came close to the gun. It was wishful thinking to believe that this guy had come from the government. There wasn't a chance I'd be that lucky.

"Holy shit!" I exclaimed. "It's you, isn't it, Bill? They let you out already? Bill Fallie! You didn't like prison or what?" I let out a crazy laugh, tried to scare him out of shooting me.

No words came from the back seat. At 90 mph, in the dead of winter, with the windows down and the engine howling, it was borderline impossible for me to hear anything anyway.

The reality of my situation set in. Fear overcame me. I grabbed my tooter, took a good rip of coke, and the powder from the open container blew throughout the interior of my 6.9 liter Benz.

"Did you sneak in at the last gas station or what?" No answer. "HUH?" I yelled. I knew that my gun was useless. What was I going to do? Did I imagine that I could make a quick move and shoot the man before he was able to pull the trigger? Hardly.

"You shoot me, Bill, and we're both dead," I said. I kept my foot fixed firmly on the accelerator. In the rearview mirror I could see nothing. I tapped the brakes and the red lights offered me a silhouetted view of the intruder.

"Jen?" I asked. "No shit, is that YOU?" It wasn't Jen. Well, not unless she'd shaved off all of her hair. "You're one of Jennifer's goons, aren't you? You're coming to collect on me or something?" I felt my adrenaline rise.

It was over. I was a dead man. The only option was to stop the car and have him do me on the side of the road. Bullshit, I wasn't going out that easy. There was something else. I had to THINK. I'd never been one to just give in. Something else... but wait... I couldn't do that. Or could I?

I casually increased the volume on the stereo, his sweaty hand pinching my neck the entire time. I took a good breath of cold Montana air, smashed the gas, and aimed the Mercedes emblem for a break in the guard rail. We'd sure make a mess at the bottom of that cliff, but suicide beat letting a cut-rate hit man have the last laugh.

The accelerator went through the floorboard and I let out a roar equivalent to the wind. I took one last glance at the speedometer: 97 mph.

It was as good a speed as any.

1

JANE

1968

THE ADMISSIONS PEOPLE AT MICHIGAN STATE COULDN'T TELL REAL FROM bullshit. The guy doing my interview was a sucker for a good sales pitch. He sat there quietly, legs crossed behind his desk, taking notes as I let loose on several mildly coherent rants about my newfound desire to achieve scholastic success.

I was coming off of a nasty winter, the worst in my life, working as a brick mason's helper, a union man, for Bershe Construction. I knew I couldn't go back to that job. The memories of the snowy sixth-story scaffolding were enough to nudge me toward a new beginning. Laboring tirelessly through daily pitfalls was not my lifelong dream, and the fear of being locked into that existence contributed unyielding resolve to my cause. I knew that my only chance at escaping that kind of labor was to attend college.

My high school transcript was a hunk of shit. It wouldn't get me anywhere but the gutter. The grades, coupled with my unwillingness to live with my father, Capt. Douglas Alexander, forced me into my first "lie or lose" situation.

Luckily, my capabilities in the field of professional deceit—probably a collection of behaviors I'd distorted from my father's success in business—enabled me to dodge the masonry bullet without having to rob a bank.

The MSU Admissions Department accepted my application and I moved from my parent's home in Lake Orion to the Michigan State campus only a short car ride away.

*　　*　　*

In college I was friends with all of the jocks—a bunch of clean faces with crew cuts and collared shirts and manicured girlfriends. I fit in for one reason: because I was obsessed with working out. Other than that, I looked like I belonged in some sort of renegade army regiment.

I wore a stainless-steel dog collar with rounded chrome studs protruding a quarter inch above the surface, and a red suit tie around my head to keep my shoulder-length hair from getting in my eyes. I also wore steel bands around my arms and a high school letterman jacket with the sleeves cut off. My jeans were covered with all kinds of symbols that some hippie chick had painted on there for me. Sunshines, clouds, trees, all that stuff. They peeled sometimes, leaving little flecks of peace everywhere.

Michigan was a somewhat right-wing establishment, but nobody ever had the balls to tell me to take off the pants. Well, I take that back: Several frat boys said something once. One went tumbling down the library steps and the other ended up in a pile of shit behind the dumpster. I had no problems with my pants after that.

*　　*　　*

It was Friday.

We were, the lot of us weight lifters, sitting like arched wing vultures brooding over a table of discarded bones. The conversation was football, weightlifting, and girls. The conversation never changed.

I caught a glimpse of this blonde. She entered the dining hall, disappeared behind a wall of bodies, emerged on the other side and disappeared again. Two quick peeks were all I got.

"Yeah, Jack. I told you about her," Teddy said. He had mentioned a blonde several days ago. Sure enough...

"Who is she?"

"If you'd get your face out of that John Sartre shit for five minutes maybe you'd have some idea."

"Just tell me who she is."

"It's Jane Cumberland. I met her the other night at a party."

"Who the hell is she?"

"She's tight with all those SAE frat boys. She's from Florida, I think."

"I think I've beaten up a few of those SAE guys." It was true. They used to jump me outside the dorms, mistaking me for a defenseless hippy because of my long hair. I often wore a quarter inch chain for a belt, which came in handy in situations like those.

"So, this blonde screws a bunch of frat boys? That's her crowd?" I asked.

"I guess. I don't really know."

"What else?"

"She drives a Jaguar."

"Come on, give me something else. I'm trying to make a move here."

"What do you mean? You saw her. Figure it out for yourself."

Yeah. He was right. I had seen her. She was perfect: blonde hair, black low cut designer dress (undoubtedly tailored), perfect body to fit inside that thing, rich tan, tiny shoes, all the little doodads that made a woman perfect.

"You think she's the best looking chick at school?" I asked. I wasn't about to take second place. Hell no.

"Yeah, Jack. Easily the hottest," he said, flexing his chest. "I've been doing those incline pushups you recommended and I don't think it's doing very much for my pecs."

"It's a shoulder exercise, Ted."

"Well, I know, but..."

Sometimes I wondered about my friend selection. Then again, they were some of the best guys around.

* * *

Several of my buddies made a bet that I wouldn't last more than 10 minutes at Jane Cumberland's table. It would have been different if there were other people sitting with her, other voices to break the ice, but Jane always ate alone. Everybody was scared of her looks, her eyes, her rings, her purses.

"Give me a break," I told them, trying to keep my image afloat. "Ten minutes is nothing. You remember who you're talking to? Ten minutes with a chick like that isn't shit! I do it all the time!"

In reality, I was scared shitless. They used to call me "Snowman" in high school because whenever I tried to get with a girl I couldn't take it any farther than a goodnight kiss. Something just wasn't there. I didn't want to sleep with them. I wasn't interested in making babies. I didn't see the point in sex. If I felt like getting a good rush I'd drop and do some pushups rather than chase tail.

Life was different for me, but none of these guys knew about my failed attempts with the ladies. I was a new man at college. My father wasn't here to smack me around, my mother wasn't here to complain about my grades, and I could make a new name for myself. I had one chance to make a play on the prettiest girl at MSU. If I blew it, I would probably never try for a woman again.

I swaggered toward her table, my nerves grinding on ice. I sat down, seemingly unnoticed. She was cleaning a giant red apple with her napkin. She would wipe it for a moment, check the napkin for stains, then move to a new spot and start buffing again.

"Hey, my name's Jack Alexander."

"Jane." She extended her hand across the table, inadvertently shoving a giant engagement ring in my face.

"You're friends with SAE right?"

"I'm a little sister. Why? Are you SAE?"

All the SAE guys were rich as shit. They drove sports cars, wore khaki pants and loafers, slung blondes around like baseball cards, went on beach trips to Florida, threw giant parties, owned boats. I wasn't bad off, but to the outside observer I was as far from SAE as you could get.

"I don't do the frat thing."

"You're your own man, huh?" She giggled, noticing the sleeves of my jacket. She was passive, a surprising trait for such a wealthy and attractive girl. I enjoyed her passivity, the way she blushed and smiled when bringing up my appearance. I felt less intimidated by a girl like this, more capable of relaxing.

"What's your story, Jane?"

"Not very interesting. How about you?"

"I'm from New Jersey," I said.

"I lived in Jersey for a while."

"I lived in Madison for most of my life."

"So did I!" Her voice rose excitedly. Things had taken a good turn. The situation was progressing. All sorts of chemicals began to seep into my brain; expectation, joy, contentment, happiness, pride.

"Where'd you go to school?" I asked.

Coincidentally enough, we had both attended the same school system. She had been there all the way through sixth grade while my family had been in San Mateo. I had arrived in Madison in the seventh grade, just one summer after she'd gone away. It was the perfect conversation starter because we each knew the same people. She had been a cheerleader and so knew the football squad and several of my ex-girlfriends. Our homes had been only a few miles from one another so we had eaten at the same restaurants, walked the same streets, played on the same sidewalks, all that.

I studied her expressions as she continued to eat. She was somewhat disinterested with me. Or no, maybe it wasn't that. Maybe she was intimidated. I remembered how she reacted when she saw that my sleeves had been cut off. This girl was from a conservative background. She had brains for money but no brains for the real world. I got the feeling that she was either very unaware or very afraid. She would hardly look up from her lunch, even with me sitting two feet in front of her.

I tried to make further conversation, perhaps something else that could lead us into a discussion.

"So, you're engaged?" I pointed to her rock.

"Regrettably." she sighed, tilting her head sideways and watching the people walk through the cafeteria. I hoped she didn't see my table of goons off to our right. One of my buddies was laughing hysterically, slapping his hands on the table like an idiot, and the rest were staring at me. I grimaced and quickly waved for them to cool it.

"What do you mean?"

"He's about to graduate law school."

"Yeah, that's good enough reason to leave him right there."

"I know."

Score one for the home team.

* * *

I heard through the grapevine, which was long, barbed, and reliably inaccurate, that Jane's father had pulled the old "run the car in the garage" trick. He had been an insurance tycoon, a big-time player with more money than he knew what to do with. Apparently, upon passing, he had left his daughter an unspeakable sum.

One afternoon, after coffee and a long conversation about the existential dilemmas of the 1960s, we sat in the front seat of her Jaguar and debated on what to do. We had been hanging out for the past few days while the Law School dweeb studied or took his tests. I didn't ask where he was, nor did I care as long as he wasn't in my face.

After a while Jane suggested that we visit her father's grave together. It wasn't my idea of a fun evening, but I think it was Jane's way of testing me, of seeing if I could be supportive under the grim and inconsolable circumstances.

The November air came down hard and cold from the Northwest. We walked the winding path through the cemetery, each step echoing inside the rotted coffins below. The wind blew the dirt and clouds so fast that it felt like you could see the earth spinning, time passing, death coming.

The brush rustled dryly, echoing ominously and remaining a prisoner of the hillsides. There was a lone headstone and several decaying flowers. Her father's name and date of birth were carved there. The date of his passing hung below as a reminder.

"He loves me," she said.

There was no appropriate response to this.

"I don't think that he meant to do it."

Again, I could offer nothing. Just a nod, a quiet, removed, backward tilt of my head. Jane was on the verge of crying. I could see tears welling up in her eyes. It was probably the first emotional response I had seen her exhibit since we met. Everything else in our relationship had been, "Yeah, sure, I guess," or, "I don't mind, we can do whatever you want."

There was never anything concrete with Jane. She was a pushover, and easy going kind of girl who had been told what to do her entire life and expected it to stay that way. I got the feeling that she loved me as a father figure, not as a boyfriend. Some nights she would tell me that she didn't want to have sex with me, that she just wanted to lay in bed and talk. Situations like this made me nervous. Now that I had conquered my fear of women, of taking it further than the doorstep, Jane girl was denying me access.

I had always assumed that once I conquered my fear that I'd be up to my ears in sex. Turns out that this was not always the case.

We stood at the tombstone for quite some time, all these thoughts running through my head. I began to think about my father. There had been days I wished he would be put in a place like this. My dad would get home from Lipton Tea Company at 6 p.m., briefcase in hand, slight stubble on his face, and the first thing he'd do was figure out a reason to slap me around. There was always something. Maybe I hadn't done well in school, maybe I hadn't mowed the lawn properly, perhaps I'd been picking on my younger brother. It made no difference. It seemed like nearly every day my father would lay into me with everything he had.

After the beating was over, the man would loosen his tie and sit in front of the television with his briefcase and a fifth of vodka. He'd watch the news, the funnies, whatever could be played quietly and wouldn't distract him from his work. He always kept his mind on the job, which is why the folks at Lipton had promoted him to Vice President of Sales. Sure, I had to respect his career, but for the first 15 years of my life all I knew of him was the palm of his hand. It had been a hard way to grow up: my only role model in business and life management was the man who was consistently putting me down, beating me, telling me that I was a lazy punk who would never amount to anything.

"My mother is in Florida. I may move back there after school," Jane said.

I snapped out of the daydream about my father. The wind groaned. She came in closer toward me, leaned into me. I felt an awkward exchange of emotion, like an ape in a cage communicating with a trainer at the zoo. Jane had never loved anyone other than her parents. Losing her father had been a critical blow. The question was, would she learn to love me, or would I merely become another bump in the road.

There was silence, then the rustle of brush. I looked around sadly at all the lonely, weathered monuments. It was a strange world.

She began to cry.

Fifteen minutes passed. We left the cemetery in virtual silence, me behind the wheel of her Jaguar. The wheels rolled through the hills and life rolled along with them. Death was a reliable reminder that I had a whole lot left to do. I damn sure wasn't ready to have my mother pay some hack to carve a set of dates into a rock.

*   *   *

Jane and I were shopping at Plum Street Jewelry Shop in Detroit. The law school fiancé had bet the farm and lost. He tried one of those: "Fine, if you'd rather waste your life with that loser I'm not going to stop you."

He didn't try to stop her and she didn't try to stop. So long, Law School Dickhead.

Jane ogled over the rings, the earrings, the bracelets, all of it. It was funky designer stuff, much more expensive than your run-of-the-mill jewelry. Jane loved diamonds and gold. She loved those things more than she loved me. It was peculiar the way her face would light up over a ring or bracelet. I had never seen her smile that way before, not even at me, not even when we talked about the marriage itself.

Jane leaned over the counter, carefully inspecting each item while thoughts of bankruptcy raced through my head. I noticed the jeweler was copping a stare at my lady. His name was Bart. He handed business cards to everyone who walked in the door. Bart Stravinsky. Made you feel real special…

"I'd like to have these two, Bart, but with several modifications," she said. I tuned her out, focusing on my own reflection in the wall mirror. Look at me: I don't belong here. I'm 21 years old! I'm not marriage material! Well, then again, neither is Jane.

Either way, with all the money involved I knew I couldn't give it up. No matter how false, plastic, or unreal she was, it made no difference. I had to press on.

My confused expression stared back at me, lips gawking, eyes twisted, red tie perfectly wrapped around my skull. The price for custom diamond work was breathtaking, unbelievable, inconceivable. She whipped out a check, filled in the full amount, and paid for it in advance.

"Don't you want to see it first?" I asked.

Bart interjected quickly, his eyes already gripping the check. "Hardly necessary, Mr. Alexander. You're dealing with the best in the world."

"Yeah…" Whatever.

I'd known Jane for two weeks and already we were signing away tiny pieces of her inheritance for the hardware that would solidify our eternal vows. In a quick way it sounded romantic, like escaping from jail or stealing a sports car. In the long run, I had no idea how it would turn out. Maybe she would come around, or maybe we'd stay strangers forever. Either way would be fine with me.

＊　　＊　　＊

My mask of dedication to academic success had long since slipped and I was in the rungs of music and drugs, playing drums for the local rock band "Revolution." It wasn't long until I quit going to school. It's hard to say if the transcript continued and they failed me or if they just marked me as withdrawn. I didn't care either way.

Jane and I rented an apartment together, a nice place that she insisted on paying for. I attempted to contribute my share of the money, but in the end gave little resistance when she filled out the checks.

I played gigs a few times a week and Jane continued with her final semester. I got a job working the assembly line at the Oldsmobile bumper factory. I just flat-out lied to the floor manager and told him I had a college degree. After a while working down there it became obvious that I wasn't the only guy who had pulled a few fast ones to catch a paycheck.

I knew that I couldn't stay in Michigan forever. My father had recently excommunicated me from his home on account of my unsociable appearance and self-professed inclination toward academic failure. Luckily, Jane didn't mind my appearance. She tolerated me because she had nowhere else to go, because I made sure that she realized that I was the strongest and smartest guy in the universe, dog collars, chains, leather jackets and all. .

We decided after she graduated that we would move to California and leave Michigan far behind. From there on out we wouldn't have to worry about money, grades, public opinion, college social drama, any of it.

2

THE BAY AREA

1969

THE TOYS AND SPORTING GOODS SECTION OF THE SAN FRANCISCO Imporium department store was trashed again. I gaped with shell-shocked dismay at the discarded boxes of packing material that lined the floor. Renaud Matheson, the sales manager above me, slid a box of Styrofoam down one of the aisles. He pushed it like a freight train, grinding the bottom against the invisible, flea-sized rocks. He dug around in the boxes for toys, tennis balls, fishing lures, shotguns, whatever he needed for the displays.

"We need more basketballs, Jack. Get back into the warehouse and see what you can do." I snapped out of my trance, his pen-line mustache and direct orders hitting me like a bucket of ice water. I slunk into the dimly lit storage cave, ducking beneath the six-foot-high employee entrance.

A college-age kid worked back there and the whole place reeked of pot. Not like he'd been smoking it in storage, but like he'd smoked so much of it that the smell hung wherever he went.

He pulled up on the forklift.

"Jack, you think I can unload the rest of those boxes from Browning over there in B-6 or should I just stack…"

I continued past, waving my hand in apathy. I had no idea, nor did I care.

"You hung over, Jack? You look tired today. What's your problem?"

"I'm not hung over, kid." I hadn't had a drink in over a week. I guess I just wasn't much of a drinker back then.

*   *   *

I was a 22-year-old college dropout from Michigan State University with little to show for myself other than a rich wife and a good sales pitch.

Jane and I had stuck with the plan: from Michigan we moved to San Francisco where we purchased a nice home in an upper-end neighborhood. Of course, my restless temperament became bored with relaxation and luxurious nothingness. I began applying for jobs after only three months of "living the life." My plan in taking a job at the Imporium was to generate my own income. I wanted something that would separate my pocket from my wife's. I was sick of surviving on her charity.

It wasn't long until my plan took substantial effect. I was soon promoted from Assistant Department Manager in Toys and Sporting Goods, which had been little more than a stock-boy position, to Department Sales Manager in Linens and Domestics. According to Dick Cleaver, the chubby old nut who had hired me, I would no longer be the fill-in Santa Claus if the normal guy bit the dust. Yes, I had done that once or twice last winter.

By the time of my promotion it was early in the year, probably February. I was just getting my feet on the ground with the company, doing everything by the book, when a shady co-worker named Greg Fenster approached me in the parking deck.

"Hey, Jack. Jack, hold on." He came up grinning. It was cold and we hunched against the wind, our breath blowing like fog. I'd seen Greg several times at meetings, in passing, but we had never spoken more than a few words. He'd always looked like a shark to me.

He shook my hand firmly through our driving gloves. He smiled sinisterly and I knew right away that he was after something other than friendship. He was short guy, much smaller than I was, and I caught myself imagining him as a poisonous snake.

"How ya doing, Jack?"

"Good, you?"

"Fine, good... look, I was wondering how you'd feel about a beer?"

"I feel fine about beer." I was weary.

"I mean, how about grabbing a beer with me?"

"Is this some kind of sick date idea, Fenster?"

"Look, I need a guy I can trust. I've got some projects going on. You seem like the guy."

"I don't want to take part in any of your crazy deals. I got enough stuff going with my wife, the new house, all that. I don't need any more confusion."

"How's the wife?" he asked, staring at my ring. Jane and I were fine. We'd made a nice life for ourselves: A respectable community, good yard, large television sets, and I had recently put in a pool. Jane was perfect-looking and she didn't have the brains to run around while I was at work. What more could a guy ask?

"Look, just come down to the bar with me. I know a good place with nice waitresses and privacy. No one will ever know we talked."

"Why can't people know that we talked?"

"You're thick, Jack," he said.

I got into my car and followed him.

*　　*　　*

"So, I don't know if I understand what you're saying... exactly." I had the Imporium spring catalogue spread in front of me on the bar booth table. A tall Heineken bottle rested half full with an empty pint glass beside it. Several dead cigarettes had been stabbed into the ashtray like crumbling tombstones. I lit one of my thin-rolled Antonio Y Cleopatra cigars and saturated the air with a darkening aroma.

Greg pointed at the advertisement and chuckled through a thick and raspy throat.

"You see those things, Jack? Instant Custom Drapes. That's my design. MY product."

I checked the cover again. Sure enough, it was the Imporium catalogue. Greg Fenster and I worked for the Imporium.

"Yeah, Jack, that's right... they're MY products and I'm selling them to OUR store." That same chuckle continued. I hated it. It reminded me of something from a serial killer movie, but something kept my attention about his proposal.

"Why are you telling me this?"

"You remember those beanbag chairs you told me about?" He dragged his cigarette exuberantly, hastily, like an hour glass leaking sand to count down the explosion.

I recalled meeting the hippie chair makers at a bar several months prior. They were great guys and had given me their number. They said that they were interested in selling custom chairs on a person-to-person basis. My initial plan had been to commercialize their operation but they seemed to think it could never happen.

"I remember something about it," I said, feigning slight forgetfulness.

"You ever thought about selling those things?"

"They're not mine to sell."

"Sure they are. Let's just find the hippies who are making them, get them to expand, buy their operation, and sell the beanbag chairs to ourselves at the Imporium. You're the one who told me about the idea, remember?"

"Why are you telling me about the drapes?" I asked, pointing at the catalogue.

"'Cause, Jack, I can't run any operations on the ground level. I'm in the Offices all day doing paperwork for Housewares. I need a guy on the floor to help me take care of things." He nodded across the table toward me. "Besides, I want your bean bag chair connection. Those things are selling like... like... shit, I don't know. I just know that other places are carrying 'em and they're selling all day long."

"What can I do?" I glanced around the bar. I'd never done anything criminal before and the idea excited me. I felt like we were in a black-and-white movie, stuck in a hole-in-the-wall bar with tommy guns and thick cigar smoke. I had been searching for a hobby to counter the sterile existence of my upper-class subdivision lifestyle. Maybe this was it? Besides, with my sort of cover, who would expect that I'd be pulling a scam like this? I was already rich. There was virtually NO chance of getting caught.

"You're my Linens and Domestics partner." He pointed at me and I shrugged. I still didn't totally get it, didn't really like him, but I was in. He kept running his mouth.

"Jack, it's good to have you on board. You gotta help me get my sales up. I need to sell more drapes! Those things cost me an arm and a leg to make. I ship 'em all the way to South Carolina, to Burlington, where they're made and packaged and then they ship 'em back here. You know how much that costs?" He lit another cigarette, blew a plume of fresh tar and nicotine into the light that hung shakily above our table. "I gotta sell more of my drapes to the Imporium. I gotta sell to stores all over the country. Where are you from, anyway?" His face was oily, tired, and deprived. He leaned in very close and waited for each response like a stray dog whining behind the butcher shop.

"All over," I said. "My dad was in the military."

"Name some places."

After each name he gave a nod, as though he knew them all very well. "San Mateo; Henderson, Kentucky; Evansville, Indiana; Littleton, Colorado; Madison, New Jersey…"

"Didn't you say your wife was from Madison?"

"Yeah, it's a long story."

"Right…" he said.

"So, yeah, I been all over this country."

"You think you could do some traveling?"

I told him about how I'd traveled in college. I used to take fantastic trips all the time—one of the reasons for my flunking out.

"Jack, this is great. You're just the guy I need. You're a good sales-man and everyone knows it." He dragged hard on the cigarette and spoke through the smoke. "Just imagine how much money you could make selling to your OWN company!" He was still trying to sell me on the idea. I hadn't told him I was interested. It was better to let him sweat it out.

"What's your plan with the beanbag chairs?"

"That's your prerogative. I'm just giving you advice on how we could make a bit more money. It's a free market out there, Jack."

"Would we start a company and buy from those hippies like whole-salers? What's the score?" I killed the beer, waved the hard body over for another.

"That's a possibility." He pushed out his lips, nodded, stared toward the center of the table. "What have we got to lose by starting a compa-ny? You got all sorts of money, man. This can be like a game for you. You used to play sports, right?" He was referencing my height and defined musculature.

"Yeah, football."

"Just think of it like high school football."

"I washed out of football after four years because of concussions."

"Then think about it like… shit, I don't know. It's going to be fun and it's going to help both of us with some extra spending cash. You don't want to live on your wife's bank account forever. Are you in or what?."

"Alright, I'm in."

He sighed and pounded his fist on the table with conviction.

"That's the spirit!" he shouted. An old man at the bar looked over and quickly turned away.

I tilted my beer toward the ceiling and watched the foam drain into my mouth. Greg was right. I needed to make my own money. I couldn't live off of a woman. It wasn't my way. I told him to keep me posted and I'd think about how to get those hippies in second gear.

*   *   *

Jane and I were in bed. She had the awful habit of asking me about my job. The last thing I wanted to do was explain my employment situation to a woman who had never worked a day in her life.

"Work's going alright... I guess." I casually flipped through the bean-bag chair pamphlet that the hippies from Clear Lake had sent me. The catalogue had been hastily assembled upon my most recent request. The products were of solid craftsmanship. There was no doubt that the Imporium would be very interested in placing an order. The only question: how could we get those stoners off of their asses to hire employees and generate more volume? We couldn't sell 15 units at a time to a market like Imporium.

I set the pamphlet on the nightstand. Maybe it wasn't worth it.

I rolled over and gave Jane a kiss. I tried for more but she pushed me away. She never wanted sex anymore. Not that she ever had been crazy for it, but ever since the marriage she'd gone virtually frigid. I rolled to my side of the bed and stared at the wall in deep thought. There was something more to life than just this.

*   *   *

I became more interested in building personal wealth and so prodded the Hippies to expand their furniture-building operation as soon as possible. The Hippies quickly complied, expanding closer to San Francisco under the supervision of Anders Thompson, the newfound president of their organization. They migrated to the neighborhoods of Santa Rosa, where Fenster and I set them up with a few storage spaces to use as makeshift production facilities.

Anders Thompson was a wild-eyed rogue. He had a giant energy reserve, bad asthma, fast hands, and a sense of under-the-table entrepreneurship legitimized by an army of willing laborers. With a little prodding from Fenster and me, good old Anders was able to organize his company and get it rolling full steam.

By the time the chairs were in production I had achieved decent pull in the Linens Department, and convinced the head buyer to take a look at the International Western Corporation Buyer's Catalogue. The catalogue and the company were, of course, one of my and Greg Fenster's creations.

The head buyer at Imporium, Harry Levin, squinted his eyes and contorted his face while reading the print.

"Interwest? Never heard of 'em, Jack. Sorry, I can't make purchases from unknown companies."

"Come on, Harry, why not check out something new?" I followed him onto the escalator. Shoppers buzzed past and the young women reeked of eight different types of perfume. "I think their furniture looks awesome."

"Yeah..." He flipped through the pictures disinterestedly.

"I think it'd be stupid not to buy this merchandise. These are hot items!"

"The company looks pretty young."

"This brochure doesn't mean a damn thing, Harry. It's all about product quality."

"Eh, alright Jack. You're a smart guy and I like your judgment. I'll give it a shot."

*   *   *

The problem then arose that once Harry ordered stock from International Western Corporation we had no way to ship it from Santa Rosa to the Imporium store in San Francisco.

"Oh shit..." Greg muttered, digging around in his briefcase at the bar booth. We had become regulars in that place, a bar called Chugger's about eight hard blocks from the Imporium. It was close enough to the store that we were on the front line, far enough away to keep our meetings from being noticed by a stray employee, and sleazy enough that if anyone saw us they'd never bring it up for fear of personal embarrassment.

"I'll be damned if UPS is on strike!" he said, drunkenly pounding a fist. The glass ashtray rattled like an angry rattler snake. UPS delivered for the Imporium, Lacy's, Ervyns, all the big department stores. Business was suffering for everyone, especially for a small company selling beanbag chairs and custom draperies. It was my first real sale and already things weren't working out.

I contemplated abandoning it: the mission, Greg Fenster, Interwest, the Hippies, everything involved. I had a decent job at the Imporium, a good wife, a nice house near Stanford, a Lincoln. Why screw it up over helping Greg accomplish dreams? Well, it was more than just Greg. It was more than his dreams. More than anything. I needed forget about all the pointless shit. Things weren't what they were cracked up to be. The wife was a good catch, but probably too good. Sure, I was a handsome guy from a good bloodline—father had been a Captain in the service and Vice President of Sales at Lipton—but if you let a passive little rich girl like Jane Cumberland walk around a town of hotshots she'll end up divorcing you for Eric Clapton or some CEO with more money than the government.

In fact, Jane was going to be gone soon either way. I wasn't around enough to keep her focused on me. It didn't matter who she met, rich or poor, just so long as he was confident and could convince her that I was old news.

"So what do we do, Greg? Delay the paychecks until we can figure out a way to ship the merchandise?"

"There's a general rule of thumb, Jack: if you don't pay your workers, you don't have a company." He was such a smart ass it made me sick. I wanted to knock him in the face but I never did.

"Yeah... well, we got the dough for the first sale. All we have to do is hope we can make another one before two weeks run out." I drained a beer, lost the tie, checked the bar for a waitress. I needed a steak.

"What do you say we drive the merch ourselves?"

"It's possible," I said. "It's a lot of shit, but it's possible."

"I mean maybe rent a few trucks and do it."

"Well, yeah. We can't fit everything in my Lincoln." I looked up at the waitress, who had a great body. She slid into the booth beside me.

"How ya doing?" she asked.

"All right." She grabbed my leg under the table. It made me jump. I looked at Greg. He pretended to be lost in a booklet of prices. It annoyed him when the women gave me attention.

"Hey, Brandy," he said, not looking up from the figures. "You guys got a phone I can use?"

"The pay phone."

"I don't have any change," Greg said. "How about that one behind the bar?" He liked to push the girls around.

"Ommm..." she bit her lip and looked at me.

"Just let him use it," I said.

"I guess. Sure."

"Who you calling?" I asked.

"I'm surprised I didn't think of it before," he said, shrugging his shoulders and exiting the booth. "We'll just start our own damn trucking company."

I sat there playing grab-ass with Brandy while Greg made the calls.

"You wanna hang around until I get off?" she asked.

"I'll see."

"Come on, Jack... please?"

"I said I'll see."

"Can I getcha something else?" She could have gotten me a number of things, only a few of which came from the kitchen or bar.

"A steak. The biggest one you got."

She gave me this long French kiss, pushed me back into the booth, ripped at my shirt and jacket. When she walked away she had my tie wrapped around her neck, dangling between her tits.

Greg gave me a look like, "I'm glad SOMEBODY is getting the work done."

I smiled and raised my beer. It wasn't my fault that he was uglier than a shaved cat.

*　　*　　*

I got sick of making the southbound drive to Stanford after work so I rented an apartment on Jones Street, close to the Imporium and Chugger's. I felt like my own man again. I told Jane that the company paid for me to stay in a hotel on nights that I worked late. She never asked questions anyway.

I used the new apartment as home base for entertaining waitresses, strippers, chicks I met at the bar, whatever. My own place made me feel successful, like I had become something in the eyes of my peers that they would never become. I walked down the street and knew that every other person was looking at me. The bums, the business men, the drug peddlers... all the men wanted to be me and all the women wanted to be with me. They were envious of my lifestyle. The boys used to call me Snowman in high school. They didn't call me Snowman anymore.

My roommate in the new apartment was Terry Kreiger. He was a huge guy, barrel chest, tree-trunk legs, arms like a pro wrestler. I'd met him at Chugger's and over some beers we'd hit it off like old buddies. We shared girls, advice, lifted weights together, and he introduced me to the world of heavy drinking.

Terry fit in well with my schemes. He worked as a manager/driver for our recently created transportation company and helped manage the Hippies making beanbag chairs for International Western Corporation. Terry wasn't the smartest guy in the world, but it was better to have him working for us than some criminal schmuck fresh out of the box.

Greg and I named the trucking company Pacific American Transportation. It was a simple matter of business: we had to move our goods from Santa Rosa to San Francisco. Damn the strikers, damn the costs, damn the legality of the whole process.

The money was good, and since I never made it home to see my rich wife it was important to keep the cash rolling in. I didn't really know exactly how much money Jane had. I estimated a number around $20 million. What I knew for sure was that, as her husband, I could walk into any bank and they'd give me a loan for 100 grand without batting an eye. Greg Fenster also knew this. He convinced me that I should take out multiple loans under my name as a way to back our companies and keep them from coming too close to the wire.

*   *   *

I became more interested in alcohol and seeing other women. I figured since my wife was cheating on me, which I was pretty sure she was, it made no difference what I did in my spare time.

Terry, always looking for a good laugh, devised a plan to hold "Stag Film Tryouts" at our apartment. The idea had been all his. Sure, I had agreed and contributed a very minor part in orchestrating it, but it wasn't something I would have thought of on my own.

The first time we held one I'd never seen anything like it. Terry and Greg posted ads all over town advertising our cause:

CASTING CALL
YOUNG PEOPLE BETWEEN THE AGES OF 18-25
NEEDED FOR ADULT ENTERTAINMENT FILMS

Then we'd put a contact number, which was usually Greg's office phone (he was the most interested.)

No one ever called, but when time came for the tryouts there was a crowd of young people that stretched down the apartment stairs and into the parking lot. Greg set up cameras in the living room—no tapes in them, no batteries sometimes.

There were hits, misses, everything in between. The whole setup was a scam to get broads into the house, get them naked, and give them a hard run without any strings attached. If the broad wasn't good enough, we just let one of the Hippies have her and sent them off with a cheap bottle of wine. And believe me, the Hippies didn't give a damn what a girl looked like. And believe me also that most of the girls were pretty rough. Greg never had a problem with them, but I was often hard pressed to stay in the same room.

For weeks I stuck around for these events on the slim chance that one of the chicks would be a knockout. No such luck. By some miracle the neighbors, the police, the landlady downstairs, never caught on. We felt no repercussions for this brazen insanity and it pushed us to take things even further.

It was the era of free love and expensive beanbag chairs; of rented Pepsico trucks and Instant Custom Drapes. The money was coming in like flood water. The chairs were selling. The drapes were selling. Pacific American had broken the UPS picket lines and was delivering our merchandise to the stores. My marriage was all but canned and I was on the path to making a fortune of my own.

*   *   *

Senior executives at Imporium had shown interest in moving me up the ladder as fast as possible. I was asked to go to lunch with Howard Carver, Assistant to the President of the company. He told me that they thought I would one day be the President of the Imporium Capwell Corporation. He explained that I would later be placed in the Executive Training Program, but for right now, "Just keep up the good work!"

Howard, after several meetings, had asked me to fly down to L.A., where Broadway Hale was based, to meet and go to dinner with him and Ed Carter. Howard had been promoted to Vice Chairman. That meeting went very well and I was flown to New York to meet other esteemed retail leaders.

There were lots of big names, big money opportunities, firm handshakes, all that jazz. In short, I was getting somewhere in life. That was all that mattered.

*   *   *

I had been promoted to Assistant Buyer of Children's Shoes and this blonde was on my lap in a booth at a bar and two guys in black T-shirts were talking to me about something to do with buying a bar near the Wharf—I wasn't paying any attention, just messing with the blonde and pounding vodka—then one guy slipped me a pebble size bag of something, literally shoved it into my palm, and they disappeared without saying anything else (well, they might have spoken but I didn't hear it) and the blonde on my lap turned to me dumbfounded and said, "I didn't know you were friends with the Beazley's?" and I said I didn't think I was but the music was so loud that she didn't hear me before Terry and two chicks came over, wrenched me out of the seat, hauled me onto the dance floor and after that song we went back to the booth where I whipped out the bag and railed some lines—I'd recently taken to enjoying the good stuff; very good speed, coke, whatever people were selling—and the first chick started coming onto me, literally running her hands down my pants. Terry's chick was doing the same. And, during all this shit, Greg Fenster came up, red-eyed, ripped-drunk, and screamed, "I just met Paul Proteus!" and I had no idea what he was talking about, just railed another line off the table while the whole bar went mad as if someone had picked up the building and was spinning it like a moth around a ceiling fan light bulb—while people approached saying my name, "Jack," one of the black T-shirt men was back, hunched in real close and asking me about lending him some capital. Everyone knew I was loaded and it got on my nerves. Again, I had no idea what these people were talking about. I was wasted, blinded by booze and powder, and so just grabbed the man by the shoulders and said, "Yeah, I'll give you all the money you want, now get the hell out of my face!"

*   *   *

Everybody had to mouse inventory at the Imporium. It was as common as dirt. There was never enough of the right stock, but we moused the records make it seem like there was so that we could generate a situation called "open to buy," which in turn facilitated the placement of further orders.

By that time I think Imporium had promoted me to Buyer of Linens and Domestics, which had been a good decision because I was skilled in that department, but a bad one because I was selling a lot of my own shit to the store.

Things were going alright, but I could feel the axe teetering above my neck. I was filling big shoes by taking over this department, and the man who had held the position before me had left a disastrous situation in his wake.

The General Manager, Dick Cleaver, the same squat gray man of 50 who had hired me, came waddling into my office.

"We rechecked the stock count, Alexander. You've fudged the numbers."

"I did not."

"Yeah, you did."

The envelope containing my final paycheck was cast onto my desk.

"You're firing me?"

"You lied about inventory. You cannot do that."

"Everyone does it! It's part of sales!"

"No. That is not our way here at—"

"Shove it up your ass, Cleaver." And I walked out of there still drunk from whatever I'd been doing the night before.

3

LACY'S

1969

ERVYN'S DEPARTMENT STORE GAVE ME A JOB BUT FIRED ME TWO WEEKS later after they realized that I'd lied about having a college degree. I was back to being jobless... again. What kind of cheap trick was it to hire a guy, give him time to settle in, then go back and do all your homework just to toss him into the street?

Well, I didn't exactly go to the street, just back to my apartment and then to the bar where I met up with a girl named Sandy. Sandy and I really hit it off. I didn't tell her about my wife, never wore my ring, and she asked me several times if I'd be interested in moving in with her. I put on the brakes in this relationship but vowed to pick it up again when work settled down.

My brother, Pat Alexander, 21 years old, had shown up at some point during all of this. He was a big guy, about as tall as I was and stocky. I was muscular, don't get me wrong, but Pat was built just like Terry. Their chests were barrels. The thing was, if you put us in the weight room I could walk all over either of them. They were hollow like giant pumpkins, I was carved out of wood.

I liked Pat being around, he was a cool guy, but the thing that bothered me was his age. He was too young for the scene. His inexperience and our lofty business plans were a bad combination. Nevertheless, he had his mind set on living with us.

To keep him out of too much trouble, Terry introduced him to the job of driving delivery trucks for Pacific American. Pat spent the next few months delivering "slightly warm" merchandise to retail stores throughout the Bay Area.

Pat wanted to know all the secrets. He wanted to get in over his head and be rich. I knew that he had to start slow. A kid that young would get himself in trouble if you gave him free cash and turned him loose on the streets.

Aside from being worried about Pat, things were going very well. From my experiences as a buyer for the Imporium I had figured easy ways to fool companies into unloading large quantities of goods into my hands without exchanging any cash. I devised scams where I would fill out false purchase orders, write bad checks, do whatever I had to in order to procure a tractor-trailer load of goods and distribute them to black-market buyers.

Whenever an opportunity like this presented itself I was the first to know and the first to capitalize. Since I was unemployed for several weeks after Ervyn's, the need for generating personal income through criminal means became a very serious endeavor.

My scam ideas were often as simple as making a few phone calls and filling out a stolen purchase order form that I'd swiped from a company like Imporium or Ervyn's. It was because of my interest with scams like these that my life rapidly became a haze of stolen merchandise, trips, vacations, suites, drunk women, and, of course, my favorite item: CASH.

✻   ✻   ✻

"We got everything we need to make this place work, Mr. Alexander. We just need a loan."

"I'm not your trust fund, Mike." Mike Beazley sat across from me. We were at Chugger's and his tan skin and Marlboro cigarettes blended him into the booth like a dirty plank of wood.

"Come on, Jack… you loan us the dough to buy the building, spend about 80k fixing it up, I'll run the bar—I worked in bars my whole life, my brother's worked in bars, everybody in my damn family knows the restaurant business. You get me that capital and I'll get you a return."

How did I meet guys like this? I really had no idea. Somehow, by some strange force, the crooks and sidewinders always gravitated to me. I guess I had an aura or a way of talking. Well, and maybe they'd heard I was loaded.

"How much you got of your own?" I asked.

"I got about 5k."

"That's shit. I got more than that in my glove box."

"Yeah, well, I been an honest worker for the past five years. I been raising a kid, keeping my place maintained."

"It's not my fault. And, on that note, I didn't come here to be reminded about being a criminal. I came here 'cause you needed help getting something going that could make me some money. You better pitch me something better than this shit or I'm leaving."

"Look, man, you get me the money and I swear to god no one will ever know you're involved, no one will ever ask you any questions, and if it fails, I'll work for free until the debt's paid off."

"I don't care who knows, Mike. That's not the issue. The issue is that the deal sounds shitty to me."

"Come on, Jack, gimme a break here! I got a kid!"

"That's bullshit. I got a wife, a brother, a sister, shit... I got things, too. Why should I give you 80 grand?"

"Just take it from your rich wife! She'll never miss it!" He slapped his hand on the table. I was his last hope in a cruel and despicable world of hard labor and low pay. His eyes focused on mine like a caged animal despises kids at the zoo.

"Don't yell at me. And don't tell me what to do. Let me think about it. I'll call you."

*   *   *

I was down in Los Angeles drinking and scouting contacts for future sales.

The night came on hard. I was with several girls. Terry had come up earlier. He told me that he knew one of the chicks with us at the bar. Her name was Lili and apparently she was into me. According to Terry, Lili was from a very wealthy family in the movie business and it'd be good for me to give it a shot.

Things with Jane were on the way out. I had known that since the beginning. It wasn't that I'd used her, it was that I'd never known her in the first place. I hadn't seen her in days, spoken to her in probably over a week, or kissed her in a month. I didn't care. The world was a big place and the flocks of women were substantial to keep me occupied.

It was evident from the start that Lili had money. She and her friends sat at the bar drinking round after round of expensive drinks; just tasting them, throwing them out, and ordering another. We stumbled out of the bar and blindly crawled into the back seat of my new Lincoln Mark IV, which I had legitimately purchased at some point during all of this.

"I've got my own ride," she said. She kissed me and lifted herself from my lap. She told me to meet her at the Century Plaza Hotel and that we'd get a room. These girls were playing it like they were loaded. I'd see about how they stacked up against a guy like me.

Terry drove my car all the way across town, somehow avoiding the countless sobriety checkpoints. The girls arrived right behind us, Lili piloting a brand new Rolls Royce. Damn, she had me way beat.

I walked in, slapped my hand on the bell, and waited. It was 2 a.m.

"Yes, sir?" The young woman asked.

"I need your best room," I smirked. Money wasn't an obstacle for a guy like me.

"For how many, sir?"

"How many you see standing here?" There were five of us. Me, Lili, Terry, and two other girls.

"I see." She fiddled with something and I sighed impatiently. "I have the Presidential Suite available tonight."

"Yeah, gimme that," I said. The girls were drunk and so was I, but I wasn't wobbling all over the place.

"It's going to be $1,199 plus tax."

I slapped my Platinum Amex on the table.

The room was gigantic, basically the entire top floor of the building. There were several bedrooms, a kitchen, all that shit. Lili and I went into the master bedroom. She began undressing as soon as I shut the door. I felt a pang of adrenaline but calmed it, pushed it away from my mind. I kept telling myself that I was different now, that the Snowman was dead, that I could do anything I wanted. I pulled out my wallet, my money clip, and set them on the table beside the sink. The cash calmed me, soothed my nerves, and in a few moments I was back to my normal self.

I could hear Terry laughing in his room with the other two chicks and I took off my watch, rolled up my sleeves, and looked down at her like a doctor.

"Hey, Jack?" She spun drunkenly across the king-size mattress.

"What?"

"I'm married," she said.

"OK." I looked across the bed and stared at myself in the full length mirror.

"I'm married to Dave Zunuck. You know who he is? The famous movie producer?"

"Oh, yeah. I've heard of him, sure," I said.

"That doesn't mean we can't keep going."

"OK."

I was still transfixed by my own reflection in that full-size, gold framed mirror.

"What's wrong, Jack?"

"Nothing, sorry." I snapped out of it and looked back at the bed, at her. "You want another glass of champagne?" I asked.

"Come here."

Those were strange days in San Francisco in the late 60s, but I was a new man and the world didn't have any bullets big enough to blow my brains out.

* * *

Lili didn't really like sex. She just didn't get into it. I didn't understand why she pushed so hard to make it happen. Maybe her friends put her up to it. She was just another one of those Jane Cumberland types who looked real good, felt real good, but when you got her in the sack it just didn't happen.

I took off out of the hotel in the middle of the night, driving like a lunatic on a head full of vodka. I ran into some lady's car on the side of the street, threw a couple hundred bucks at her, and kept driving toward the coast.

About halfway to wherever I was going—I had no idea where to end up—I pulled into an abandoned dock and parked the car. It was still night, around 4 a.m., and a hooker banged on my broken window.

"You looking to get screwed or robbed?" She peered through the cracked glass.It must have broken when I hit the lady's car.

"Getouddahere, lady," I said.

"What's your problem? I'm trying to help you." She dragged on a Newport cigarette. I knew they were Ports because I could see the pack shoved in her cleavage.

"Gimme one uh them smokes." I reached out. She slid one through a hole in the glass.

"You want some company?"

"You got a light?"

"Yeah, hold on." She stood up, fiddled around in her bra some more, handed me a pack of matches. All of this was going on through the cracked window.

"You wanna unlock this so I can get to know you?" She jostled the handle.

"Don't have time." I slipped her a 100. She said thanks, told me to get some sleep, and took off down the sidewalk. I started the car, turned around, headed toward the freeway and shouted songs with the radio.

The windshield shattered and water rushed in around me. Damn, it was really pouring in! Hell! Shit! The damn car was vertical in the water, spiraling down toward the bottom. I struggled with the seatbelt, snagged it on something, the damn thing wouldn't come off!

I finally got out, opened the door, which was near impossible, and swam to the shore beneath the pier. I walked up to the nearest motel, sopping wet, no idea how I'd gotten there. I filled out a form, got a room, and went to sleep in my clothes.

*　　*　　*

It was the following morning.

I spent some time in the hotel making phone calls. I spoke with Mike Beazley, the guy I had just entrusted with 80k. Mike was starting his bar and a few investors—myself, included—were helping him with the conceptualization. The place was going to be called Zipples, and according to Mike Beazley it was going to be the hottest bar on the West Coast.

Hours passed in the hotel room with the sun slanting through the blinds. I thought about everything: the grass out there being cut, my old man, mom, the people in cars on the freeway going different places, the studded dog collar I used to wear in college, the wife, old ladies shuffling with canes past my window. All simple shit, but it kept me from spiraling off the grid.

I found Lili outside the Plaza Hotel.

"Where's your car, Jack? What happened to you?" Questions, questions, questions...

"Om, yeah... I got arrested last night. Drunk driving. Cops took it."

"Oh..."

"Yeah. I'm going to go buy another one right now. Where's Terry?"

"He's still in the room. We're going to breakfast." It was 2 p.m. The hotel had probably nailed my card for another night. Shit.

"Where are we going?"

"I don't know. Why did you leave last night?" she asked.

"Personal stuff. Don't worry about it."

"I just wondered."

"I said not to ask me any questions, alright?"

"Jeez."

We got into her Rolls. I drove. We went to the Beverly Hills Hotel and met some of her other friends for lunch. They looked about as bad off as we did. Their clothes weren't still damp from a swim in the Pacific, but they were visibly roughed up from a hard Friday night.

Lili introduced me to the bartender, a guy named Tommy. Tommy was clean cut with a pretty face and perfect hair. He seemed too pretty to be a crook, but Lili said he had a very good network among the white-collar types.

It turned out Tommy was a loose cannon. He stole me away from the table after the meal and told me all sorts of shit about how he was buying and selling diamonds, rubies, emeralds, any type precious stone or metal.

Did I want in? It was great money.

"Sure as shit I want in."

"You got the capital?"

"What do I look like?"

"Good. I'll get you connected with some guys I know. They've needed a friend like you. The thing is, when I get you the connections you have to cut me a percentage of the dough."

"That's how this game works?"

"Worked this way for centuries, Jack. The bartender sees everything." He laughed and patted me on the back. This was a good move for me. I needed to separate myself from Interwest and Pacific American. I had a feeling that Fenster had been using me for my money. He was such a sneaky guy and his jealously bothered me. Every time a woman started hitting on me Greg would make a snide remark or leave the table. I couldn't help it if I had charisma. Why couldn't he understand?

"I'm fine with giving you a cut, Tommy. Just let me know when you get some deals lined up."

"I'll call you," he said. We were in business, definitely.

* * *

I was hired at Lacy's Department Store by Fred Pinkelstein as the Assistant Buyer for Housewares. Nobody seemed to give a shit that I'd messed up at the Imporium, that I had no college education, that I was a perpetually recovering from a speed and booze hangover.

I walked the walk at Lacy's, talked to the right people, made a few strategic business trips to the Orient and bought the right shit. I kicked off the Lacy's Cellar in SFO and was promoted to Buyer of Perfume and Cosmetics. I don't think I realized it right then, but I had stumbled into a hell of a job. I was traveling all over the place on jets and in limos, in and out of the United States nearly every week for business.

It was after a trip to Paris that I took a side trip to Nairobi, Kenya, and got a room for a few days under the advisement of Tommy the Bartender. The view from my room was wild. The hotel was called Treetops and it sat in a huge banyan tree. Every night they would put food out and turn up the lights so guests could watch the animals outside their windows. This chick came up to my room and she insisted that we go to a bar rather than smoke cigars on the balcony all night.

I went downstairs and called Greg Fenster from a payphone to check on our companies. He assured me that everything was alright.

"We're working on the Starlight Laundry plan," he chuckled. "We pick up our first load tomorrow."

"Great..." I said. I had a feeling that their plan wouldn't work, but I didn't have time to talk about it right then. "I'll see you guys when I get back. Don't screw it up."

The girl and I entered a derelict watering hole that some native insisted was "the best in town," and took a booth far off from the rest of the world. A group of people arrived and walked disinterestedly toward my table.

The people in that place were sharks, con men, thieves. You could tell it by the way they sat with their eyes peeled and focused, by the way the mood changed when certain men came through the doors. Her friends took the booth with us, each of the men with a girl and each of us smoking a cigar.

"You buy perfume?" one guy asked. He had bright blonde hair and a strange accent. I couldn't place it. Each of the men wore several rings, bracelets, necklaces. Their girlfriends were similarly decorated.

"Yeah, I do," I said, gulping a glass of vodka and OJ.

"You buy anything else?" He was hinting at something—a bag on the table. They must have heard who I was, figured out that I was fresh in the business. I got the feeling that maybe Tommy had orchestrated it.

"What you got?" I asked.

He flipped it open right there. No one was around to see it except for the waitress, and she was necking with one of the goons so I figured the whole place was on the take.

Inside the case were a bunch of stones. I took a close look, picking up the box and inspecting each one.

"We know you through Tommy Stillwell."

"I don't know who that is." I lied.

They remained uneasily silent.

"I'm kidding," I said. "You guys aren't cops?" I knew they weren't, I just asked to gauge their reactions.

"We are not." They spoke very precisely, careful not to make a mistake. I realized that perhaps my sense of humor had been out of their comfort zone.

"Good..." I inspected the stones. "Well, here's the deal: I got cash, but I gotta talk to somebody in town first." I went back to my room after that, made a phone call to a guy in New York, a Jewish guy who knew Tommy and who knew whether or not I should make a deal with these people.

He didn't answer so I called Tommy and he assured me that the whole thing was straight. I went on down there with a briefcase, counted out some bills, and offered them a price.

"This is what I got." I put a stack of bills on the table, about half of my cash.

"And what else?"

"That's it."

"We don't like it," the European guy said, pushing the money toward me. The table was filthy and the bottom bills became wet from beer sweat. The girl I had been drinking with gave a strange vibe like she was sleeping with one of the other men at the table. She'd served her purpose. Forget her, Jack, there are more fish in the sea.

"Well, it's all I got. You want more and you'll have to give me the stones on the front. Tommy says you're good guys, that I can trust you."

"He told us you were coming, asshole. How do you think we set up the deal?"

"I don't know. I figured I just looked like a bad guy."

"You're not funny."

"Yeah, and neither are you," I said.

There was silence. Everyone stared at me.

"You want to buy or not?"

"I told you, this is all the money I've got. You wanna make the deal—make it. If not, stop wasting my time."

"On the front?"

"No. Forget the front. Just give it to me for the money on the table." I pointed to the stack.

He counted it and slapped the bills against the wall. He turned toward his friends and they spoke in a different language. Maybe they were Middle Eastern—it was hard to tell. The guy was bright blonde but it sounded like the Semitic language of Arabs.

"We'll do it."

"Sorry to inconvenience you." I grabbed the case. "Prick."

He flipped open a knife. One of his goons prevented me from exiting the booth. The girl came in real close to me like to whisper in my ear.

"Don't mess with us, baby," she purred against me, fondling my tie and collar.

"Feeling's mutual."

The girl kissed me on the neck. I pulled away from her and exited the bar. In 15 minutes I was back in my hotel drinking from a fifth of a Stoly Silver and waiting for the 5 a.m. to Frisco.

*   *   *

While I was out of the country doing diamond deals, Terry, Greg, and my brother had taken a few steps forward with Starlight Laundry, the newfound sect of Interwest.

Two weeks prior to my departure to Kenya I had brainstormed the insane idea to con the Navy into a signing a contract with us to do their laundry.

Terry, Pat, and I had been sitting around drinking, jabbering, smoking cigars on the balcony. Terry had at one point told me about his experience in the laundry business. I said something like: "I bet the military does a shitload of laundry."

They all agreed.

"Why don't we see about doing the laundry for them? Terry, you know a bit about the laundry business, right? We'll rent out a space or something."

"Hell, we could just do their laundry at the mat and charge them out the ass; you know, like we're a professional company."

"We can start it through Interwest," I said. So, in a nutshell, that's how Starlight Laundry got started.

Next we rented three giant Pepsico trucks and I took a limo to the Navy docks, to the USS Pittyhawk. I got on the vessel and gave them a pretty good offer for doing their laundry. The Navy haggled a bit, nothing serious, and I got out of there with a signed deal. I had never thought for a minute that it would work.

It was that same afternoon that I left for Paris on business for Lacy's. From Paris I had taken the detour through Kenya, where I had picked up that case of stones from the folks at the bar. I had left very abruptly after signing the deal with the Navy and so had delegated the fulfillment of the laundry processes to Terry and Pat. I had a feeling that this wasn't a good idea, but there was no other choice.

I was back in the states now, riding home from the San Francisco airport, which is just south of the city. On the ride I noticed three abandoned Pepsico trucks on the side of the southbound freeway.

At first, I thought nothing of it. Moments later, however, suspicions began to mount. My ride rushed me home and I burst through the door to find Terry, Pat, and some other Dumbo passing around a near-empty liter of vodka.

"What in god's name happened?" I yelled, throwing my arms wildly and snatching the jug.

"Jack, calm down. It wasn't our fault. We got the laundry, right? Took it down to the mat to run it through the machines. Then, when we got to the mat all the garment bags were locked. We didn't have the damn keys to open 'em."

"So…" I said, still wild with disbelief.

"So, we just figured we were supposed to wash them in the bags. And we did. Then we found out that the damn 'dress whites' are supposed to be pressed."

"Yeah…" I was waiting to hear the bit about the trucks being left on the side of the freeway.

"So, there was no damn way we could press the dress whites, so we just washed 'em, threw 'em back in the truck, and took off."

Pat looked up out of his drunken daydream. "Yeah, bad part was we couldn't dry 'em."

"What?"

"Yeah, they wouldn't let us put 'em in the dryers because of the locks," Terry said.

"But they'd let you put 'em in the washers?"

"I don't know, man."

"My god…"

"So, yeah, that's it."

"No, that's NOT it! Why the HELL are MY three Pepsico trucks abandoned on the side of the freeway?"

"We got scared, man. Lost it. Froze. I don't know."

"You better go get that shit, take it down to the Navy yard, and tell those bastards what happened before they start shelling the apartment." I stuffed my case of stones into a kitchen cabinet, into a safe I had mounted there, and locked it.

It was likely that highway patrol had already ticketed the trucks, which would add an extra grand or so to our mounting bills. I boiled around the apartment for a while after sending the guys out to finish the job. I got a bit drunk myself, started answering phone calls from girls and all sorts of people and before I knew it there was a brunette on my lap and I was at Zipples throwing back drinks, laughing, high as gas on speed.

*   *   *

Yes, Zipples had opened.

Mike Beazley had come through. Not a night went by that the place wasn't packed. I felt good there; gold chains around my neck (the rock business was going well), shirt open down to my chest hair, good muscles, Pat and Terry always close by. My clothes were all tailored, expensive shit from Bergdorf's or a good suit I'd dug up in Saks. I smoked cigars, nodded at the important people, and put off the vibes of a big player. People in that bar respected me. I had quite an image. Sometimes there were a couple of broads with me, sometimes just one, sometimes a vodka rocks, other times a bottle of something being slung around my table.

The waitress came up and handed me another drink. All the waitresses had huge tits, so naturally everybody called the place Nipples. Mike hired the most busty girls in the city to serve drinks. That, along with Zipples unique "X-Rated Bathrooms," ensured a packed house. You see, in front of each urinal was a television screen. When a patron stepped up to take a piss the television would begin playing a porno. The same was true for the women's bathroom, only on the backside of the door the projection was Burt Reynolds doing a striptease.

I was feeling rough that night; freshly arrived in San Francisco from Florida where I had been staying at the Breakers Hotel with Gaye Squires. I had met Gaye about six months back on a buying trip to New York. She had been sitting in the lobby of my hotel in a leather easy chair with her hands over her eyes and tears pouring down her cheeks. All I could see was blonde hair, beautiful legs, high-heeled shoes that set her calves perfectly against the chair, and perfect little hands wiping away the tears. I had immediately approached and taken a seat beside her. I set my business briefcase between my feet.

"What's wrong, sweetheart?"

She looked up. I think at first she didn't know how to receive me. She was silent, just stared.

"Can I do anything to help?" I asked.

"He left me here alone... with no money. And he just left and went—"

"Don't worry about it." I said, I stood up and reached into my pocket. "You need money for a plane ticket?" I removed my bills. "Where you headed?"

"Florida... what?" She didn't understand what I was doing. I peeled off $500.

Her mouth dropped. She was wide-eyed and unable to comprehend her luck or my generosity, whichever was more unbelievable.

"I can't accept this," she said.

"It's fine. Trust me."

"I'll pay it back."

"No big deal."

She gave me a hug. She was model material; had the eyes and hair and whole package like something you'd see on the runway or in a magazine. Gaye Squires was one of the most perfect women I had ever seen.

"Here," I said, scribbling on the back of one of my Interwest business cards. "This is my address. When you get the money, you can mail it back to me." I knew it wouldn't happen, I just wanted to give her my contact information in case she got lonely down there.

"I will. I'll mail you the money."

And I'll be damned if a month later I didn't get a letter in my Interwest office PO box from Gaye Squires. The money was inside the envelope along with a note requesting that I come to visit.

So, that night in Zipples I was tired—I took a giant slug from my vodka rocks, slid it across the table, reached for the next fresh one, let off a plume from my cigar, closed my eyes and leaned my head back against the wall—because I had just gotten back from Florida.

The women were hunting me, as was typical in Zipples. I was busy, though. I was thinking of Gaye in Palm Beach, a girl named Mary in Kew Gardens, Casey in Dallas. I was thinking what a shit I was to be ignoring the storm of drunken females circling my table like hammerhead sharks. I had too many girlfriends to be starting something new on a night like this.

Well, maybe not. I looked around but didn't see anything that interested me.

I stabbed out a cigar, removed another one from my leather sheath. They were the same smokes as always: the Antonio Y Cleopatras with the dark leaf wrappers. Some things change, some things don't.

*　　*　　*

I acquired a trailer full of 00BK shotgun shells and my buyer fell through. I was stuck with this huge load of ammunition and no place to dump it off. It was, of course, stolen. It would be about two days before Remington or whoever it was figured out that they'd been rooked for 15 grand. About that time they would begin the hunt for someone who could ID the buyer, who could pinpoint the contacts who had arranged the deal, etc. I was pretty sure that they wouldn't trace it back to me. At least, they hadn't been able to do it yet.

In the newspaper there was all this shit about the Black Panthers walking the streets with shotguns and I said to Terry, "Hell, why not drive down to Oakland and sell a bunch of shells to the Panthers?"

Pat was eager to do it. He thought it was funny as shit. I didn't know if I wanted him in charge of the sale, but I couldn't waste my whole day being jerked around Oakland with a truck of stolen goods. He and some other guy who worked with us drove up to Santa Rosa, picked up the ammo, took it to Oakland, and unloaded the whole thing in one afternoon.

*　　*　　*

In addition to buying truckloads of shit and selling it under the table, Terry and I were running Cadillacs down to Mexico almost every weekend. I had a sweet scam worked up for this.

I was in the dealership one afternoon, preparing to make a big hit, when a salesman approached me with great anticipation.

"How do you like it, sir?" He leaned into the car, took a big whiff. "That new car smell. You just can't beat it," he said.

"Yeah."

"It's the Eldorado model."

"Yeah, I know what it is. I'm a dealer."

"I see…"

"Let me get two of them." I pointed at both Eldos. "And at a fair price or I'll walk out the door."

"I'll see what I can do."

"I'm telling you, don't jerk me around or I'll leave here without thinking twice."

You had to act like the price mattered, that way in a month when the bank draft didn't clear he'd put the gun to his head wondering why the hell you haggled so hard if you were just stealing the car in the first place. There was a simple, angry, displeased etiquette that had to be followed. It was the same type of behavior I'd learned from watching my father pace for half an hour across the showroom floor at the Chevy dealership when I was a kid.

"Two cars, sir. And at a MORE than fair price." He handed me the papers, a pad, a pen, a price, all the "P" words that I didn't really give a shit about.

"Yeah, yeah…" I said. I signed everything, filled in a fake name, filled in the same information on the bank draft. While I worked on the papers he marked both cars with temporary tags. I handed him the paperwork along with my ID and a phony credit card that he could use as a secondary form of ID. He took them into his office and returned with a smile and two sets of keys.

The bank draft could take up to 30 days to clear. For 30 days these cars would not be reported stolen. They would be completely legal, their titles and information lost deep within the politics of the automobile distribution business.

*   *   *

We came back from Mexico by jet, as usual, and the limo was there to pick us up. I made it to Lacy's an hour late, stumbling out of the limousine with a couple of empty airplane bottles of vodka still in my pocket. I got on up to the office without being noticed, crept behind my desk, and began making phone calls.

Gaye Squires had left me a message: "Jack, it's Gaye… I don't know if you realize this or not, but the Cadillac you rented last month from Hertz is still parked in the garage on Route 1. I figured I'd call and tell you just because I know they've got to be charging you all sorts of fees and—" I erased the message. They could bill me for the whole damn car for all I cared. Hertz fees… if that's all I had to worry about I'd be doing great.

My superior, Benjamin Irving, came into my office. He dropped a stack of papers on my desk. I momentarily forgot his name, almost called him Greg. He left saying something about going out of town that evening and did I have my bags packed? I did not.

That evening I was back in the airport boarding a jet. One of the same stewardesses from that morning was on the plane with me. She smiled, nodded, nothing more than that.

There were some issues with the engine, something about oil, and we landed in Phoenix for the night. I had no bags, no luggage, no extra clothes. It was 4 p.m. and I headed to Goldblatz to peruse their selection.

The stewardess from both flights was in a payphone booth on the sidewalk. I walked past casually, pretending not to notice her. I stood on the corner even though there was no traffic.

"You been doing a lot of flying," she said.

I turned around. There she was.

"Business."

"What do you do?"

"I buy perfume and cosmetics for Lacy's. My name's Jack."

"Wow, a Lacy's perfume buyer."

"Yeah, that's me. What's your name?"

"Heidi."

"Nice to meet you."

"You like it?"

"What, the perfume? It's alright." I got a good look at her: she wasn't a Gaye Squires, but she was good-looking nonetheless.

"I've got a room at the Hilton if you want a glass of champagne," I said.

"Sure."

We went back there and after three or four drinks…bingo, bango, bongo.

*　　*　　*

I spent the next few days in Mexico City. I made some deals, met with some people in the airplane business, bought some diamonds, shoved them into my carryon luggage, made arrangements to meet an arms dealer in LA who would trade the diamonds for a truck-full of guns that I could then sell to a guy in San Francisco who was always on me about finding firearms. And that guy, the gun guy, stupid as he was, would take the arms at an absurdly high price and probably be willing to give me a tip as to where he suspected the other guy, the one in L.A., was buying the stolen weapons in the first place so that maybe I could get in on that and cut him out.

From Mexico City I flew to New York City, where I met with Aron Alprim, the President of Canel. Alprim had the most incredible office I had ever seen, literally the entire top floor of the Avon Building. We had lunch at Le Cote Basque where he introduced me to Zsa Zsa Gabor and Johnny Carson. What a trip.

Then, I met with Dr. Banger von Bangendorff, the creator of the Evyan White Shoulders fragrance. We went to his house/laboratory where he gave us a tour. He strolled the floors in a lab coat testing chemicals, showing us processes, handing over lists of ingredients that he special ordered from across the globe.

"I made this fragrance for Eve," he said. She was his wife, deceased.

Nobody said a word.

I was drunk, so I looked right at him and said, "Very thoughtful, Dr. Banger." What else could a guy say?

The Baron had floral arrangements placed all over the house. Eve's office suite was just as it was when she was alive: the bathtub was filled with hot water, rose petals sprinkled on top, fresh cut soaps, mountains of feminine decor everywhere.

People at Lacy's seemed to think it would be a valuable experience if they sent a couple of us out there to meet this guy. It turned out to be nothing worthwhile. Don't get me wrong, the guy had a best-selling perfume line, but his personal life was something I'd expect to see in the beginning of a high-budget horror movie.

*   *   *

I was in Lacy's, going over prices, straightening out the books, making phone calls, arguing with people, etc.

I got a call from someone downstairs on the floor.

"Jack, this is Lisa at the front... yeah, there are a bunch of guys here to see you, a few of them just walked past and went upstairs."

"Thank you." SHIT! Must have been the Feds, the Gestapo, the mob... who knew. I checked my peephole. There was no lock on my office. Damn Lacy's cheapskates! I took a hurried rip of Scotch from a bottle that I'd been given as a present. I never did like Scotch very much.

I walked out, figured that they may not recognize me with a three-day beard.

There were about five of them, each one in a military uniform. They were speaking with the secretary. She pointed at me and I froze like a shot duck.

"Hello, sirs," I said, extending my hand to the one who appeared to be in charge.

"You're Jack Alexander." He didn't ask, he informed me.

"Yes, sir."

"Captain David Borror, United States Navy. Come with me immediately." I followed him down the quiet staircase, the sound of boots pounding against the carpet like a death march.

There were at least 20 of them down there crowding the sales floor, all the employees staring dumbfounded at the glittering Navy uniforms. (Obviously they'd found someone else to do the laundry.)

We descended the escalator moving at twice the pace of a normal man.

"You're the CEO of International Western Corporation?" he asked. I nodded. "Starlight Laundry is a division of your company?" I looked around. Somehow, no one of any importance had noticed all of this.

"Yes."

He handed me a release form, a notice that Starlight Laundry's contract with the United States Navy would be terminated immediately.

"Just sign here, please." He pointed to a line.

I signed it. They left. No one noticed a damn thing. What a relief to have those suckers off my case.

*　　*　　*

Terry, Pat and I, were at a table in Zipples at 1 a.m.

This chick came up, sat down on my lap, started talking about nothing and I wasn't listening. Thankfully, Greg wasn't around to throw one of his fits about me getting all the attention. I was getting sick of that guy. I had talked to Terry about leaving Greg altogether, maybe starting a company of our own. Greg was good at what he did, sure, but he acted like a girlfriend the way he pouted and griped over the stupidest shit.

What really got to Greg the worst was how easy it was for me to get money. No matter how hard he tried he couldn't beat my numbers. This maddened him, often driving him to argue with me about unimportant nuances of business.

Greg was getting to be too much for me to deal with. There was a fine line to draw: I didn't want to ruin our relationship in case I needed him in the future, but I needed a break.

"Can I finish this?" the girl asked, picking up my drink.

"Sure," I said, coming back from my daydreams about Greg. "I'll get you another one." I raised my finger and the waitress leaned her ear close to my lips. "Lemme get a bottle of vodka over here. Tell Mike it's for Jack." She was a new girl, probably didn't know about me. Hardly anyone knew I was an owner. The fewer people knew, the fewer people hit me up for money.

The chick on my lap was a good catch, probably one of the best in the crowd. After a while I started to get to know her a bit and we went into the kitchen for 20 minutes.

We were back at the table when my brother leaned over next to me, a very distressed look on his face.

"What's the problem?"

"I got this Playboy Bunny, bro."

"Yeah? What's wrong with that?"

"I got no ride, man."

I flipped him the keys: Snap, ching.

"You're the man, Jack."

He took off. I felt weary about giving him my keys after what had happened with the Pepsico trucks. I sighed as he walked away, that blonde thing pressed tight against him. In order for him to grow up he needed responsibility. By lending him my car he would realize that I respected him. Maybe he would behave like an adult. Maybe he would feel more accountable for his actions with Starlight Laundry.

Terry disappeared from the table with some girls. I went outside for a breath of fresh air and handed my half-burnt cigar to a good-looking woman at the door. I think she just picked up smoking it.

The chick waited a few seconds and followed me out. Her name was Mandy. She told me she'd been watching me.

"I think you're a sweetheart," she said.

Hadn't my mother told me that my father had been a sweetheart? Didn't something happen to us after a while that ruined it? Mandy was drunk, probably had no idea what she was saying.

"Your name's Jack, right?"

"That's right." I stood there on the sidewalk and eyed my limo.

"You're a big shot at some company, aren't you?"

"So?"

"I've just heard about you, that's all."

"Let's get the hell out of here."

"Where's your car?"

"I gave it to Pat. We'll take my limo."

The driver, a young guy named Dobbs, was asleep in the front seat. Dobbs was a Hell's Angel I'd picked up fresh out of jail. He was a fairly honest guy but couldn't catch a break. He was in need of decent wages so I figured I'd take him on as a full-time driver. You could trust the Angels not to open their mouths about crime, and you could also trust them to have your back if things turned sour.

Dobbs was probably drunk. Who wasn't? I tapped on the window loudly, the safety glass vibrating against his head. He jumped from the steering wheel like he'd just come from the minefield.

"I gotta go," I said. "Let's get this bus moving."

"Sorry." His voice was raspy, thick. "Hop on in."

*   *   *

My brother showed up the next day, ranting. I could hear him in the living room, through my bedroom door. It was something about jail.

"What's the problem?" I asked, emerging from my cave in a pair of boxer shorts. I was still wearing a couple of chain necklaces; the rest I think I'd given to some of the waitresses. My hair was disheveled from a rough evening and I ran my hands over my scalp, futilely attempting to untangle it.

"Dude, Jack, I was in this hotel over on Van Ness this morning and the cops busted in there. I was with that Playboy Bunny, remember? And they pinned me down, started to arrest me and I was like, what the hell are you guys doing? And they said, 'Jack Alexander, you're under arrest for...' And I said hell if I'm Jack Alexander! And they said, 'Show me some ID' and I pointed to the dresser and they checked the thing out, man, and it wasn't you, Jack, you know? So then they took off; just left me on the bed with that chick."

I swallowed and headed to the bathroom for a long piss. The feast was over. The hunt was on.

4

SAN DIEGO

1969

I HAD PHASED OUT OF LACY'S BECAUSE OF LONG NIGHTS. NEVER MADE A conscious decision to quit, I just stopped going in. It was probably a good thing since the fuzz was on me and the second place the S.F.P.D. checks is your job.

I decided that I was done with Greg Fenster and that I'd leave town with Terry. Greg wouldn't mind. In fact, he'd probably take it as a good thing. He would be the sole controller of Interwest and Pacific American. It would be his show, his head trip. Good riddance.

Terry and I went to a dealership and legitimately purchased a late model Pontiac convertible under his name. We loaded it up, packing what little we cared to bring: cash, magazines, case of beer, fifth, liter, bag of shirts, extra pair of pants, etc. We headed to San Diego.

We exited Route 5 near La Jolla and rolled into an apartment complex right by the beach. We had cash, which everybody liked, and so got a good deal on the place. It had a swimming pool, balcony, and was completely furnished.

We went out and bought a couple of stereos, some extra clothes, a couple pairs of shoes, bathing suits, and a few television sets. Gradually, the new apartment began to feel like home.

My brother was no longer with us, opting to stay in San Francisco. He had a good thing going with Pacific American. He was orchestrating truck runs, driving trucks, helping Fenster with the management aspects of the business. The cops weren't onto him... yet.

Speaking of Fenster, I gave him a call after arriving in San Diego and asked about getting my paycheck from some deals I'd made for Pacific American.

"Oh yeah, Jack, I've got all sorts of stuff pending..." It was probably bullshit. "The tax sleuths are riding my ass, Jack. You know how it is."

I said a few nice words and hung up the phone. What a bullshitter.

*　　*　　*

I called Jane Cumberland, my wife.

"Yeah, yeah... I know. It's rough... it's not that, baby... it's not that... I'm in Coral Gables on business... nope... long days... I don't know what they could have wanted... no... no problems here... I'll call back soon...tell them I'll talk to them when I get back. It's probably about Pat. I think he's gone bad... sometimes... this is a payphone... I just don't want to..."

The pigs were all over my house in San Francisco. It wouldn't be long before they found the apartment, the office I had rented in the Trans-America building, the paper trail of stolen automobiles, the missing trailers of shotgun shells, televisions, lamps, furniture, tires, purses, diamonds... my god, shit was crashing. I was safe, though, far removed from all of it and down at the boardwalk pay phone smoking a cigar and watching my money roll in like waves.

There were hundreds of thousands of people all over the beaches. It was something they called the "Over the Line" competition. There were literally hordes of three-man teams out there playing each other for the international title.

Over the Line was just like softball without all the players; just three guys playing softball against three other guys. One guy would pitch, another would catch, the other would field.

I stood on the boardwalk and looked down at the scene. There was the ocean far beyond the beaches. Nobody was on the water except for guys moving oil and trash.

A bicycle cop rode by. A kid dropped his ice cream and cried. A bunch of queers pranced around and one of them called out something to me.

I took a long walk and watched the seagulls. They ate the discarded food, snatched bread off tables, circled the trashcans. It was the free-market concept. Everybody was at it.

The drunks from the tournament stumbled up the stairs from the beaches and mopped the floors of bars with their bodies. I circled around the area, walking slowly and talking to a few girls but seeing nothing that made me want to drop everything.

I went inside a bar. A bunch of old guys were drinking. It was quiet in there. The air conditioner hummed above the bartender's stereo. Cool breeze. A beer came and I slammed it. Something had to give. My break had to come. A score was coming; a good one—something that could set me up forever.

Well, maybe not... but who knew?

Some old Jew sat down at the bar beside me. It was a pretty nice joint. Nice and quiet but no girls, which was unusual for any bar on the beach, especially one filled with old guys carrying fat wallets.

"What's your story?" he asked.

"Don't have much of one." I stayed vague. It was the best I could do with a casual acquaintance.

"I like that chain." He pointed to my necklace, took it in his hands, named several of the stones and guessed where I had gotten them. Good show.

"What's your line?" I asked.

He nodded at the necklace. The bartender refilled his drink. Straight tequila.

"Me too," I said.

"Who you work for?"

"Myself."

"It's the only way."

He set me up with some folks around there who knew some men I'd dealt with in Madrid. He was buddies with a diamond wholesaler out of Rome I'd worked with six months back.

The connections were forming tighter. I could feel that I'd soon be plugged into the pipeline permanently and with the potential to generate excessive income.

*   *   *

On a whim...

I drove up to San Francisco in a stolen Mark IV—the bank draft scam never failed—and scouted out airplanes. I had a scam worked out where I leased airplanes from businesses in Northern California under the names of fake companies and flew them south where I sold them to friends in Acapulco.

I was able run this scam twice before I felt the heat get too close. I had been in a Learjet rental facility filling out paperwork when I caught a vibe that the receptionist was sizing me up. A few moments later she was on the telephone. I knew what it was about. I was gone in a matter of seconds and vowed to stay away from Learjet heisting until things cooled off.

The Mark IV hummed along toward San Francisco. I was headed to a private airport on the water just north of the city. All the planes in that dock were seaplanes, only capable of landing and taking off in the water. I got the idea that maybe I could run a bank draft scam on one of them, or maybe I could just get an idea of their prices then rent one and pull same trick I'd been working with the Learjets.

It would be a nice day either way: a good drive, no stress, a vacation from Terry and all the madness of La Jolla.

I parked the Lincoln in a parking deck and called a limo for a ride to the airport. The driver got there and I'd had him before.

"How's it going, Mr. Franklin?" he asked.

"Pretty good," I said.

He took me up to the airport. We passed Lacy's, the Imporium, all those familiar stops. I stared through the tinted windows at the masses of people stutter-stepping between traffic. What the hell did the Lacy's crowd think? Where did those chumps think I'd gone? The PD had probably convinced them that I was a murderer, armed and dangerous, a renegade and lawless bandit. That's the way the authorities got people to tell them things.

"Mr. Alexander killed his family, his cousins, an entire church, every last person in the town of Abilene..."

Then, some face of chattering teeth and teary eyes would spill the beans on where you were hiding out. The key was to lose the chattering teeth and teary eyes, which is what I had done by leaving Jane Cumberland, my ex-wife, in her pretty home on the south side of the city.

A woman would get you caught. Too often had history told the tale.

*   *   *

"You can take the keys to the planes and have a look around for yourself. Is that alright? No one is here to help you right now. That's the best I can offer." The old secretary smiled pleadingly, hoping that I would agree to this option.

"Yeah, that's fine. No problem." I took the clipboard and ring of keys onto the dock and walked the line of airplanes. Several caught my eye. I located the respective keys, checked the prices on the clipboard, opened them, got inside, rustled around and checked all the specs.

It was a dull day. Boring as shit. The sun would soon be setting. I milled around, nearly heading back to the dock house several times.

Then, on my last inch of curiosity, I entered one final plane. I dug around the interior feeling the seats, the upholstery, the controls, everything. It was the nicest one yet. I opened the glove compartment and there it was: the title. I picked it up. Hmm... That's right, Jack. It's the title. Just sitting in the glove box.

Right off I thought it was a setup—like the secretary knew me from a wanted poster and rather than risk having her head blown off she gave me the keys to all the planes. It seemed too perfect. I walked through the gate toward my ride. I told my limo driver to take the day off and handed him some bills. He thanked me and drove through the gate.

I strolled back onto the dock. I was alone out there and the plane cranked right up. The engine purred. Right as rain. I pulled the throttle and the thing tugged against the ropes. Bingo.

I knew how to fly a plane... sort of. I'd paid one of my Learjet pilots to teach me on one of our runs to Acapulco. We'd trained in his Cessna 310 for a few hours. Flying was a cinch. I had never flown something with pontoons before, but so what?

I jumped out, untied the ropes, snatched a look at the sleepy dock house, climbed back in, and taxied the thing into open water. The secretary appeared in the doorway, her weak form wobbling with disbelief.

There was no real runway out there, just a bunch of Styrofoam pyramids anchored in the water. I aimed the nose between all that shit and yanked the throttle. The plane took off nicely; not too incredibly different than a normal airplane.

Once in the air, the reality of my situation hit me. I had done this thing on an impulse. I really didn't know what I was doing. I had no idea where to go or what to do. Also, I hadn't checked the gas tank. That was the stupidest mistake I could have made. Lucky for me it was on FULL and the oil levels and everything else seemed in order.

There was San Francisco, glistening in the gray afternoon beneath me, and I was powerful and in control of the situation. The Earth was so small.

I navigated along the breakers, edging the compass northwest with the sand and white water. Time passed and I watched the redwood trees and the wilderness. My sights were set on Alaska. It was the only reasonable destination when piloting a stolen seaplane. Besides, I knew the perfect spot on Lake Washington where I could stop and refuel mid-trip.

*   *   *

Several days passed and I was back in the Mark IV heading south on Highway 5 thinking about Jane and the meaning of life. I had become something great. I was living on the edge of the world and people respected me. And to think, just a couple of years ago I had been a failing college student.

The interior of my car was pitch black and my pockets were shoved full of cash from the plane sale. I was fully blown on cocaine, rocking my head from side to side and singing along with the radio, a song by the O'Jays.

Long drive...

Where was Jane? Where had everyone gone? Pat? I hadn't seen my parents in a few years, probably since the time Jane and I had visited them and things fell through with Dad.

I needed to call Sandy. I'd dated her for a few weeks several months ago. Maybe I could get things figured out with her. Maybe we could get married, get a house near La Jolla, live off the fat of the land.

Who knew how far Sandy and I could go? I really liked her. Granted, I hardly knew her, hadn't really thought about her in a while, but I could tell that she was something worth clinging to.

I railed some toot and focused on the highway. No pigs yet, just a hoard of geriatric Oldsmobile drivers taking up both lanes. I could tell the truckers were as pissed as I was the way they honked, flashed lights, braked erratically, swerved as though to knock cars into the ditches.

Maybe one day there'd be a road for guys like us, a road where the weak were cast into the hillsides and the scared were forbidden access. A paved segment of flat land where you could burn down the coast hard, at top speed, with blazing wind and a .38 hanging out the window firing shots into the rest of the world.

I woke up with the Lincoln symbol from the steering wheel branded on my forehead. I was trapped in the middle of the damn jungle! Someone had tossed the car, searched through it and torn it apart. My shit was everywhere. The grocery bag with my change of shirts was gone. (I'd long since lost my briefcase.)

Where was the cash? Good... still in the pockets. I struggled with the door. These damn Mark IVs always gave a guy hell when it came time to exit the vehicle post-accident.

I had bites covering my body. Mosquitoes, horse flies, desert gnats, sand fleas, whatever they were—all of them had descended upon me after the wreck. And glass...

The Lincoln was totaled. I kicked it, popped the trunk, grabbed a dreg from an old fifth of Belvedere and shoved the rest into the front pocket of my suit, which had also been through hell and back and showed it.

It was a solid 100 yards to the highway through mud, snapped branches, leaked gasoline, and poisonous snakes. Judging by the distance, I'd say I hit the woods at 60 mph.

Well, I thought, if I had to go flying off the highway while sleeping I'd rather do it here than somewhere else. It could have been far worse than this. I finally reached the road, the cool wind evaporating the sweat from my neck. The cars fired past me like tracer bullets. I watched in disbelief. How had I managed to make such an awful mistake?

I straightened the tie, tugged on my jacket, shoved out my thumb, and waited for a miracle.

*　　*　　*

We were in Wallbangers Bar at 4 a.m. What was new?

Each morning around this time they would line the counter with old-fashioned glasses, fill the bottom half with tequila and top with 151 rum. Then, the bartender would light the drink on fire. Anybody with hair on their ass was supposed to drink one. Terry and I always took a couple, sometimes three if we were feeling exceptionally good about the night to come—meaning, if we had more speed.

We picked up our second glass and I blew mine out. I noticed that Terry hadn't extinguished his, but I was too drunk to warn him. He kicked it back hard, the 151 running down the sides of his mouth and the flames burning off sections of his eyebrows.

"Terry! My god, man! You're on fire!" the bartender yelled at us. I stood there, fascinated, stunned, laughing. Terry smacked at his face, quickly smothering the purple flames.

The glass was still flaming. His giant arms slung it clumsily at the waitress's tray. She wasn't paying attention and her tray became unbalanced and flames engulfed her arm, the floor, everything.

Several men moved in and stomped the fire, tossed their coats over the poor girl. Terry was sitting at the bar, checking his face in the mirror behind the liquor bottles. Everything was moving fast. I was on a shitload of speed and trying to get out of there before the Harbor Lights hit me.

Then, Terry and I started laughing and couldn't stop. He stumbled, fell onto a chair, and smashed it flat under his enormous weight. We laughed even harder. We had a couple broads with us, a couple guys and their girlfriends were coming back to our apartment to do some coke, drink some more, screw, whatever.

We piled into the Pontiac convertible and I wheeled it back to the pad.

The girl I was with was a knockout. She said she was from Russia but I couldn't be sure. She was all tan and dark hair, which I didn't picture as Russian, but she had a perfect accent and her eyes stood out like blue fire. Apparently she had been modeling for several designers. A model… it was possible, but I doubted it just by the way she held herself.

The two of us went over to the couch, spread a line of cocaine on a palm-sized mirror and split it. Someone cranked up the tunes. Terry jumped off the balcony into the pool and several of the guys followed— fully clothed or naked. Neither would have surprised me.

"So, Natalia? You're from Russia, is that right?"

"Yes," she said, edging closer.

There was a thump, a shrieking crash, the sound of wood and metal breaking. The big white door flew onto my lap, smashed my forehead. Natalia screamed, jumped from the couch and rushed into the corner. I stood up, threw the door back at them, and was tackled to the floor. I was removed from the apartment in handcuffs.

5

JAILBIRD

1972

I WAS IN SAN MATEO COUNTY JAIL; A FRESH TURD MAKING HIS WAY through the pipes. The first thing I did was buy some commissary: a few candy bars, toothpaste, several other "luxury" items. I returned to my bunk, shoved the goods beneath my pillow, and headed for the shower. What a shitty day, week, month, damn it...

The cell was about 20 feet wide and 40 feet long. Two showers, two shitters, two sinks, two mirrors, and 30 bunk beds like shelves on the wall. I walked past everything, past all the brothers as they pretended to ignore me. They waited until I wasn't looking to take a good stare, size me up, figure how hard I could be taken advantage of.

The shower sucked. Weak stream, semi-cold, one of those plastic stand-alone units, nothing good about it except that it got me somewhat clean. It was jail, what did I expect?

When I returned to my bunk I found that my commissary items had been stolen. No real surprise. I moved slowly without making too much of it, trying to pretend like nothing happened while I secretly scanned the room and plotted my next move. I knew I needed to act, but act on whom, and with what?

I stood there for a moment soaking in the various scenarios and running my fingers through my hair. I had stopped hiding from confrontations, and for the first time in a few years someone was engaging me in a real brawl. I needed to take my stand against these creeps. I had one shot to take them down and it had to be just right or I'd miss the target and wind up dead or in the hospital.

A voice came from behind me, quiet and deep, directed but dissipating among the others.

"You see the Blood with the red doo-rag on his head? The big one— don't look right now. That's your man." I turned to the bunk above mine, as mine was the middle of three. A thin man was lying there reading. We were the only two whites in the cell and he kept his eyes on the book as he spoke.

"You don't do anything now. You just sit down and act normal. He knows you noticed it, but he figures I was asleep and didn't see him."

I turned slowly and caught a glimpse of the bastard. I leaned against my acquaintance's shoulder-level bunk. The big problem in a place like this is that you never know who you can trust. For instance, how did I know that the old man hadn't taken my stuff?

"I'm Jack Alexander," I said.

Nothing from this guy. He had long greasy hair, like he hadn't been to the shower in six months. He hadn't made his bed and he was fully dressed in his bright orange jumpsuit just like the day he got there, which I would learn had been a month ago. His giant beard was ragged and grey, garnishing his shoulders and chest, which were painted black with tattoos. He was a Hell's Angel.

"How can I get my shit back?"

He took his eyes away from the print like a bothered librarian.

"Take this, Jack." He pulled a tooth brush out of his boot. Funny, he was the only guy in the whole jail allowed to have his boots on; everyone else was issued shower shoes. The brush was sharpened to a point at one end. He slid it deftly toward the edge of his bed. I took it, inserted it vertically into the pocket of my orange jumpsuit sharp end down.

Doo-rag was over there playing cards, no idea what was about to hit him.

"Not now," he said. His hand clasped my shoulder. "You wait until lights out. You take that rig over there and shove it up his nose. Once it's up there you rip it UP as hard as you can." I gulped. "You do that at 10 p.m. after lights out... which will be in a few minutes." He cleared his throat and stretched out. "You better get him good, hard enough so that they drag him outta here." He rolled over as if to go to sleep. "Do it like I said or they'll be on us before midnight." I laid down in my bunk and heard him whisper: "If you don't follow through, you'll have ME to deal with."

*   *   *

I was being tried for hundreds of fictitious checks, multiple counts of theft, fraud, and embezzlement. I was transferred between institutions around the Bay Area to attend court on a regular basis. The days wore on and after a while I began to abandon hope. More than abandoning hope I just forgot it existed and lost sight of the end.

The charges mounted, leaving me to wonder how I'd possibly committed so many crimes. Where had I found the time? It seemed like I was taking the charges for 100 men. No matter, they connected me to even the most obscure locations and dealings.

One of the conditions of each sentencing, no matter the county, was to make full restitution before my release. Restitution, I found, would be extremely costly and virtually impossible to generate.

*   *   *

I had been busted in San Diego, so I started my incarceration in San Diego County Jail, a place called "The Snake Pits."

We were hustled in there like dogs, each man separated, stripped, showered, deloused, forced into a uniform. They handed me a roll of wool bedding and a sheet.

The lone guard strolled me down the barred and crowded hallways.

"You new kids got the penthouse suite," the guard said. He laughed and opened the stairwell door. I read his nametag: BUCK.

"Keep forward! You turn your head around again and I'll smash it."

Buck... I'd remember that guy if the shit hit the fan and I had an opportunity for revenge.

We kept going down and down the stairs. If the smell was any indication, it was shaping up to be a Grade "A" Hellhole. I was at first wondering if we were passing a bathroom, but a few moments later I realized it was the stench of the cells. It wafted up the darkened corridor, hung stagnant among the damp walls of the depths.

"Go on in," the guard said. He shoved me down a ladder. It was dark down there and stank of breath, sweat, bodies, and excrement. It felt like I had entered another world. The temperature changed and the humidity rose. It was cooler down there, and black. The door slammed behind me.

In the center aisle there were shallow puddles of stagnant water, and several men grunted as I stepped on their toes. Several others made no sound at all.

There was nowhere to sit, to put the bedding, to lean against a wall, nothing. It was dark and the bodies seemed to have been piled on top of one another. What the hell was this place?

I finally found a clear spot and used my bedding as a stool, leaning my back against the rounded tunnel walls. Water dripped from every direction. In less than an hour I was sopping wet from sweat and condensation.

"Is this the sewer system?" I asked a man with a long mustache and hair similar to mine. He looked over at me, nodded through no light. "Why are we down here?"

"You from Portland?" His voice was deep, resonated off of the cement.

"No."

"Oh, never mind then."

"Why are we down here?"

"Oh yeah…" He took a long look around. The hours did not collapse in a place like this. Time became a placid beach to the prisoner; he spoke slowly or not at all. "I don't know why you're here, man. I guess this is how they're doing shit now. Too many people to fit 'em upstairs."

"Is this the sewer system?"

"Yeah. They blocked it off, shoved bars onto the ends of the pipe. There are several tunnels stuffed full of these guys." He nodded around at our company. Virtually everyone was a Mexican immigrant, probably illegal aliens.

"I see…"

"That's why they don't give a damn about the conditions."

I closed my eyes and prepared for a long stay

*   *   *

Usually a man will fight extradition like there's an alligator on his leg. This case was different. I used my extradition to get me out of the

Snake Pit. Several detectives came and picked me up, drove me to the air-port. I had been down there for only about three weeks.

"It's a nice day to fly," one of them said. His nametag read BILLY. I could hear their conversation through the chain between the front and back seat. I was sitting upright, my wrists aching behind my back and my knees cramped against the metal divider.

"Hey, Billy, you wanna loosen these cuffs up or what?"

The driver picked at his teeth with a toothpick.

"You see the Dodgers game?" Billy asked the driver.

"No."

"Dodgers won. Pretty good game."

"You know I don't follow baseball. Not a New York team anyway."

"Yeah. Just a way to pass time, I guess..." Good old Detective Billy, a sad sort with a single-story house in Rohnert Park and two kids halfway through school and the wife in and out of the nuthouse. He car-ried the .45 to work every day and she moaned about making peanut butter sandwiches.

We took a PSA jet, the same ones I'd taken when coming back from Mexico sales trips. I laughed quietly to myself as a familiar stewardess poured drinks for the dicks. Wait a second... I gave her a long look. It was Heidi, the girl from Phoenix who had come back to my room. She noticed me sitting there: long hair, beard, a grim smile. She pretended not to recognize me.

I must have stunk like hell; worse than anything most people had ever smelled. And even with the stench they sat me in Coach like I was Joe Shmo vacationer.

*　　*　　*

I was housed in the West Block of San Quentin State Prison. The men in West Block were mostly angry parole violators who had been picked up and brought back inside for something trivial. It wasn't a bad spot compared to the Snake Pit. In fact, San Quentin was paradise compared to a wet hole in the ground.

West Block was segregated into three basic groups: La Familia, Black Panthers, and Hell's Angels. I was white and therefore gravitated toward the Angels.

Rick Moss, my old toothbrush buddy from San Mateo County Jail, introduced me to Bennie. Bennie had a swastika tattooed on his fore-head. Both he and Rick were Club Members, and both had decent pull.

I spent some time doing my homework and watched the way those guys acted in the yard, at the weight pile, in the cell block.

The days moved by slowly at first, but with time they melded into one another and I soon forgot how terrible conditions had become. The outlandish became commonplace and my affiliation with the Members was legitimized through Bennie. He and I worked out together, ran, lifted, did pushups after dinner, that sort of thing. In prison, friends were the only thing that held me back from the final, hopeless, depraved charge at the razor wire.

*   *   *

I was watching prison baseball one day, milling on the bleachers with a crew of guys. One of the guys was from Death Row; he had recently been converted to a Lifer. I had lifted with him once in the Lower Yard, but had never known what he was in for. Still didn't, for that matter; just knew it was bad enough that they had planned on burying him.

We sat there watching the game.

"You see they got the hand-me-down jerseys from the pros?" he asked. He was an older guy. I pictured him with a long chute of wheat sticking out of his mouth on the high seat of a John Deere tractor. He was tall, not quite as tall as me, but up there around 6'2".

"I noticed. They look good," I said.

"That's what those boys need. It keeps 'em motivated."

"Yeah."

"They look like champs out there." He spoke despondently, I guess because he had been on his way out for so long. Every sentence was formed like it could be his last.

"It's bothersome to see you young guys in here."

I didn't say anything.

"You're what, 25?"

"26."

"Yeah..." We watched the game. "You know, Jack, I hurt a man real bad once, back when I was your age. I think it followed me. I think things like that follow anyone who does them."

Again, there was nothing to say.

"I got him with a broken beer bottle right in the eyes. Both eyes. Bam. That was it." He moved the hair from in his face. "I think that man's still on me for that. Like a living ghost or something, if he's still alive." The laughter of men on the ball field washed over the bleachers. "You ever hurt a man like that?"

"I stabbed a guy up his nose with a sharpened toothbrush once."

He nodded. The ball game rolled on.

"How long you been with the HA's?" I asked him.

"Oh, about seven years. Give or take. How about you?"

"Since I got here, basically."

"Yeah... a lot of times that's the way it happens."

"Yup."

"You wonder sometimes if it's real, you know? If there's really anything after all this shit. You hear 'em talking about life after death... sounds like an oxymoron to me." He adjusted himself on the bleachers, leaned back and took in the whole scene. "Life ain't nothing worth crying over." He spit. "I expect I'd do just as good as a rock on the hillside as I would a man in the cell."

Someone cracked off a line drive. Dust flew, men hustled around the giant diamond. The Earth flew through space and we sat on the bleachers staring at the San Quentin water tower propped and silhouetted against the barbed wire sun.

Thinking: a man is nothing more than a rock on the hillside.

*　　*　　*

"You know, Bennie, I don't think I'm normal."

"What do you mean?" He looked back at me, removed the 45-pound weight that had been strapped around his waist.

"I mean... I just don't know if I think like everyone else."

"Maybe you're insane," he said, not joking at all.

"Yeah. I'm going to ask someone about my head. I think I need to get it checked." I felt strange, on edge, wild. All this time away from booze had shocked me into semi-understanding of the depraved workings of my mind.

I spoke with someone about it. One of the doctors believed me, I guess because it was true, and I was sent to California Medical Facility in Vacaville for psychological evaluation.

*　　*　　*

The good people at Vacaville determined that I was, in fact, a crazy person. It wasn't that I was drooling all over myself or smashing my head against the walls; no, I wasn't crazy in the normal sense of the word. The doctors gave me a new label, one that I had never expected to hear. I was diagnosed as a "Criminal Genius." They offered little help for this problem other than prison.

And it wasn't a good idea to give a guy like me a title like that. No matter how repentant he was (and I wasn't repentant in the first place) calling him a Criminal Genius gave him a new lease on life, new confidence to walk out there and take over the world... one bad check at a time.

I was kept in Vacaville for a weeklong "surveillance period," during which time I got to know several lunatics who lived in the cells surrounding me. My roommate was a 350-pound monster serial killer who had the brain of a four-year-old. It was scary, but he left me alone for the most part. I just kept saying really nice things to him all the time and he stayed to himself.

There were guys in there who were too messed up to read their own case files, so I took it upon myself to help them. I read maybe six or seven cases, advised the guys on what to do. I wrote letters to their attorneys and requested that their cases be reopened.

Right before I left, one of the crazy men handed me a thick, quarter-sized piece of metal. I took it in my hand and studied it carefully, unsure at first what it could be. It was a ring; a stainless steel ring. It had been fashioned from a nut taken from one of the cell doors.

"How the hell did you get that thing off?"

"Time," the man said. It must have taken a week of loosening it up with his bare hands or his heels. Then, after that, he had rubbed it smooth on one side so that it wouldn't be abrasive to the wearer's hand. It looked good, really good. I felt a sense of honor that those men had taken so much time to put together a gift for me. It was at least a two-week process to make a ring like that. Grinding down the nut on smooth cement, getting it even, polishing it on metal and then on fabric.

I put it on, balled my hand into a fist, and the man gave me a hug. Sure, I'd helped him with his case, but the gift meant more to me than he realized. Certain things about prison don't make sense unless you're there.

*   *   *

I went to a work release facility and was transferred to someplace down south near San Jose. After a couple months at that place, working hard labor each day, I was transferred to a sister institution where I was forced to find a real, "outside-the-walls" job.

Somehow my father, the man I least expected, came to my aid. I received a letter detailing his plans to help me pay my restitution fees and get me back on my feet. Through some of his connections he got me what he considered a "good job" working the night shift at the Kaiser Hospital.

Each evening I would leave the work release institution and head to Kaiser dressed in my blue janitorial outfit. The hospital was quiet, except for the ER, where the Mexican janitors and I spent hours each night mopping up puddles of blood from the surgeries.

One night we were in there, in the surgery room or whatever, taking a squeegee to the blood and guts, when I heard the abnormally fast rattling of stretcher wheels. The head nurse shouted: "The material seems to be rubber, Doctor!" That's when the thing clattered past the doorway, IV tubes in tow, a man on his belly naked and moaning, arms writhing and gripping the nurse's wrist. None of the Mexicans spoke English, so when the nurse said, "And Doctor, the shaft must be 14 inches long! And that's the part that's still inserted!" nobody laughed but me.

Sure, some nights in the hospital were amusing. But that didn't make them tolerable. I've heard even the Nazis found ways to laugh. True stuff: a man could go stark raving mad if he kept a straight face and let the reality of imprisonment stab him in the gut. Every now and then bits of anxiety would sneak through my guard, but less and less with time. Or maybe I just felt it less and less. Either way.

I had revelations late at night in the Kaiser Hospital. I often spoke them aloud because none of my co-workers understood English.

I would be cleaning, saying things to myself like, "I'm Jack Alexander, the notorious stolen jewelry salesman, airplane thief, trickster... a professional con artist. It's still me standing here, mopping up this shit. It's the same guy who three years ago blew 50 grand a month on whatever he wanted, usually shit he used only once. I'm just not rich anymore... I'm the ex-millionaire from San Francisco, the EX-badass who dated waitresses from Zipples and had one night stands with airline stewardesses."

Sure, I had lost most of my important titles, but the boys at Vacaville had given me my new label, a different but not altogether unimpressive identity. I was now the Criminal Genius of San Quentin. I liked that title.

And there I was, completely under the radar: a quiet young man cleaning up some doctor's failed attempt at open heart surgery.

Damn if I hadn't seen some horrible shit.

6

STINSON BEACH

1974

PAT AND I WERE STANDING IN MY PARENT'S GARAGE IN SAN MATEO
County drinking glasses of orange juice and thumbing through our
life stories. Pat was still young, around 23 or so, which made me 27.

"What's your plan?" he asked.

"Stick it out here, I guess."

We stood side by side, about 2 feet apart, facing our new room on
the back of the garage. I was trying to figure out how the hell Dad
thought we'd be able to live in there after all those years on our own.

"Dad picked you up at the jail?"

"Yeah."

"How was that?"

"Alright. What more can I ask?"

"Yeah."

"That was lucky. It was nice of him," Pat said.

"Yeah."

He looked at me hard. "So, what are your plans, man?" I could sense
that he wanted to latch on.

"I just answered that. What are you talking about?" I was irritable, in need of a good drink—something I hadn't had in a couple of years.

"I mean, what do you plan on doing with your life?"

"I work at the Kaiser Hospital, Pat. I'm a janitor. I signed away my life to the Parole Board and 'promised' them that I wouldn't look for another job."

"That's horse shit."

"What isn't?"

"So it's the justice system that's screwed you?"

"In its own twisted, unintentional, backhanded way... yeah." I killed the orange juice, reached into mine and Pat's fridge and grabbed two Green Meanies.

"You're smart enough to get a better job than the hospital, Jack."

"It's not like you gotta tell ME that." I shook my head at the situation, the futility of my predicament. "Nobody hires ex-cons. They just don't do it."

"True."

The neighbor was mowing his lawn. The hum grew louder, then quieter, then louder as he drove right next to our wall. Great location...

"What have you been doing for the past few years, Pat?" I downed half the beer in just a few pulls.

"Same old. Working with Fenster. Tax fraud's brought him down a lot. I was up and down the coast driving merch. You know the deal."

"That guy never sent me my money." I shook my head. "I don't really care anymore. I guess we all had it bad for a while."

"He was on the edge of losing the business when you call from San Diego. He did the best he could. He's really not a bad guy." Leave it to my brother to be duped just like I was.

"You're fine with moving back here?" I pointed to the sheetrock walls, the 2x4 rafters, my parent's garage, our new home.

"I don't know. I'm fine with whatever as long as I don't end up in jail," he said.

"Yeah..."

The conversation dried up. There's not much to talk about when you're fresh out of prison working as a janitor and living in your parent's garage with your younger brother.

*　　*　　*

Terry and I rented an apartment in the Fisherman's Wharf area, moved a bunch of furniture in, and began using the spare bedroom as a headquarters for our new company, Papillion Productions International. We had plans to hold rock concerts for bands affiliated with Biker Clubs, and with the connections we had in the San Francisco area— Hell's Angels, conmen, businessmen, you name it—Papillion Production's success wasn't a matter of IF so much as HOW, WHEN, and for how much MONEY.

"I got a great connection in New York, Jack. If you're interested in talking to him we could fly out there," Terry said.

"Eh… we'll see." Terry had never been much of a businessman but I figured maybe we could give it a shot. I was tired of doing all the work and maybe this would show Terry something about how to take control of a situation. Terry had been working for a telecommunications company in San Francisco and had applied for a job in Hawaii. He kept joking about us moving to the island if he got hired. It was a possibility, but I never saw any reason why a man would want to leave the continental United States. Life is about opportunities and outlets, not being trapped on a rock.

*   *   *

Some patient in the ER had lost a limb and I was on disposal duty. There was this bag in the corner of the room—this giant white trashcan covered in blood and a thick white plastic bag inside of it. The bag was opaque; opaque because we all knew what was in there. It was that guy's ARM.

Yeah… I don't think I ever went back to Kaiser Hospital after that. Just sort of faded away… again…

*   *   *

The folks at Oakland Coliseum were interested in working with Papillion Productions. Papillion, by the way, was the name of a '73 prison movie starring Steve McQueen. It was about a guy locked up off the coast of South America for a murder he didn't commit. Horrible conditions, near death, crocodiles, solitary confinement, bad shit any way you looked at it. Anyway, I thought the irony was too perfect to ignore.

Terry and I flew to New York City and met with Dan Poindexter about lining up another show. The three of us met at Friday's. It was the original Friday's, the one at First Avenue and 63rd Street. I hadn't been there in several years. It was in the neighborhood of so many good places I used to frequent when working for Lacy's. Places like Adam's Apple, Maxwell's Plum, The Palm, and a few other pick-up joints. Friday's was on the other side of the town from our flea-bag hotel. What the hell, Terry and I couldn't be too picky at that point.

Dan's connections were sounding less and less impressive as the ride back from dinner wore on. Dan was the sleazy type, also very sloppy. He wore a thin gold necklace, fake watch, overly gelled hair, and smiled too much. Terry told me that Dan had a reputation half-ass hustler. It was just like Terry to know this about someone and not tell me until we flew all the way across the country to meet him.

Dan had a girl in the cab with us from Friday's.

"So, who are your friends?" she asked Dan.

I smiled, flipped her a business card. I had been waiting to hand one of the new cards out. She liked the name Papillion Productions. She said it reminded her of the movie. I told her that Papillion was my father's name, that it had nothing to do with the movie.

We bullshitted for a few minutes and then she and Dan made out while Terry and I discussed the rainy weather, our business prospects, the plans for booking a gig at Madison Square Garden, etc.

I had to pay the driver because Dan, as it turned out, was a cheapskate and had "left his wallet in the room."

It was cold and I was wearing a trench coat, a cap, carrying no umbrella. My luggage was minimal, all of it fitting inside one large briefcase. I also carried a business briefcase filled with the Papillion papers. I peeled off a few bills and gave the driver a tip.

A Rolls glided past, a blonde running her mouth in the back seat. I don't know why, but I thought about Gaye Squires. Damn, what a girl. Where had she gone? I had never resolved that thing with the rental car that I'd left parked in Tampa. Or had I? Probably Hertz just charged me for the whole car and more than likely I paid it off without realizing it. I chuckled just thinking about it. Those were the good old days.

But what had happened to Gaye? I hadn't heard from her in what felt like eons. I'd been down to her place about a month before I was incarcerated. She was living in a trailer near Tampa and I hadn't stayed very long. After a while she turned a bit crazy and started demanding more and more of my time. It wasn't money she wanted; no, she'd never had any money. She wanted ME (for some stupid reason). The whole relationship sprung a leak and I abandoned ship.

I thought about my old girlfriends while the Rolls cruised past and the bad parts of New York City got worse and the rain began to soak through to my scalp.

"You boys ready to go upstairs or what?" Dan asked, huddled beside his chick. She was decent looking, but what was the big idea? Who gave a damn about pretty girls at a time like that? We were out to make Papillion Productions a success, to schedule a gig at The Garden, not to flip-flap around the city with a halfway–decent-looking drunk hard body golddigger. There was no time for these sorts of antics, yet somehow Dan Poindexter found ways to indulge.

I was in the bathroom shaving, the dank humidity from the shower hanging heavy with the door closed. I could hear Terry and Dan out there laughing. They were messing with the girl. Not having sex with her, but probably coming close. She didn't mind. She was egging them on. Some girls enjoy that sort of thing; especially the types that go back to hotel rooms with strangers at 6 p.m. and lie on the bed drinking straight liquor.

After a while it became apparent that this chick thought she was going to get paid for messing with them. It was apparent to me, anyway. Terry and Dan hadn't picked up on it. I remained in the bathroom getting ready, altogether uninterested in fooling around with a semi-hooker. I figured that they'd pay her 100 bucks and that would be that. I would rag on them about it for a while and it would be forgotten. Big deal.

An hour passed and we went downstairs, the four of us, and hailed a cab to the bar. We were planning on hitting Max's Kansas City, one of the craziest nightclubs in town. I figured that maybe we'd be able to make some REAL connections for Papillion.

"John!" Terry yelled. I went by John Rison whenever I was with Papillion clients. The name change was to protect myself in case the company was ever placed under scrutiny by the IRS, the Feds, a weary customer, bounty hunter, etc.

Terry kept yelling my name.

"What?" I was annoyed with them by now, all three of them, for piddling around in the hotel for so long.

"The chick's not coming to the bar. She wants money. You got some money on you?"

"Hell no, I don't have any money! Why the hell would I pay that girl even if I did?"

"Look," he turned to the chick, grabbed her hands like he was telling a kindergartener goodbye on the first day of school. "It was nice, but we'll have to catch up with you some other time. Goodbye." Terry turned and headed for my cab.

The girl was livid, began screaming at us. The cab hummed off and we were gone.

"Stupid decision to talk to that girl in the first place," I muttered.

"Lighten up, John."

"Just listen to me from now on. When I tell you we're here on business, it means we're here on business. At the club you can do whatever you want." I stared out the window. "You have to learn to play it straight sometimes in order to get shit done."

*　　*　　*

Max's Kansas City was something out of a damn Rock Star's bathroom magazine. There were chicks everywhere, tons of booze and drugs, loud music, all sorts of crooks and millionaires. I felt right at home.

I ordered up a vodka rocks, took a seat at the bar, laid low for a few minutes and surveyed the scene. It was good to be back in the ballgame, away from the San Quentin water tower, the Snake Pit, the endless river of county jails and courtrooms. I sipped at the vodka slowly, precisely, like the glaring and cautious Russian, in no hurry to make a move or not to make one.

Here I was, a month out of the slammer, free from hard time, my own man again. I was the president of a production company. Things were shaping up. I was crouched and ready to make another hard uppercut at the world's jaw.

I lit up an Antonio Y Cleo, tried to look as uninterested in women as possible. The old plan worked. Sure enough, a chick came right up and took the stool beside me.

"People don't sit in this bar alone, buddy," she joked.

"What do they do?" I said, turning my head away from her, implying that I didn't see very much going on.

"You wanna dance?"

"Not really. No."

"Come on."

"Give me a break. Can I buy you a drink or something?"

She took what I was having and moved in real close beside me. The ancient methods of attracting women were simple as butter on bread if only you knew how to hold your cool. They call it "having the touch." And I guess I had it.

"I'm Valerie."

"I'm John."

"What do you do for a living?"

"I'm the president of a production company. Papillion Productions International."

"That's cool." She was a beautiful girl with tan skin, deep brunette hair, and eyes that sparkled in the neon bar lights. She had a small smile and outgoing gestures. It was like she had been the center of attention her entire life and knew how to take it modestly.

"So, you from around here?"

"I've lived here about a year," she said.

"What do you do?" I asked, making sure not to stare at her too long.

"I dance," she said. I chuckled through a mouth of ice. "Not like THAT!" she laughed, slapping me. "I'm a dance instructor."

Valerie was my third brunette in just two weeks of freedom. Not bad. Not bad at all.

*   *   *

At 3 a.m. the call came from the front desk that the police were downstairs and wanted to speak with me.

"Is this Mr. John Rison... of San Francisco?" The front desk asked through the crackling phone line. I went on down there, drunk as the next guy, and there were police in the lobby. Terry and Dan were with me.

One of the cops flashed my business card as if to say, "Yeah, John, we caught ya." Then there were handcuffs and all three of us were in the back of a cop car.

"On what grounds are we being detained? What's the charge?" Terry shouted, his giant body barely fitting in the cramped space.

"Rape, you freaks," the cop growled.

"Give me a break, man! No one even got CLOSE to that dirty—" The door came crashing shut, It was me, Terry, and Dan Poindexter all riding in the back of some jarhead's squad car with pictures of his kids playing baseball on the dashboard and a tactical shotgun vertical between the two front seats.

The street lights reeled by like a movie, like I was watching the car from the outside and violin music was playing.

Goodbye, Valerie... while you're still passed out in my bed, me and the boys are on the way to the station to be thrown into the hole, showered, printed, booked, housed, harassed, dicked around for the next 30 years.

What the hell was new?

*   *   *

They called it Manhattan Detention District South, or "The Tombs." And I'll be damned if they weren't right on the money when they came up with that one.

Terry and Dan Poindexter had rolled over on me. They had given me up in exchange for freedom. Terry spoke to me on the phone, tried to convince me that he'd been loyal.

"She had the John Rison business card, man. You gave it to her in the cab, remember? It was hard evidence."

"But I didn't even TOUCH her!"

"There was nothing we could do. She said it was you."

Bullshit. I knew he was lying but I didn't care enough to argue about it.

I was back in the cell doing pushups, staring slanted down the long hallway by smashing my forehead against the bars. My cellmate was black and I don't think he understood a word I said. I didn't understand him either, but sometimes we spoke just to hear the sound of our own voices.

"I'm not going to make it out of this one," I said. He stared at the ceiling from on his back. "They'll figure out who I am once they finish running the prints. The fake name won't last. It's all a farce, man. All bullshit. I'm headed up the river...to Attica... 30 years at least. I'll be 57 by the time I get out. IF I get out..."

He didn't respond. We ticked the time away and away and away.

*   *   *

I listened complacently as the judge commenced the preliminary hearing for the bullshit rape charges. The police hadn't done a full background check yet. Everyone still assumed that my phony ID's were real. They had no idea that I had skipped parole in California and was operating under a fake identity. I needed to get acquitted before the trial or else the fingerprint search would come back. If they found out who I really was they would lock me up forever.

"John Rison, please approach the bench." I went on up there, placed my hands firmly on the long wooden railing and stared up at the judge. The girl was there—the hooker or whatever she called herself.

The proceedings continued with her crying, screaming, changing her story each time my court-appointed attorney asked her a question.

"Your Honor, Ms. Ratcliff has responded differently to the same question all three times it has been asked. Her testimony is shoddy at best."

"Objection!" the District Attorney shouted. The courtroom remained silent except for the bustling feet of late arrivals being turned away by the bailiff. The judge waved off the DA and continued to listen. For a court appointed, this guy wasn't half bad.

"Your Honor, we have evidence of past accusations by Ms. Ratcliff that fall directly in line with the accusations presented against Mr. Rison. All previous charges were dropped for lack of compelling evidence. I ask that these charges be dropped for the same reason."

The judge turned to Hooker Ratcliff. "So, how do you explain the absence of semen post-incident?"

"I don't know! I guess he didn't FINISH in me!"

The judge stared, disgusted. I think he actually cringed at her. "How do you explain, Ms. Ratcliff, the previous incidents where you have alleged rape and the accused was found innocent?"

"Your court system SUCKS!"

"That language will not be tolerated, Ms. Ratcliff." The judge went through several papers. The Hooker cried, sobbed, slapped her hand against the wooden bench. The judge was not jarred by her antics and continued flipping casually through the folders of evidence, statements, whatever.

"Mr. Rison, please stand." I stood. "John Rison, the State of New York hereby finds you innocent of all charges presented. You are free to go." I shook my lawyer's hand. Ms. Hooker Ratcliff screamed.

"Look at him and look at you," the judge said to the girl. "You think I believe that a young, successful, good looking businessman needed to rape a girl like you? There are too many holes in your story." The judge turned to me. "Mr. Rison you will need to appear in this courtroom in 30 days to have the case formally dismissed and your record expunged. You are free to go. Thank you."

If I were to come back in 30 days I'd be coming back for 30 years. One more week in that town and the fingerprints would return from California; a direct match to Jack Alexander, former inmate at...

I did what any sane man would have done: I hit the road south.

*   *   *

Terry, Dan, and I took off in Dan's Oldsmobile junker from New York State to Wilmington, Delaware, then on to Rehoboth Beach.

I didn't know Rehoboth all that well but had heard it was a party town, a place where a few guys could blend in without being questioned by the locals. We arrived totally unsettled and out of our minds; worst of all, we were on a limited supply of cash.

Papillion had crashed. Dead. The End.

We got a hotel room right on the beach and Terry and I tallied our losses. The plan was to hit the bars, but first we needed clothing. We took what little money we had and scrounged up some shirts, some new shoes, things that could keep us on track for the first night.

We made a long, slow drive up the beach and stopped at one of the larger bars. Dan was drunk and high in the backseat singing along to the radio. I let it go and parked the car.

Nobody in the bar had a face. Everybody stared at us sullenly and crowded around their friends like wolves. There seemed to be mist hanging over the lights, something eerie was floating everywhere but I couldn't place it. I got strange vibes, the same vibes you get from being in jail. Jail messed with your head. Any gathering of people automatically reminded you of something from the yard.

I played my old game and took a lone stool at the bar. I drained a fast shot. Terry began yakking at some chick on the dance floor and I kept ordering vodka rocks until I'd had about three. Then a girl with really long hair came up and sat beside me, running her arms around my shoulders and leaning in real close.

"My boyfriend's a dickhead," she said.

I nodded.

After a few quiet moments she spoke. "You wanna come back to my place and have a few drinks? This bar sucks."

We left, taking the car without telling the guys. Bingo.

*   *   *

I spent the rest of my time on "vacation" shacking up with various women, all of whom I met at the Rehoboth Beach bars. Terry, Dan, and I lost touch during everything and we met up back at the hotel some weeks later. We drove back to SFO in Dan's junker. I was afraid of the airports anyway, and with no money to charter a plane I felt better on the road.

Back in San Francisco, Pat was finally owning up to his responsibilities. He had cleaned out the Fisherman's Wharf apartment the day I was released in NYC so that no one could piece together where we had been staying. Five days later, the cops had stormed the place and found no prints, no documents, no money, nothing. When we arrived back at the apartment there was hardly anything left other a few old letters. The cops had forgotten to clean out the mailbox each day and so had Pat. From the looks of things the apartment was still vacant. We grabbed some papers from the box and hit the road.

I stopped at a payphone and called a few numbers looking for my brother. No one knew anything about where he was. I hadn't heard from him since New York, since he called to tell me that he'd cleaned out the apartment.

Terry thumbed through the giant stack of envelopes as we drove south.

"Hey, man!" he shouted excitedly. I glanced over from the driver's seat as he opened an envelope from some company. "Look at that! I got the job in Hawaii. They want me to fly out there as soon as I can."

"That's great, Terry." I said dryly, focusing on the freeway and lighting one of my cigars.

"This is awesome, man. Hawaii! I'll be set for life." He laughed. I kept on driving and we headed south, far south of the city, down to Fenster's new place.

When we got there Greg answered the door in a pair of sweatpants and a t-shirt. I hadn't seen him in a few years and he looked a bit worse for the wear.

"You still at Imporium?" I asked.

"Lost that job a long time ago. Thought you knew that?"

"Maybe I did. I don't remember. How's Pacific American?"

"I had to sell the other house. This one's not as nice." He turned and looked up at his house from the front doorstep. "The pigs raided the Trans-America office. I set up shop in my house. I do all the work from here. There's not much work these days..." Greg seemed different now, like he was tired of the business. He was getting old. I could see the creases from stress in the fragile skin around his eyes..

"You seen my brother any?"

"Pat? Hell no. I heard he's up in San Mateo living with one of the strippers that used to work the orgies over at the Byrd House."

"Yeah, I heard the same thing," I said, mildly disgusted.

Fenster's face was tired and I knew that he didn't feel like talking. The way he slugged a beer you could tell he needed it more like medicine than anything else.

"So the business is done?" I asked

"It was all tax problems. They started uncovering my shit and then, BAM, the whole company collapsed."

"I'm sorry."

"At least I didn't get sent up the river like you did."

"Eh, it's alright."

"Can I help you out with anything? I don't have much money, but I can spare a bit."

"How about some money for drinks? I'm not trying to start any stuff around here, just wanna head to the bar for a night. I know a place I can go where I can find a rich girl." I laughed.

"You gonna get another girl to take care of you?"

"There's nothing wrong with that. They got extra money." Fenster laughed at me. We stood on his front porch looking out at the street and the rest of the suburbs.

"Jane doesn't live too far from here," I said. "A nicer area, but not far."

"Jane's got herself another man, Jack."

"I figured as much."

"She didn't write you?"

"She did. I think she left that part out. She sent me ONE picture. My own damn WIFE."

"What can you do. You guys weren't really married anymore. You knew that."

"Mhmm." I shook my head.

"Bet the cops are knocking her door down every day," he said.

"Probably will be at it again once this trace comes back and they find out I was in New York on trial for rape." We laughed. I had mentioned the charges to him on the phone. Anyone who knew me knew I wasn't a rapist. The whole thing was a laugh.

"Yeah, anyway, Jane lives with that rich old codger. They've got a house somewhere down near the beach." He pointed southwest.

"I see." We looked off in that direction, as though we could see 50 miles through the houses, buildings, trees, shopping malls. "You need help with anything, Greg?"

"No. Forget about me. You're welcome to stay here for a while if you need it. My place isn't much, but it beats the street."

"You know me, Greg. I don't end up on the street."

"Times are getting rough for guys like us."

"Yeah, well... you gotta adapt to the climate."

"So, Terry's going to Hawaii?"

"Yeah."

"Why don't you go with him?"

"I'm thinking about it. I'm on the run... I don't know if hopping on a jet in the San Francisco airport is really the best idea."

"Never stopped you before."

"True enough."

He fiddled around in his wallet, took out three C-notes. "It's all I can spare. Buy yourself some drinks, whatever you want. Find a girl to take care of you and give me a call if there's anything else you need."

"I will." I took the money and folded it carefully into my pocket. In my mind I was called back to that cold winter day in the parking deck at the Imporium, our hands shaking firmly through leather gloves.

The old dialogue echoed in my head, "Is this some kind of sick date idea, Fenster?" We laughed. Without Greg where would I be? Probably still at Imporium and probably still married to a millionaire. Now look at me...

"Stay clear of the police, Jack. You and I both know they'll put you away for good next time."

"Yeah," I said. I hoped that maybe I'd never see him again.

*　　*　　*

I was joking with the three girls at the table, slapping my second bill down for another round of drinks. I had $100 left. One more bill to make this night work. Which girl would it be? I couldn't decide. I reached into my pocket, felt around for a tab of speed. It was Black Beauty Speed, the only stuff that could keep me focused.

I tipped it back secretively. The bartender brought me some change. Usually I wouldn't have taken it, but I was on my last leg and had to stretch the dough. Without money I risked losing my position at the table and in turn losing my ability to go home with one of the girls.

The bar was owned by some of the San Francisco 49er's football players, and through the grapevine I'd found out that one of their girlfriends was at my table. I paid special attention to her, giving her one of my Beauties and buying her double shots of tequila.

The speed kicked me in the ass. I was in high gear and it was early, only around 11 p.m. I was jittery, pulsing with adrenaline, but outwardly I remained calm and relaxed.

"How about another shot!" I slid one toward her.

"You trying to get me drunk, cowboy?" she asked.

"I just like to share."

She leaned over and kissed me. Things were progressing and I could feel the speed working on my brain, gearing me up for the drive back to her house or a hotel, wherever.

I was on the way to the pisser when Terry came up. "Hey Jack, that chick lives with one of the 49er's. You need to watch out."

"I know who she is, Cupcake. Just keep cool. I'm working on something."

"I just met an old friend of mine. I got a place we can stay in the city. You wanna crash there tonight?"

"No."

"He might have some chicks over."

"Eh, tempting, but no."

"Where are you going?"

"Probably to this chick's house."

"Even though she's dating a professional football player?"

"Yeah, Terry. You should get a girl and come with us."

"I'm not going home with some chick that's tied up to a millionaire linebacker."

"The boys are away with the team right now. It's the best time."

"You're crazy."

"Grow some balls, kid."

*   *   *

Terry took off to Hawaii for his job. I remained on the mainland at Stinson Beach, a bit north of the Bay Area, living with Barbara Wherry. We were staying in her boyfriend's house, a million-dollar beachfront villa with a pool, hot tub, cobblestone driveway, professionally manicured lawn, rock sculptures, all the good stuff.

She was bored, tired, lonely, the same symptoms as everybody else. The relationship with the NFL jock would have never worked if he hadn't been worth millions. I guess that's why they pay those guys so much.

I asked her if she was with him for the money or what.

"He's got an aura. Pro athletes have an aura."

"Just like a rock star, eh?"

"You've got an aura."

"I guess we all do."

"See, it's not just money."

"But there are good auras and bad ones."

"You've got a bad one but I like it."

"Yeah. How about all this stuff?" I pointed around at the house. "Does IT have an aura?"

She laughed, shook her head. "My mom told me that money couldn't buy happiness. All I wanted was a chance to test her advice."

"What'd you find out?"

"I don't know. She was right and wrong all at the same time."

"Yeah...."

"What makes you happy?"

I took a sip of vodka and a drag from the cigar. She slept and I looked out over the ocean, stared off toward Japan or whatever rich and lonely stiffs were around the other side of the planet getting ready to wake up with the light from my sunset.

An old saying came to mind: "It is darkest just before dawn."

It was.

*   *   *

I abstained from stealing any vehicles in the San Francisco area because I thought that perhaps my face had been plastered on dealership walls. It was possible that I was a marked man, and there was no sense risking a collar when Barbara was more than willing to let me drive her husband's "extra" Cadillac Fleetwood.

I tooled that behemoth down to the city, a good little drive on five shots of Stoly, to the pharmacy. I walked to the back of the pharmacy, leaned over the desk casually. A young woman approached me, smiling.

"What can I do for you, sir?"

"I need to have an emergency epileptic card made."

"Alright. Would you like your photo included on the card?"

"That would be great."

"Come on back." She took me into the rear of the pharmacy, past the aisles and aisles of prescription drugs that would all inevitably end up inside somebody's stomach. I eyed a few of the names. I wasn't into that stuff like some people.

"Sit here, please." I took a seat. She snapped a photo. There was some question about my risk level. I made up an answer. It must have sounded correct because she nodded, filled something out, and handed me a clipboard.

"Fill in your personal information." She left me back there in the chair, alone with all those drugs. I filled everything out and a few minutes later she came back, took the clipboard, and entered the information into a machine. Two minutes later she handed me the ID card.

Carver, Jay Lee
EPILEPTIC
Prone to Epileptic Seizures
If you find this person in a state of illness
please contact emergency services immediately.
Do NOT attempt to perform aid.

           *   *   *

"It's been good Barb, but my time here's up."

"I don't want you to leave! Let's go get lunch first."

"No can do, Honey. Gotta go right now. I got all sorts of shit to do in the city and it can't wait. The driver's already out there."

"Alright…"

I took the money she'd given me and got into the back of her husband's Cadillac. The driver drove me south toward the city.

"You like Mahler?" he asked.

"I don't really listen to classical," I said. He had something in the tape deck. I let it play without protesting.

"Whadda we gotta go to the library for?" he asked. He was an older guy, thick hands and a hook nose. He stared out over the wheel. He kept very cool eyes but they were glazed. I stared at him for a while, studying all the deep scars on his face. Who was this guy?

"I need to take care of some personal business." I cleared my throat. "Late fees."

"Oh, late fees, eh?" He nodded. "I used to spend a lot of time in libraries."

"Oh yeah?"

"Yeah. I read all of it."

"Oh yeah?"

"Yeah. I used to go in and just sit there and read every day. I didn't like the kids I went to school with."

I was silent, watched the ocean go past, then the trees.

"I used to get these giant boils all over my body—HUGE boils, man. Everywhere. I had to go to the hospital for it. Kids made fun of me. Shitty time."

I studied his scars.

"Where are you from?" I asked, trying to change the subject.

"L,A. Ever heard of it?" He laughed. I could smell wine in the car. Strong, deep, rich, cheap wine. It smelled as if it had been poured like syrup all over him.

"I've heard of L.A.," I joked.

"Yeah… Harness season's coming up." He turned up the tape, a German woman belted and he hummed along out of key.

"Harness season?" I shouted from the back seat. The radio was blasting.

"Horses. Don't worry about it. Never mind. Night harness racing. It's sort of my thing." He swerved across several lanes.

"You been a driver for long?"

"No. Never done it before. I'm filling in for some guy. Sick or something. I don't know."

"I see." He didn't look much like a driver. Didn't talk much like one. He had pretty hands, soft but calloused, veiny but thick-skinned and long.

"So you're leaving the legs or what?" he shouted.

"The legs?"

"Your girl. That thing up there. The one in the stockings."

"Yeah, I'm leaving her."

"She's married isn't she?"

"Beats me," I lied.

"Yeah, I think she is. She seemed like a prude, like someone hadn't laid it on her in a while."

I was silent.

"You laid it on her, right?" he asked.

"Something like that."

"How about we stop for a beer?"

"I don't have time."

"I got a bottle of port under there." He gestured toward the passenger seat. "All yours if you want a slug."

"No thanks."

"Alright. Suit yourself." He kept staring out at the road, contemplating the music or the world or something more than just driving.

"You're driving me all day, is that right?" I asked.

"As long as you're paying me all day."

"I thought she already paid you?"

"I'm kidding."

We were quiet. The car rolled along.

He sighed, turned down the music a notch at the end of a symphony or whatever it was called. He looked in the mirror, those sparkling and glassy eyes penetrating my soul. "Beautiful women are just like beautiful daydreams. Neither seem to last very long."

"I'd agree with that."

"It's a war out there." He pointed to the city, the San Francisco skyline from the Golden Gate Bridge.

"Who's winning?"

"Hard to say. You think you're doing alright?"

"I'm doing pretty good," I said. "You feel good about it?"

"Well, no pains to speak of," he chuckled. "The lack of pain is as simple as the end of feeling it." He pointed at the city again. "Suckers and assholes. Whores and animals. It's a zoo, a jungle, a shotgun nightmare."

"What do you mean?"

"You get a little bit of joy out of it and you got it made. That's all I mean." He was drunk.

"I don't know what joy is." I thought about that. Did I? "Well, maybe once in a while I feel something."

"Every small shard of happiness is a contract with the devil."

"You think so?"

"I think that it's war, Jack. I think that we're fighting muzzle to muzzle and that there aren't any angels on the battlefield."

"What's your name, man?" I asked. He was a strange guy.

"Henry." The music began to play again. He leaned back. "Call me Hank. What's your name?"

"Jay Carver."

"Jay Carver..." he repeated. "I'll never remember that name."

"What do you mean?"

He laughed, turned up the music, and rocketed into the city taking long pulls from a near-dead bottle of port.

* * *

I got a library card under the name Jay Lee Carver and filled out a phony vehicle title with the same name. I went to the bank and opened a bank account with the vehicle title and a fake business card I'd procured from the office supply store.

It was 10 a.m. and the beauty shop was bustling with crazy ladies in curlers and tinfoil wrapped all over their heads. I went in there and told the woman to bleach it.

"All of it?"

"Yeah. Bright blonde. Even my eyebrows. Even my mustache."

"Alright..." She was unnerved.

Two hours later Hank waited in the parking lot while I stood in the shitty DMV line for a new ID card.

The woman finally called me to the green desk, handed me my card, took my money, and sent me on my way. So simple, yet so hard.

Hank was out in the lot smoking cigarettes and laughing with some woman. They were leaning against the hood of the Caddy. I walked toward them and overheard Hank saying something about wanting to pull her skirt up and something else.

"Good god, man!" I yelled. The woman laughed. I noticed that Hank had gone across the street to the liquor store for a bottle of J&B. He held it like a beer and drank from it with the same concentration.

"She's a hooker, Jason. She doesn't mind," he said.

"Get a life, you jackass!" I said. "You're too drunk to drive me anywhere. Give me the keys."

"Alright, Carpenter, just relax."

"It's CARVER."

"Alright, CARVER! I KNOW your damn NAME!" He was blind drunk, hanging onto the woman and slinging that bottle all over the DMV parking lot. We were a beacon for cops. I took the car, went to the airport, left it in the parking deck, and used my fake ID for tickets on a plane to Hawaii.

It had been a hell of a day but finally Jay Lee Carver had become something more than a name on an Epileptic ID card.

7

HAWAII

1974

TERRY WAS WORKING FOR A TELECOM INTERCONNECT COMPANY CALLED the Hawaii Corporation that sold Stromburg Carlson Communications Systems. I thought about taking a job there, but decided against it. I wouldn't have minded working for Stromburg, but I did my own thing, found my own jobs, paved my own golden roads.

There were plenty of jobs in Hawaii, but almost all of them were dependent on tourism and didn't pay much. Another big problem for island employers was that no one would stay for very long. If you were interested in making something of yourself in business you'd do 10 times better on the mainland. The only people who stayed in Hawaii were women. Five or six of them would team up and divide the rent of a single apartment. Otherwise, it was like working for the average wage of a guy in Flint, Michigan, while living in Manhattan. There was no way anyone could afford it.

I applied for two jobs and received phone calls that very same evening requesting that I report to both. I couldn't make up my mind so Terry and I drank.

My drinking and drug expenditures alone would have been a logical reason for me to take both jobs. However, I did it because I figured I would size them up for a few weeks and ditch the dark horse. The first to call had been the Feonard Company, a Hawaii-based advertising firm that handled the advertising for hotels, condominiums, tourism and in-flight magazines. The second and more interesting offer was with the Yell and Bowell Company, who sold microfilm technology to banks. Microfilm was the new and secure way to photograph checks and important documents. I could smell the opportunity for bank fraud a mile away.

Monday morning I went on down to Feonard Company and they set me up with a company car (white Ford sedan) and a list of phone calls to make. I took the list, organized my office, made a few calls, and headed out to canvas the territory.

I also stopped by the Yell and Bowell offices that day. They too gave me a white Ford sedan as my company car. I shadowed a guy named Robert Chen in order to learn about my position. I would have to fly to Texas for formal training, but it would be a few weeks before that was necessary.

Yell and Bowell was impressed with how well I did. After a while I hardly had to come in as long as I kept my numbers up. Later, I took time off from the Feonard Company (told them I had to tie up loose ends in Nevada or wherever I lied about being from) and flew to Texas for training.

In Texas I learned all sorts of applicable skills. They took the trainees behind the scenes and into the simulated backrooms of banks and other financial institutions. I learned exactly what happened from the time a check left your checkbook to the time it was processed by the bank staff and filed away for eternity.

I was given instruction as to the methods used to create and store financial documents (bank drafts, checks, bills of sale, cashier's checks, money orders, etc.). They taught me how to use the perforation machines, which I found could be ordered direct from the company and required no license.

All in all, both of my new jobs worked well together. Sure, I was working all the time, but there was nothing else to do other than sit around the beach, pick up chicks, talk about Terry's horrifically depressing early 20s, or walk from his shit-hole apartment to the bar.

It was a remarkable life. Just several weeks ago I had been a dirty jailbird circling the drainpipes of the justice system, now I was rolling in fat paychecks, driving new cars, and frequenting night clubs where chicks literally threw themselves at me.

"Hi, I'm Melody. Wanna go back to my place?" Or, "Has anyone told you that I'm the best dancer on the island?" I'm serious. They even bought me drinks.

That sort of stuff was happening every night. There were times I was home during the day on the weekends, sitting on Terry's couch, and the craziest shit would happen.

We'd be watching the game together, me in my silk boxers, which was all I wore around the apartment. It could be morning or mid-afternoon and girls would show up unannounced, undressing down to their underwear, or less, to get comfortable, or to show us their tan lines, or to show us the scars on their bodies from enhancement surgeries.

The girls would shower every so often and as one group would leave another would arrive. They were delighted to do whatever we wanted and seemed very eager to please. At times I imagined that making us happy was a contest for them.

Times were strange. And strange times were good times in my world. I was fresh out of the hoosegow and following the coveted path to Hawaiian greatness. Things were looking up.

*   *   *

I gave one of my company Fords to a girl who was a regular at my apartment. I guess I hadn't needed the car anyway. I would see it every few days, just driving up and down the street like it was a total stranger. I let it go.

I bought a Lincoln Mark IV and a Porsche 911 and rented a house in Kailua.

It wasn't just any house. I had been speaking with a realtor about whether it was a better investment to rent a house on the island or purchase one and he had told me to rent.

"I know the perfect spot for a guy like you," he said. Whatever that meant.

As it turned out, the house was owned by the Hawaii District Court Commissioner. He had gotten Rock Fever, the legendary claustrophobic disorder caused by living in Hawaii for too long. The Commissioner was taking a year leave on the mainland and his vacation had opened up a ripe can of worms for me. I now was residing in an upstanding man's home, using it as a command center to plot my seasonal "rip-and-run."

"Commissioner Jameson told me not to rent the home to anyone with a penchant for alcohol, clumsiness, or disorderliness," the realtor told me, jotting my name down on the rental receipt and gingerly removing the yellow copy. "I'm glad I found a man like you," he said, nodding his head, flicking a business card into my hand. I initiated a firm handshake. "If you hear of anyone else in the market…" he said, gesturing at the card.

"Certainly," I smiled. He drove off down the road. Terry pulled up in his black Monte Carlo—company car—and stumbled across the lawn, waving goodbye to the realtor.

*   *   *

I was at the Infinity nightclub, which is a colossal showroom with three bars, stadium booth seating, a dance floor, rock bands, well-endowed waitresses, drugs, razorblade mean Samoans, beautiful drunk women in heels, mirrors, lights, noise, people falling, you name it.

Terry and I used to stand at the center bar, in a very specific and conspicuous spot, to keep an eye on the entire scene. This particular evening there was a wet T-shirt contest, and from our spot we couldn't see extremely well but we agreed that the show wasn't worthy of us abandoning our post.

There was wild applause and there they went: all that water poured over all those T-shirts. We pointed, cheered, popped a few more Black Beauties.

There was commotion onstage. The winning girl got to choose any man from the crowd that she wanted. Any man… I stood there real calm and watched. Terry was beside me, leaning over the railing and looking down some waitress's shirt. The crowd waited in silence. Then, the girl pointed.

I remained still, calm, like a bear in the hunter's sights.

"Come on down here, buddy!" The man with the microphone yelled. Everyone cleared away from me. I pointed at myself in question, pretended that I didn't know she'd chosen me.

"No way!" I said, putting my arms out in disbelief. Who would have thought she'd have even been able to see me up there?

I walked downstairs and she hugged me, pressed those giants against my chest.

"You're a tall one," she said. The man with the microphone laughed and clapped, moved the crowd's attention to something else and the night continued. We got drunk together and went up to her room. Amazing night.

* * *

I met Leslie at Infinity a few nights later. She was a nice girl. Tall, thin, facially one of the best-looking I'd seen in a few months. I had stayed a few nights at her apartment several weeks ago and thought nothing of it. Tonight she seemed more interested in me and I was willing to give it another shot.

I was drinking with Terry and Dan. Yes, Dan Poindexter had arrived from New York. He was eager to drink up the spoils of whatever war I was conceiving against the island state.

"You got a good thing going here," Dan said, patting me on the back. He slugged at the drinks and pointed at the girls. He tried making conversation with Leslie but she ignored him. Dan put too much gel in his hair for anyone to take him seriously. In all honestly, it looked like he'd dunked his scalp in a bucket of donut glaze.

Leslie was bored with the loud music and Dan's ceaseless blabbering. She asked if we could go hang out at my place.

"Sure," I said. We left immediately.

The police commissioner's home was desecrated yet again by an endless night of drugs, booze, sex, inane conversations, and general all-around debauchery.

* * *

Leslie was an airline stewardess. She was quick with a joke, fast on her feet, and intelligent in certain ways that are unnamable but give a girl the stamina to travel on airliners for 15 hours a day and not lose her sanity.

She had a very rich ex-boyfriend who lived in Seattle and still called her continuously. She also had plenty of attractive friends—planeloads of female friends, in fact. And all of her ladies needed a place to stay.

"You know, Jay, I've been thinking..."

"I hate when you do that," I joked. She gave me a look.

"I was thinking that since Elise and Casey have no place to sleep on layover that they could crash here, you know?"

"How long?"

"I don't know, they're off for three weeks." Her head bobbled when she talked. Big pink bubble-gum lips opened and closed, telling me all this stuff.

"So you have two friends who need a place to stay?"

"Well, then in two weeks I've got Erin and Pauline."

"So four total?"

"Jay, this place is HUGE. You can EASILY fit everyone in. They're all girls, too."

"What's that have to do with it?"

"You're saying you'd be opposed to having five women sharing a house with you?"

"I'm not saying that. I'm saying—"

"Just what I thought! You don't KNOW what you're saying!" She laughed, jumped into my lap. We were on the back porch drinking rum swizzlers or some other type of overly sweetened drink that she loved. I was high on speed, preparing something for work on the table while trying to force down an epic steak that I had seared on the grill.

"All I do is work and all you can think about is how to cram more expenditures down my throat," I said.

She laughed ostentatiously, threw her head back in the Hawaiian sun and for a few fractions of a second everything was perfect, just like a photograph: her head and hair flung backward, the warm breeze, the steak, my finances, the sunlight, my hand supporting her as she leaned over the arm of the chair... hell, even the rum drink was alright.

I remembered what the driver had told me: every moment of happiness is a pact with the devil. What the hell did that mean anyway? I hadn't bargained with anybody for any of this. (I looked around at my house, the girls, my two cars, the stack of cash in my safe, bags of drugs, endless liquor, all those blondes...) I'd WORKED for my lifestyle. There was a big difference in selling your soul and hustling, grinding, getting out there and making things happen. The devil probably thought the same way. I didn't give a damn. That was enough.

I looked off into the yard, deep into the brush behind my house. Something rustled around, a small dark figure, probably a dog. I eyed it suspiciously but dismissed it as nothing.

"They got enough strays around here," I said to Leslie.

"Is there one down there?" She walked to the edge of the deck.

"I think I saw something... there!" I said. He rustled in the bushes, desperately seeking even the smallest morsel of trash.

"I don't see anything, Jay."

"Eh, never mind. Forget him."

"I wanna see it, where is it?" She kept staring and I walked over to the edge of the deck. Had the thing disappeared in thin air or what? Where had he gone?

The doorbell rang and I forgot about the dog. It was probably Terry; then again, I was a wanted man, so there was also a chance that it was the Gestapo ringing just to see if I'd answer. If I was dumb enough to meet them head-on they would catch me in the perfect scenario: unarmed and naked, except for my silk boxers, and they'd spring several leaks in me with the 9mil and some guy would jot down something about "Mr. Jay Carver, case 83792-983, was killed while resisting arrest...trying to stab Deputies Halbucks and Davis with a steak knife... fired multiple shots at the suspect, 17 of which hit him in...." and so they'd file me away and no one would bother with a funeral.

If that failed—if I was too fast and headed for the bedroom—they'd surround the place, riddle it with bullets, tear gas, pepper spray, napalm, high explosives, whatever they use to oust somebody from a potentially fortified ex-police stronghold.

I gave them their chance and walked right in there and opened the door wearing only my boxers. It was some kid. Well, not a kid, but a young guy in a suit. He was an insurance salesman.

"Alright, punk. Gimme your best pitch and maybe I'll think about it."

"Well, Mr. Carver, you buy from me and you have a guarantee that the big corporations can't give you."

I stared at him.

"We can give you, um—"

"Out!" I yelled, shaking my hand at him like I would shake it at a dog. "You hesitated, kid. You stuttered. Bad tactics. Beat it." I flipped out a bill, slapped it in his palm.

He stared. Confusion set in; awkward tension and dumbfounded lips quivering.

"Jay? Who's that at the door?" Leslie called from the back porch.

"It's just John Lennon, Honey. He's looking for England and got lost." I shut the door real slow in the guys face, saying something like, "Don't ever stumble again, kid. Don't EVER stumble..."

I was high and the day hadn't really started yet. I had two jobs, not to mention I was selling and running small-time test scams on the side. My fingers ran anxiously through my fake blonde hair. I stared at the floor, picked a point and focused.

The rum came on hard. 9 a.m. It was the perfect snapshot of my perfect world: drinks, girls, drugs, and the serrated but continuous bargains with sanity.

*   *   *

It was about 2 a.m. They had recently come out with Automatic Teller Machines and there were about six on the island. I was high on speed, racing around in my Lincoln Mark IV, hurrying like a madman to find one. I had a little machine of my own, a handheld electronic device I'd snatched from Yell and Bowell. I'd heard about the ATMs, about how they worked, and I knew that my electronic pulse generator could crack the codes and net me some extra cash.

I spotted one! Ah-ha! Through a drunken haze of erratic lane switching I tooled the car into the lot and pulled up beside it. What a machine! A giant cashbox just sitting in the parking lot waiting to be ripped off! My theories were confirmed: the human race was reversing, becoming more naïve as the years wore on.

I attached the electrodes to the keypad and fooled around with the device for about10 minutes. Then, just like magic, it began typing codes into the machine through tiny electronic pulses.

I lit a cigar and waited. Five minutes. Ten minutes. Forty-five minutes... still nothing. I began to feel awkward, like someone would drive past and report me. Chances of that were slim. The only sobers driving around this time of night were cops, and I imagined I wouldn't get arrested for sitting at an ATM unless I was taking a crowbar to it.

At 50 minutes the thing flashed a message at me:
GREETINGS GENERAL MANAGER
WOULD YOU LIKE TO
- CLOSE-OUT
- REFILL
- CHECK BALANCE
- LOCK
- SET TIME

I pressed the button for CLOSE-OUT.
STEP ONE: ENTER YOUR BRANCH I.D.

I reset the pulse generator and put it to work. This combination came much more easily.
THANK YOU. PLEASE CHOOSE FROM:
- TOTAL CLOSE-OUT AND COLLECT FUNDS

- PARTIAL CLOSE-OUT AND SHUT DOWN FOR EMERGENCY
- EMERGENCY DISPLACEMENT OF FUNDS
- SYSTEM RESTART

Obviously...

The thing spit out about 10 grand into a tray and I had to keep removing the 20s so that they didn't overflow into the lot. I shoved them into my briefcase. I had a bottle of beer in the cup holder and I knocked it over, spilled it all over the floor while fumbling with the cash.

I used a skirt that I found in the back of the Lincoln and tried to clean off the front seat. When I looked back at the ATM there was money spitting out into the wind. I cracked the door, reached down, clawed at the bills which were blowing beneath my car. I pulled up a few feet and got out, chased a few 20s into the grass, picked them up, loaded my pockets, and left in a frenzy toward the next bank.

I spent the rest of the night skidding from ATM to ATM. The fourth combination took forever, and at around 5 a.m. I abandoned the heist and headed home. I had nailed three ATMs in just under three hours. Not bad for the first time out. Not bad at all.

* * *

I was outside the Feonard Company's office complex at 6 p.m. talking to Freddy Tavenport's nephew. The Tavenports owned the Feonard Company, and so befriending the nephew of the owner seemed like a reasonable idea.

"You feel like getting a drink?" I asked.

"No, I can't. My son's got a ball game. I gotta run."

"Oh, alright, see you later."

I walked to my car and settled into the driver's seat. The sun was beating in on me from the west. It had been a long day, all ATMs considered. My house was full of women and my briefcase, still in the beer-drenched passenger seat, was on the verge of exploding open with cash.

I was in a dilemma: I needed sleep, but going home was like going to the circus. I needed a break. I had long since taken my last dose of amphetamine. I could theoretically drive over to Waikiki and re-up on the Black Beauties... no, forget that, I'd be better off taking it easy for a few hours.

I sat there, stoned from exhaustion, just staring out at the palm trees.

"Jay!" There was a knock on my window. "When did you get this ride?" It was Peewee Tavenport, the nephew. He was referencing my new Lincoln. Damn, I'd forgotten to drive the company car to work...

I played it cool. "Oh, this old thing? It's a friend's." It was brand new.

"It's nice. Sure beats those damn LTD's they give us."

"Yeah..."

"Where is your company car? You trade it in?" he laughed. What the hell did he mean? I couldn't understand people anymore. Somehow I had separated myself from them. People couldn't identify with me, and I certainly couldn't identify with them. I felt very few emotions besides lust, aggravation, greed, and hatred.

"Yeah, I traded it in," I laughed. "No, just kidding. My Ford has a flat."

"Oh." He lit a cigarette, offered me one. Camels... eh, I didn't love a Camel but I figured what the hell.

"My son's game isn't for a couple of hours. You still wanna grab a beerski?" Yeah, Freddy Tavenport often called them "beerskis." Kind of like brewski only with a strange nonsensical Hawaiian twist that suggested Rock Fever... or perhaps Rock Idiocy. His tie dangled inside my window and I studied the design. I was confused. Was there really a Santa Claus on his tie? A Santa and eight reindeer chasing a beach ball? I was so stoned and gone... the speed had really let me down hard. Santa's warped voice yelled down to me from the North Pole, something about how I would get a giant black horse for Christmas

"Yeah. I guess, Peewee. Sure, the bar it is..."

"If you don't want to it's alright. I just forgot what time the game was when you asked."

"No, it's fine. Let's go."

"No, forget it, Jay. You look like you had your mind on something else."

"Just follow me, Gene." I don't think he heard me call him the wrong name.

We went on down to the bar, sat there staring at the television, ordered some tall ones, drank 'em, got two more, drank 'em, started jabbering about football. He had played for a Division II team in college. Running back. After a while he left and I put my head down on the bar. At 2 a.m., the 24-hour anniversary of my ATM heisting career, someone jostled me.

"Jay... Jay..." I woke up. 2 a.m. Shit... I had work to do before I went to sleep. The bartender knew me there so he didn't mind that I'd slept for six hours on his bar. That was lucky. What wasn't lucky was that I was falling behind at both of my jobs and was out of speed. I called my usual connection. No dice.

Everything crashed down on the drive home. To keep myself sane I kept saying, "no matter how bad it is on the outside, it's better than the best day in a prison cell."

It was almost always true.

*   *   *

Terry and I scoured the island for ways to invest my newly procured cash. I got the idea to invest in a bar, another Zipples type thing, and it turned out that I could purchase a nice place for just under what I had in my stash. The bar was in the International Market Place and the concept was simple: Oysters, Booze, and Broads.

Through the bar I made several valuable contacts and began a small loan-shark operation. Nothing too serious, but every now and then someone would pay me back a good sum when I didn't expect it.

We spent some time and money sprucing the place up. We hired decorators, purchased new furniture, had the walls painted, the floors cleaned, sealed, waxed, put in new televisions...

*   *   *

My house was packed with five topless, attractive, drunken stewardesses. Despite the noise, it wasn't so bad. I finally re-upped on speed and life came back into focus. The days passed slowly. Each night became a montage of drug-induced recklessness.

I was at Infinity, at my usual spot in the back, watching a rock show, drinking with Terry and some friends, running on high RPMs. There was a girl at one of the booths, a really attractive Spanish or South American type. I couldn't tell which. She kept waving me over, giving me the eye. She was at one of those semi-circle booths with the high backs, the type you can't see over from behind.

After two or three waves I went to the booth and peeked in to see what she wanted. WHAM! A greasy Samoan fist cracked me right in the forehead. I spun around, flew a few feet backward and braced myself against the bar. There was this chick on the other side of the bar. I saw her gorgeous face, her long and mysterious hair, and she stared at me like a precious stone. She sipped a drink, blushed, giggled at my confused expression. Terry and Dan were hot, over at the table in a flash and ready to throw down. The Samoans were carrying. It could get bloody.

I went over to the booth, put my hands between them, and stared down at the Samoan men. The girl in the booth had tricked me, duped me into getting punched in the face. I scowled at her and she looked away. One of the men had his hand on a piece, a chrome snub-nose revolver. Probably a .38.

"Look, you guys need to cool off. It was your girl's fault. I didn't do shit. You don't wanna start anything. Not in this bar and not with me."

They yelled something. The bouncers had seen what was happening. They knew me. I knew them. It was good practice to tip those guys. They came rushing over, dragged the Samoans out of the booth, even the girls, and carried them downstairs and out of the bar.

The girl from across the bar, the one with diamond eyes, walked toward me very gracefully, tactfully, directly. She was tall, slender, impressively constructed like a Polynesian queen or someone who could cut your throat without thinking twice. She was obviously powerful, which usually meant that she wouldn't like a guy like me. I had a strong personality, and often times two strong personalities had a way of working against each other.

The feminists hated me, despised me, called me a womanizer. The submissive women were sucked in by my charm. This wasn't my choice, it was the chemistry of things.

The girl introduced herself as Jennifer and I introduced myself as Jay Carver. She lived with several people in Waikiki, in a condominium complex called Yacht Harbor Towers, which overlooked the Waikiki Yacht Harbor. We went back to her place and while we were drinking on her balcony, taking in the sight of all those giant boats, she spread me a line of cocaine.

I took a deep one, a thick one, and everything felt right about it. In fact, for a minute, it felt too right. I looked up at the harbor, all the lights and the ships with people drinking, dancing, entertaining, playing music. Man, I loved my life.

I felt like the building was creeping up from behind me. I turned and looked back. It seemed to stretch upward forever, even though we were only two stories from the top.

"You alright?" she asked.

"Yeah, sorry. Just got a bit of a head-rush."

"This is good, huh?"

"Oh yeah." It was the best cocaine I'd ever had. Probably as pure as it could get without taking a trip to Escobar's ranch (which I imagined wasn't out of the question for whoever was responsible for bringing this stuff).

"Who else lives with you?"

"My boyfriend, his friend, and his friend's girlfriend live here, too."

"Your boyfriend? He won't mind if I'm around?"

"He's out of town. He doesn't mind, though. He lets me do what I want."

"I see…"

We went inside to the bedroom, did this amazing thing, and fell asleep after a few hours. I had never been as impressed by a girl as I was with Jennifer. I felt a strange connection, like we were meant to be together. I thought to myself, lying in that dark bed, that I wouldn't ever let that feeling go away.

*　　*　　*

There was a noise in the hallway like someone moving furniture. I sat up in bed and checked the clock: 4 a.m.

"Jennifer, get up." I nudged her. "Jennifer!" She stirred, sat up beside me.

"What is it?"

"Somebody's out there in the hallway?"

"What?"

I felt my adrenaline rising like a boiling pot. I stood, grabbed my underwear from beside the bed. "Somebody's out there." I crept toward the door, cracked it and looked into the hallway.

"Oh, Jay, wait…" she said, fumbling with something, probably an assault rifle or hand grenade. God only knew what was happening.

I put my back against the wall, fearing the worst.

"Jay, relax. Get off the wall—CARLOS, NORBERTO IS THAT YOU GUYS?" Jennifer yelled. She turned on the light. I put my hands up, trying to silence her. Damn, this was it! And I had no gun…

"NORBERTO! Is that YOU, baby?"

"JENNIFER!" Someone yelled. I prayed that it was Norberto. Then again, I prayed that it wasn't Norberto.

He burst in the door, whoever he was. She jumped up, ran across the bed, down the three stairs at the edge of the bed's platform, and gave him a giant hug, a long kiss. Yeah, and there I was, standing in my underwear.

"Berto, this is Jay."

"Nice to meet you," he said. The guy was young and good looking. He extended his hand. "Norberto."

"Jay Carver."

"Good to have you at my place."

"Thank you."

"I brought gifts," he said, smiling, chuckling, heading into the hallway with her on his shoulder. I searched frantically for my clothes, hoping that—what? Hoping that he hadn't noticed that I was naked? Was this my cue to leave? I couldn't figure it out. Why hadn't the man socked me in the face for sleeping with his girl? Were these guys more subtle than Americans? Would he wait for the right moment? Perhaps shoot me in the temple after I fell asleep?

Carlos, Norberto's partner, opened two Samsonite Hard Body briefcases in the hallway. Both were chocked full of cocaine. I didn't believe my eyes when I saw how many kilo bags could fit inside those things.

"Try some," he said. He reached down, removed a bag, took it into the kitchen, and spread a pile on the granite countertop. "You like cocaine, Jay?"

"Sure," I said. He handed me a gold tooter and I railed a line.

"You like it?" Carlos' girlfriend asked. They all studied my expression.

"Damn!" I said, standing up hard and straight, feeling that brand new rush like the world was on fire and my brain was running a drag race.

"He likes it," Carlos said. The five of us laughed. We were deep beneath the radar of the feds, the DEA, the average citizen, huddled around some kind of holy light. We poured drinks and got higher and higher, slapping each other on the back and cracking jokes.

Linda, Carlos' girlfriend, was talking about certain cocaine binges she'd seen "the boys" go on, when she relayed this message to me: "And sometimes, after about three days of binging, Jennifer and I would have to take turns 'helping' Carlos and Norberto get to sleep..."

Carlos spoke about the duo's recent buying trip to Tahiti. His joys and fears poured out of him with the help of our tequila. It was like we were best friends, the five of us, and when the sun rose they were gone. They'd left a kilo in the drawer for Jennifer and were on a long-distance run with the rest of their work.

We slept until evening.

*   *   *

A kilo of cocaine, or 1,000 grams, was worth a lot of money in 1974. Each gram, if sold in that unit specifically, especially since it was of exceptional quality, would bring in $100. I learned that Jennifer would be selling most of it in quarter, half, and full ounces. She also stepped on it a bit by combining the pure coke with Minit (a baby laxative that was baked in the oven on cookie sheets to make it look and shine like ice crystals.) These crystals were then ground up and sprinkled into the powder to add weight.

Jennifer was entitled to as many of these keys as she could flip. I became very interested in dating her, not just because of the cocaine but because she was incredibly beautiful. She was interested in living together, so I suggested that she move into the Police Commissioner's house. It would be good for the relationship. We could get to know each other a little better and in the meantime I could learn a few things about the drug trade.

Leslie didn't like it. Neither did the other girls. They kept giving me looks like "what the hell do you think you're doing?" But I didn't care. Jennifer was a dime, a "10," and I wasn't going to let a woman like that slip through my fingers.

Leslie and the other girls faded. Maybe a few ill words were exchanged. Nothing serious. Who cared anyway? All's well that ends well, right?

In addition to the craziness at home—Jennifer always insisted on being naked, especially swimming naked, cooking naked, entertaining our guests in the nude. Her constant nudity annoyed Jennifer.—my jobs began to meld together, becoming scarily undistinguishable from one another. Several times I took the wrong paperwork from one to the other and almost got busted.

"Jay, how's it going?" the boss would ask.

"Good, Dick..." Or was it Ted? I'd always say the name quietly just in case it was wrong.

"You got anymore word from Bank of Hawaii as to how many units they're interested in?"

"No." I had forgotten to check my mailbox. No doubt they had called me back.

"Really?"

"Yeah, let me re-read my messages and see if I missed it."

"Do that." He'd begin to walk away. "Oh, and Jay?"

"Yeah?"

"Are you coming to the cookout this weekend at Kapono's place?"

"Om..." Of course I wasn't. "Let me check my schedule."

"Are you feeling alright?"

I made sure to look him right in the eye, high as gas, burning up inside. "Yeah, man. I'm feeling pretty damn good. Why?"

"Oh, nothing. I just thought you sounded a bit hoarse. You out late last night?"

"Not too late. Maybe 7 or 8."

"Look, Jay…" The boss came in real close, leaned on my desk, spoke quietly and peered around the office. "Ernie said he saw someone in the parking lot last night while he was reconfiguring the filing system upstairs." He looked at me puzzled. "He said the guy had long blonde hair, a good build, and was driving a tan Lincoln."

"Yeah?"

"And this guy, whoever he was, keyed into our building, came out with a briefcase, and then he pissed in the parking lot, right under the second light pole, and drove away." He was indirect, staring into the corner of the room.

We sat there for a minute.

"Was that you, Jay?"

"Hmm." I put on a face of cosmic befuddlement. "It doesn't sound like me…"

"And what, you don't remember?"

"Tom, of course it wasn't me. Are you kidding? I don't even own a Lincoln." I had driven it to work that very day.

"Peewee said you were driving a Lincoln the other afternoon."

"That guy's a nutcase, Dick! You and I both know it!"

"Keep it down! That's the boss's nephew you're talking about." He hushed me. The funniest thing was that he didn't protest my remark.

"Look, Dick, if you think I was up here last night drunk and pissing all over the lot, you don't know me very well. If I'm drunk, I'm at home where I can't drive. My girlfriend takes the keys, hides them, and puts a limit on my beers. I can only have four beers, Dick; and those are on FRIDAY!" I looked down and saw the fifth of tequila in my desk drawer. It could have ruined me. I slid the drawer shut very slowly with my knee.

"Alright. Relax, Jay." He threw his hands up in surrender. "I'm sorry. I didn't know…"

"It's fine, Ed."

Close one, but no sweat. It didn't matter either way… caught or not. Who needs a microfilm job when your girlfriend's purse is the Bird's Nest?

*   *   *

I began to line up purchase orders and ways to swindle companies out of merchandise. My house was stacked full of papers detailing my plot, and for several weeks I did nothing but drink, get high, and file my scams. It would all happen very quickly, in a one- or two-day period, and then I would be gone.

"You want me to come with you?" Jennifer asked.

"Well... I wouldn't mind it. You've got a good thing going, though. I don't blame you if you want to stay."

"I don't want to stay. I'm sick of this place. I want to go with you."

"Alright, but I gotta warn you, it's not always roses out there."

"It seems like an adventure."

"Yeah, maybe right now. All we do is party all the time."

"Don't put it like that."

"I'm just saying."

"Don't make it sound so... worthless."

"I'm not. I'm telling it like it is."

She came over to the couch. Her couch, Norberto's couch. We were in Carlos and Norberto's condo so I guess it was his couch. Strange. I had papers spread everywhere, including all over the couch. I stared at the couch, felt something twitching inside my head, maybe even in my brain. I squinted my eyes at the papers and continued reading. My plan was to hit the dealers where it hurt: shipments of diamonds, ammunition, watches and necklaces, household appliances, and guns. It was an all-out war: Dealers vs. Jay Lee Carver. And damn if I was going to let them take me alive. (Much less broke...)

I knew that the score would be a resounding success if only I could keep my head straight. Along with the copious amounts of cocaine, my little snowbird Jennifer had me knee deep in more amphetamines than I knew what to do with. Everything from Black Beauties and Bombers to various designer pills. The new drug she had for sale was very potent. It went fast at the night clubs. I was on it at that moment, stoned out of my mind, literally hovering in the air above the couch. It was great stuff, very different from anything I had ever tried. Jennifer called it Molly.

*   *   *

I woke early for a Sunday, probably around 11 a.m., and went down to the Beach Bar at the Hilton. It was one of the only bars that was packed pre-noon and I knew that I could get a table and drink while going over my soon-to-come scams.

The Beach Bar was full of Wall Street guys—at least, that's how they presented themselves. They drank from 11 a.m. to 3 p.m. and went to bed in the afternoon in order to get up at 3 a.m. and play the New York Stock Exchange.

The guys in that bar always gave me looks. They were older, the youngest being somewhere near 35. I had a feeling that a lot of them were doing it for the chicks. Girls liked guys with money, and if you had a few bucks for drinks and didn't care how early you got wasted, the Beach Bar was a pretty decent place to hunt tail.

I sat alone, reading and re-reading documents and studying my papers. I was virtually 100-percent prepared for Monday's Big Hit.

*   *   *

I made several purchases, rallied a number of trucks full of stolen merchandise, and distributed them to predetermined buyers. That was day one. A slow day one, but it was a start.

On day two, using fake papers, I went to virtually ALL of the major jewelry wholesalers and bought high-priced items to resell at a later point. (Rings for $30,000, necklaces for more than that, anything I could get my hands on… all with false checks.)

By the end of day two, my full-size briefcase was literally packed with gold and diamonds. In the evening hours I collected several debts for drugs, specifically Jennifer's cocaine debtors. We had fronted work all over the city in a last-ditch effort to round up cash.

I went to several dealers' homes and with a bit of prodding was able to collect the money in full.

Lastly, I unloaded the remainder of my speed onto an old friend of Leslie's who worked for the airlines. The guy had very little money, but he had given me a connection that had made me thousands. I figured what the hell and just gave him what I had and prepared to leave the island.

*   *   *

My jewelry briefcase was waiting in the foyer. My other briefcase, the one in my right hand, was chock full of $100,000 cash, each brick of bills wrapped in aluminum foil to fool the airport scanners.

We had plane tickets to Los Angeles and I was on the horn with the train station trying to get the departure times from L.A. to Phoenix. They weren't cooperating, had me on hold for 10 minutes, so through a haze of cigar smoke I slammed the receiver and headed out the door.

I carried both briefcases with me into the rear of the limo and shut the door myself.

Jennifer had a gold tooter in her purse and was taking sniffs.

"I'm going to miss having all those goodies from my guys," she said.

"Yup." Whatever, we had to get out of town.

Carlos and Norberto had shaken my hand two days prior when I had told them my plan to leave.

"Congratulations on Jennifer," Norberto said to me. It was strange how he had no hard feelings. It was an amicable split. I guess there was a culture difference that I just didn't understand.

"Thanks, man. You're sure you're alright with everything?"

"Jay, she is not for me. There are other women. Plenty of others. Trust me, I am fine." We shook hands again. "Good luck."

We got to the airport and I ran my briefcases through the security detectors. There was a pause. The woman at the machine called for assistance, removed a bag from the line. I couldn't see which one they had selected, but I knew it was one of mine.

Jennifer gave me a look.

"Sir!" one of the managers yelled, looking in my direction.

"Yes?" the man behind me in line said. I remained frozen. Hell, maybe I could pass the briefcase off as his and get the hell out of there before they could prove otherwise.

The manager walked over, set a briefcase on the table behind the divider. I still couldn't tell which bag it was; the money or the jewelry.

"Sir, do you have a permit for this?" the manager asked, not being clear on exactly who he was speaking to.

The man behind me answered. "Yes, I do." He fumbled around in his pockets, removed his wallet.

"Sir!" A woman yelled. I turned toward her. There was no one in front of me in the line. The mass of humans had waddled through the gates and I had remained frozen.

"Sorry," I said, hustling toward the metal detector. I sniffled back a runny nose, removed my belt, and stepped through porthole.

"You've got such wonderful hair," the lady guard said.

"Thanks."

"Tell me, honestly, do you bleach it?"

"Never touched a bottle of hair bleach in my life." True enough...

"Wow, really?"

"Really."

I moved along. Both of my bags were on the floor at the end of the security check-in line. I grabbed them: diamonds and jewelry in the right hand, cash in the left.

We sat down on the plane. It began rolling. It was a rainy Hawaiian afternoon but the planes were taking off anyway.

"It's not a big storm," the pilot assured us. "We'll be out of the clouds in no time and arriving at Los Angeles International Airport at 9:35 p.m. Right on schedule."

I downed two vodkas before the plane left the runway. Jen leaned her head against my shoulder and we moved up through that storm and into the very familiar tropical sunlight. The higher we got, the more you could see that the clouds were only over the island. It was funny: a clear ocean everywhere else but rain on all those people.

I looked at the overhead bag storage. The strap of my money briefcase had been closed in the hatch.

"Can I help you with something, sir?" The stewardess asked, noticing my stare. She fixed the strap, stuffed it neatly away.

It is strange how people come within inches of their fortunes... and miss.

8

ATLANTA

1974

FROM THE LOS ANGELES AIRPORT WE TOOK A TRAIN TO PHOENIX. IT WAS a nice ride through the desert and gave me time to piece together a plan, which I began to execute upon our arrival at 11 a.m.

I got my hair, eyebrows, and mustache dyed black with gray highlights. I purchased some high-end non-prescription glasses, a new suit, a new briefcase, new shoes, and rented a hotel room and got drunk.

The second day I went to a pharmacy and got an epileptic ID card.

Phoenix was alright, but after a few days I had to get out. I set my sights on Atlanta and boarded yet another airplane—cash wrapped in aluminum foil. We arrived in Atlanta and there was a driver waiting in the terminal. He let us off at the Fairmont Hotel.

"Will you be needing my services again this evening, sir?" he asked.

"No," I said. I didn't want to keep renting a limousine. I wanted to buy one.

There was a tall, skinny young man behind the desk with vibrant blue eyes and blonde hair.

"Hi, I need a suite for two," I said, nodding my greetings. "The name's Redding. Lance Redding." I handed him my fake ID card from the Arizona DMV.

"Sure, Mr. Redding," he said, sorting through several drawers and passing me the appropriate paperwork. The bellboy took my bags, loaded them onto his cart. "Those go to Room 312, R.J."

"Wait, please," I interjected, putting a hand up asking the bellboy to stop. "I need a safe deposit box. I have several important family items that I need to secure under lock and key."

"Yes sir. What size box would you like?"

"Preferably your largest."

"Sure."

He handed me another form. I filled it out and passed it back.

"American Express, BankAmericard, Master Charge?" he asked.

"I'll be paying with cash."

"OK."

I counted out the bills, laid them on the marble countertop. Several old squares walked past, gave me the nod. I was Lance Redding, the lawyer. I was a respectable salt-and-pepper guy with a good vocabulary and sharp eyes behind a new set of Benjamin Franklin spectacles.

Lance also had a foxy girlfriend and a couple hundred grand in jewels and cash, but none of the squares knew about the loot. The good guys were notoriously blinded by the expensive business cards, the personal limo, Jennifer's body, my platinum Rolex watch with the triple-diamond bezel and face, hundred-dollar hairstyles, tailored suits, all the gizmos I'd grabbed in Phoenix.

My story was vacation: visiting family. It was generic but what the hell else was I going to say? "Yeah, I'm here to start a scam operation and maybe rip off a few companies." I think not.

"Your box, Mr. Redding." He led me to the back. I carried the briefcases with me. He stood over me like a vulture. I gave him a look and he exited the room. I removed half the cash from the briefcase and two-thirds of the jewelry. I locked the box, secured the key in my pocket, and headed into the lobby with considerably lighter luggage.

"Is everything in order, Mr. Redding?"

"Yes. Perfect."

"My name is Mervin. If you need anything, just dial the front desk." He handed me a card.

MERVIN C. WHITCOMB
GENERAL MANAGER
FAIRMONT HOTEL, ATLANTA

I signed another paper and R.J. wheeled the bags up to the room. We ordered dinner and drinks and spent the night watching television and taking lines of what little Hawaiian cocaine we had left.

*   *   *

"...so then I got out of prison and that's how I ended up in Hawaii with Terry, who was working for Stromburg Carlson selling phone systems." That was basically the end of my story, and I had told her all the parts before it.

"You ever thought about us selling coke together?" Jennifer asked.

"Well, yeah, maybe. It crossed my mind."

"You seem like you'd be perfect for it." She took a pull off of one of my cigars. "Norberto and Carlos asked me if you had ever been a dealer. Have you?"

"Not really."

"Carlos does well in that business."

"What kind of deals does he make? Like how much money?"

"Well, I mean, you saw some of it. He usually has about 500 grand to buy with. He makes good profit but he spends lots of it. They've got a house in Aspen and that condo in Hawaii. Then there's the yacht, an airplane, some other stuff. And I think he's got another place somewhere in South America, and a new place on an Island in the Caribbean, in the Bahamas I think? But he and Norberto will never discuss it."

*   *   *

We were at the bar, a nightclub a couple miles from the Fairmont, drinking. It was a quiet night, a Tuesday at around 10 p.m. and already I was beat.

"I used to have an office in this town."

"Oh yeah? For what?"

"I had a company called International Western Corporation. We sold merchandise to department stores. Drapes, furniture, chairs, stuff like that."

"I would've never guessed."

"Yeah. I used to work for Lacy's. Did I ever tell you that?"

"No!"

"Yeah, I bought perfume for Lacy's for about a year."

"What happened? Why would you ever quit a job like that?"

"I don't know. It just wasn't for me, I guess."

She took another pull from my cigar and we worked at the drinks. She pushed her lips out and exhaled the smoke; white smoke, a giant plume that clouded the booth.

A slutty waitress walked past. I noticed her, but I quickly brought my attention back to the table. Jennifer was too perfect for me to be bothered.

"You miss the island?" she asked.

"No."

"What did you like most about it?"

"How easy it was to rip off the ATMs."

We laughed. More drinks came and went and came and went.

"You miss partying all the time?" she asked.

"We've only been gone a week."

"I know, but you seemed so into it. You were ALWAYS at Infinity. I used to see you there seven nights a week."

"You were there, too, usually climbing out of someone's limo... alone."

"Well, I was... but usually it was because my boyfriend was gone. What's a single girl to do? Sit around the house alone all night?"

"Oh, don't get me wrong, I'm not blaming you for being in that bar."

"I wasn't there HARDLY as much as you."

"I don't think many people were."

She laughed. "Except for the waitresses."

I fixed my eyes on the ice in my glass, stirred it around.

"What's the plan?" she asked.

"I don't know." I kept stirring. "Wait it out here for a bit. Get our feet on the ground. Maybe look for property... a house?"

"You want to get a house together?"

"Why not?"

"I didn't know you were that serious."

"What do you mean?"

"About us," she said.

"Only if you are."

"But you're Jay Carver," she said, nudging me under the table. "You're the ultimate playboy. All the girls told me about you."

"You'd heard about me before?"

"Who hadn't?"

"Who told you about me?"

"It was some girls I knew from the Hilton."

"What'd they say?"

"That you ate steaks for breakfast, that you were always high, that you knew how to get a girl in bed. You know... that sort of thing."

"Those days are over." I clinched my teeth with resolve. I was trying to be serious about that. "Now it's you and me, Jen. We're business partners. We're just like Bonnie and Clyde."

She laughed. She liked the idea.

"Are you IN or what?" I asked.

"Absolutely."

"Good," I said, finishing off the drink.

"You seem tired." She studied my face, took her thumb to the corner of my eye and wiped something away.

"Let's go back to the room. I need a shower."

*   *   *

Outside the bar was my personal limousine. I had purchased it several days prior with cash and hired an ex-con as my full-time driver. He was a nice guy, a former Angel who was trying to go straight. They never lasted long. And they especially didn't last long driving a vehicle with four wheels.

I knew that chauffeuring me around Atlanta was only a temp gig until he could afford an old Sportster and black jacket. He'd be gone after that, back into the wild blue with the rest of those soldiers. Hopefully, he'd give me some notice. Hopefully, he wouldn't sell my ride for start-up cash and take off one night while I was sleeping. (Highly likely.)

The Angel opened the rear door for me.

"Did you have a good time inside, Mr. Redding?" He was a young guy, probably around 23.

"Good as it can be in a place like that."

"I gotcha."

He shut us in the back, blasted The Who in the cabin up front, and took off for the hotel like a speed-fueled madman.

Jennifer and I rode the elevator to the third floor. The doors opened and we traipsed into the long hallway. I followed the red carpet with my eyes, stared up toward our room. Twenty yards down the hallway some guy was fiddling with the handle, trying to break in.

He was the straight-edge type: a fresh razor taken to the face every day, pin-stripe suit and tie, polished shoes, never cheated in school. Probably he was carrying a .45 under that sport jacket.

I grabbed Jennifer by the wrist. She hadn't seen the man. We slowly turned around, backtracked a few paces, caught the elevator door, and headed downstairs. We took the rear exit and jogged into the parking lot. The driver was still there, stretched out in the back seat of the limo. I'd given him money for a room but I guess everything was being saved in the Harley Fund.

"Joe, get up! Let's go!"

"What?" He looked up wearily and I pulled him out, stuffed him into the front.

"It's time to move. Take me to the Sheraton."

I darted into the Sheraton Hotel, asked to use a telephone. The man behind the desk led me into a booth. I inserted some change and dialed.

"Fairmont Hotel, Mervin Whitcomb speaking, how may I direct your call?"

"Mervin, this is Lance Redding. I'm in room 312 over there."

"Yes?"

"There was some guy snooping around my room when I got back, probably a burglar or something. Could you send security up to check it out?"

"It was not a burglar, Mr. Redding. It was an agent with the FBI."

"FBI?"

"Yes, sir. It is hotel policy to call the Bureau when a client checks in with cash instead of credit."

"What kind of a policy is that? I've never heard of that!"

"Sir, I'm sorry. Is there anything you need to be concerned about?"

"Gimme a break!"

I slammed the receiver.

I was outside, shoving Jennifer back into the limo. "Joe, take us back to the hotel. The Fairmont. Drive in the back way, through that gravel truck entrance or whatever it is. You know what I'm talking about?"

"Yes, sir."

"Park there and we're going to let Jennifer out. We forgot something in the room."

"Are you guys switching hotels or what?"

"No, no... don't worry about it. Nothing serious."

We pulled back up at the Fairmont. I noticed a government-issue vehicle parked in the rear lot. From what I could see, the agent was not in the vehicle.

"Jen," I whispered in her ear. "It's the Feds. They're onto us. Get in there and get whatever you can. We can't go near the safe deposit, but you can get in there and get the stuff we have in the room."

"But Jay!"

"Just get the hell in there and hurry up!" I shouted through a whisper.

"What are you going to do?"

"Well, if I had a gun I'd go in there and raid the deposit box and shoot up the place. But, I don't have a gun, so we're getting the hell out of here. Now GO!" I pushed her out the door. She had left her tooter in her purse and I picked it up, shook it, breathed in what little dust I could scrounge from the bottom.

"What's going on, Lance?" the driver said. "Did I hear her call you Jay? Is that your middle name or something?"

"No. I go by Jason sometimes. Love joke... don't worry about it."

"What's the problem with this hotel?"

"Nothing, it's a great place. She forgot something."

"Why are you leaving?"

"Good god, man! Stop asking me questions!"

He shut the divider and Jennifer returned.

"Hey, Joe," I rolled down the divider. "Take me to the airport."

"You leaving?"

"No, damn it! Shut up! I'm MEETING someone. Who the hell told you to ask me about my business?"

He let us off at the terminal.

"We'll be back in half an hour," I said.

"Alright. Do I just wait out here or what?"

"What you think, Big Guy?"

"Why are you taking those bags with you?"

"I'm throwing them away, Joe." I looked at them: perfectly good bags.

"They're... moldy."

"What?"

"Just SHUT UP!"

"Throwing luggage away at an airport? At midnight?"

I walked away, furious. I would never see him again. Or the limo. Or my jewelry. Or Mervin Whitcomb's pallid face behind the desk at the Fairmont Hotel, who was happy about all of it. Mervin had trotted back to my safe deposit box like a snake behind the counter of the liquor store sneaks drinks. I knew it in my bones.

Mervin had grabbed up 50k, easy, a box of diamonds, maybe a few watches. He took the stuff home to his girlie. She had dreamed of traveling the world on Mervin's dime but never thought it possible.

I could see him laughing maniacally, gripping the bills and tossing them into the air, showering himself in fluttering green and smiling, smiling, smiling. It hurt me a bit. All I'd worked for was gone. I was back to circling the drainpipe, a spider drowning in the sink.

I glanced back at the limo. Smoke from the cigar hooked over my shoulder like a cape and snapped off into the orange streetlight. A plane growled and skidded onto the runway. We walked through the airport, past all the ticket windows, downstairs, out the other side, and into a cab.

"I need to book a private jet," I told the cabbie. "Where do I go?"

He drove.

"Hey, man, you can't smoke in here. Company policy."

I flicked the glowing cigar butt out the window at a light pole. It flew through the air in slow motion, ricocheting with sparkling luminescence into a deep and dark puddle.

Psshhhh.

9

FORT LAUDERDALE

1975

THE JET LANDED, WE EXITED, AND I CALLED A LIMOUSINE SERVICE AND had the driver take us into town. We cruised around for several hours surveying the neighborhoods.

Backstabbing was a common occurrence in Florida—I had learned this from what Gaye Squires had told me about several of her business associates. I'd picked up on the ways of those rich Tampa Bay types from marrying Jane (whose family was from Tampa) but the Miami crooks with their Star Island homes and Rolls Royce Phantoms were a league all their own. It was too much, and I could sense from the get-go that I'd need to keep my eyes on the meal ticket in order to make it through this one alive.

"Driver, please stop here!" I yelled, pointing at a home on the golf course. We had about 60 grand in cash and jewelry. It was enough to rent a nice home and still have money left over for me to secure an office and fund all the expenses that go with setting up an operation.

I was going over names in my head, flipping through a mental Rolodex of all the people I'd ever known and trying to come up with a fake identity.

The AGENT ON DUTY sign was hanging from the mailbox of the home.

I was muttering names while walking up the driveway. "David Rancher, David Blanchard, David... I like David..." I needed a phone book. Stuff was moving too fast and the brake lines had long since been cut.

I wondered where Pat was hiding out? Still with the parents? Maybe he re-enlisted?

"Hi, Damian Scott. I'm the Realtor for this property." He held the front door open, extended his arm and first shook Jennifer's hand, then mine.

"Hi," Jen said, looking up at the impressively large chandelier in the foyer.

"David Hutton," I said, giving him a good hard strong one. "This is my wife, Carrie."

"Hi, David. Hi, Carrie." He was one of those super artificial bastards—the type that the real estate companies lock in a $500k house with no television and a box of files. He gave me a brief tour of the house and spent most of the time jabbering about wood grains and granite countertops.

"This is my dream home, Damian. For my money, there's not another one like it in the world." It was a golf course community. There were 90 other houses that had been designed on the exact same floor plan.

"That's great," he said. "I'll be here all week if you'd like to come back and take another look."

"No, Damian, I mean it's my DREAM property. I can't let this one go. I'll take it."

"You'll just... take it?" he gulped.

"Yes. How long has it been on the market?"

"About a year. It will be hard to move this summer. I can get you a good deal."

"Good. I want a lease for $2,500 a month, with an option to purchase in one year for the list price. I'll pay $2,000 for the option. Present that to the owners and let me know what they think. Is it a family?"

"No, it's owned by a corporation."

"Good. Please get the offer presented today."

"I see, well..." He fumbled nervously with the paperwork, handed me something which I immediately signed and returned to him. Something, a quick shadow, dodged across the back yard.

"You guys have stray dogs out here?" I asked.

"No. Why?"

"I just saw a dog run across the back yard."

"That's impossible, sir. The back yard is entirely fenced." He tilted his head sideways to straighten his uneven smile. I went to the back door and peered into the sunlight. Sure enough, there was no dog.

*   *   *

We had landscapers out back installing palm trees and staghorn ferns around the pool. Several of the ferns hung from the ceiling in polished brass pots. The living area of our new home was round and tapered up to the center. Everything was glass. We had a giant staghorn fern in the middle of the high ceiling and it hung from an enormous chain. Spotlights shone on it.

Probably because we'd been living in Hawaii for so long, Carrie (that's what we were calling Jennifer) and I had unwittingly turned the house into a makeshift version of a Waikiki night club.

Our plan was to set up a lavish appearance for entertaining guests and possible business associates. It was necessary to come across as though we had money to blow.

I was in the kitchen one afternoon, my head in the crevice of my elbow, waiting on hold for someone at the property leasing office. David Hutton—my new identity—was a lawyer, and his office was soon to open in the Fort Lauderdale area. Attached to the rear of the new office, coincidentally, was a warehouse for rent.

A woman answered, "Jergenson Business Properties, this is Blanca."

"Hi, Dave Hutton. I'm looking to rent the 2010 property just off of East Commercial."

"One moment please." She typed something. "Yes, sir, you spoke with William yesterday?"

"Yes, he was supposed to call me back but hasn't."

"I see." She typed something else. "The property is still available and you could begin your lease on the 1st."

"It's the 12th, ma'am. I don't have that kind of time. How about we begin the lease tomorrow and I'll just make that my rent date."

"This particular facility needs minor renovation, Mr. Hutton, and—"

"Forget that. I'll do it myself. Start the lease tomorrow and I'll pay a full month this month."

"Sir, I can't do that."

"I'll pay double this month, I don't care. I need the office. My life depends on having a place to work. Just as I'm sure yours does…?"

She was silent.

"I'm an attorney. Attorneys must have desks. We've got to have leather chairs for clients and files and racks of books. Where am I going to store all that stuff if you don't give me an office? I've got truckloads of files parked outside my house just WAITING to go somewhere!"

"Sir, I cannot do it."

"Where's William. Get me Will. Billy. Whatever you people call him. Get him on the phone… NOW!"

She put me on hold. I waited and put my head down on the counter. There was no more cocaine and we were thousands of miles from any trustworthy connection. The speedy stuff would have to wait a few days until I could begin the law practice.

"Mr. Hutton?"

"Billy, hey, Dave Hutton here. I need that property tomorrow. No question. I got trucks of furniture and files. I need to get in there."

"And you're willing to pay a full month this month?"

"Of course, however, a decent human being would give me the month for free, compensate me for any necessary renovations, and insist that I move my things in whenever I please."

"I can't do all THAT."

"Yeah, I know Bill."

"I'm sorry to be so difficult. What can I do to help?"

"The lease starts this afternoon," I said.

"Come by my office and pick up a key. We'll discuss the terms."

"I knew you guys would come around."

"Look forward to doing business with you, Mr. Hutton."

I hung up the phone in utter disgust.

*　　*　　*

I rented another office space in addition to the office/warehouse on East Commercial. I had two young ladies as secretaries, one in each office, and I could tell that they had a hunch that something funny was going on but seemed to be fine with it. College students were cool with anything if you paid them 10 bucks an hour more than the competition.

I was in my East Commercial office going over paperwork, thumbing through several documents that needed to be forged in order to create my latest money-making brainchild: a promotions company called International Eastern Corporation that would develop sales contests for major corporations.

My phone buzzed. It was Lauren, the blonde who worked the desk out front.

"Mr. Hutton?"

"Yes?"

"There is someone here to see you." What? A law client? Give me a break.

The guy came on back.

He reached across my desk and shook my hand. The way he gripped I could tell he was a working man, someone from the shovels and pick-axes and mud; a true-grit tobacco-spitting laborer with big teeth and a Georgian drawl.

"Ernie Hagar."

"Dave Hutton."

"Pleasure, sir."

"Take a seat," I said, opening my palm to the rented furniture I'd strewn all over the office. I walked past the mirror and checked my hair, which was still colored very nicely and made me appear much older than I actually was.

"I'm in a bind, Mr. Hutton."

"Dave, please."

"Dave." He picked at his teeth with his tongue, thought up the best way to say what he needed. "I had an accident at work and threw my back out." I nodded. "Giant crane tilted half an inch and I went off the side of the platform and when I got up things just weren't right."

"Mhmm," I said, overly concerned.

"Now, my employer is claiming that it's not their fault. They say they ain't going to be responsible for compensating me while I'm out of work."

"That's a tough situation, Mr. Hagar, and I wish I could help you with it. I am not, however, the best personal injury attorney for your case." I opened a book on my desk. I'd taken 20 minutes the other day to jot down a list of lawyers from the Florida Bar Association. I didn't think I'd get many potential clients, which I hadn't, but from time to time people were stopping in and Lauren was sending them back.

I mulled over the list, ran my finger along the names, stopped at Pullard & Bobbitt.

"I'd call Pullard & Bobbitt, injury attorneys, tough fighters, great people."

"Are those the guys from TV?"

"Yeah."

"Are they going to charge me an arm and a leg?"

"They'll charge you whatever they charge you. Probably not body parts. Whatever they want, I'd advise paying them. They're good, especially that Bobbitt guy." I was talking out of the deep blue.

"So, I should get Bobbitt to handle it?"

"Your call. Meet them and make a decision."

"Where are they located?" I was getting annoyed, edgy. I had things that needed to be done and Hagar was clogging up the office. My personal line had rang-out once, and the business line went off like a time bomb. I heard Lauren in the other room.

"Sorry, Mr. Hutton is with a client right now, can I take a message?"

"Alright, Mr. Hagar. Good luck."

He stood up slowly, stretched his aching back, and headed for the door.

"I ain't gotta work my other job—the register down there at the Chevron—until 12," he said, turning toward me and gripping the handle with rough hands. He turned it wearily, moving the door slowly out of his way. "And when I don't have to go in until 12, I can see my little girl. She's not in school yet. Damn... I don't know where I'm going to get the money—"

"Wait," I said, lifting my eyes from a folder where a bunch of fake bank documents had been filed away. I realized how pathetic his situation was. Maybe I could help him. "Mr. Hagar, sit down. What is your employer's name and phone number?"

"The boss's name is Ken Strong. He's the president. His number is..."

The phone rang quietly in my ear and I waited, quickly throwing together a plan of attack.

"Hello, my name is David Hutton, I need to speak with Mr. Strong." Silence, a few clicks. "Hello, Mr. Strong, my name is David Hutton and I am an attorney representing Ernest Hagar. Are you aware of the fact that Ernest has sustained a serious job-related injury?"

Strong jabbered at me.

"Would you prefer that I take this up with your insurance carrier? The suit we are planning to file will be for $2,000,000. Are you interested in making an offer? Mr. Hagar is sitting right here?" Strong ran his mouth. "Mr. Hagar, Mr. Strong would like to offer you $250,000."

I pressed the MUTE button, twiddled the phone in my hand. "Mr. Strong? Yeah, Mr. Hagar said he would rather file if you won't consider $500,000 as settlement." He hit me with another offer. "Let me see if Mr. Hagar will accept $400,000..." I pulled my ear away again, pretended to be in conversation. "Ernie, I suggest you take it." He nodded.

"Ok, Mr. Strong, you've got a deal. I will send the papers over in the morning. Please make that check out to my firm: David M. Hutton LLP. I will draw up a release and have Mr. Hagar sign it. Thank you, Mr. Strong."

I placed the phone in the cradle on my desk.

"OK, Ernie, sign here." He reached across and signed. "Stop by tomorrow afternoon and I will have your check for you. The amount will be for $300,000. I am taking less than my normal fee since this matter was handled so expeditiously."

"Thank you, I appreciate it, sir."

He was gone. Lauren, the secretary, came in with a note and laid it on my desk without saying a word.

"From now on just tell people I'm busy. Tell them I'm not taking any new clients."

"Well, which do you want me to say?"

"You're a big girl. Make it up yourself."

She laughed and headed back into the front room. She was a fox, a striking, blonde college girl with all the right moves. I was a good five years older, probably 50 years ahead of her in real-world knowledge, but liquid intelligence isn't everything.

My office door hung open and the light from the outside world leaked in, a horrible reminder of the magnitude of Earth. If the sun could find me, so could the enemy. And the sun could virtually always find a way.

I put up the barricade against humanity, closed the door softly, the sun disappearing like the world's last sliver of decency. I went back to making phone calls and stabbing cigars into the marble ashtray. The ashtray was full after a while, so I dumped it into the trashcan beside my desk. All the little ashes plumed up volcanically, resting on the desk like snow. I leaned back in my desk chair and spit into the can.

PING.

*   *   *

The money came in at the end of the month and Carrie and I were delighted that we had more than enough funds available to pay the bills.

"So wait, David, I don't understand how you acquire these goods in the first place?" I was funneling goods into my warehouse.

"It's all about purchase orders, looking legitimate, writing checks, sometimes paying for things… It's what I do best," I said, cutting a steak, sipping wine, enjoying dinner with Carrie at Hubert's.

"Moving goods is what you do best?"

"It's kind of like my calling," I said through a bite of steak. Carrie still knew very little about me. It worked well that she did not mind my penchant for criminal ventures.

"I see…"

"You remember those few trucks I had in Hawaii? All that stuff?"

"Yeah."

"Yeah, well, I used to pull stuff like that all the time."

"How do you do it?"

"Well, I'm going to start a company just like the one my friend and I started back when I worked at Imporium. It was called International Western Corporation."

"What are you going to call this one?"

I thought about it for a moment. "International Eastern Corporation. InterEast."

"Really imaginative…"

I laughed.

"I still don't understand how you get all those trucks of merchandise." She studied her wine like there was something wrong with it. I curled my lip and swallowed a bite of meat.

"The company's purpose is the transportation of goods." I chewed another bite. "We'll work in conjunction with my other companies to move merchandise to sellers."

"Right…" She didn't understand. She didn't need to. The waitress came up, poured me another glass of wine. I nodded my thanks.

"I've got that warehouse space in the back of the East Commercial office. I've been using it to store all kinds of merchandise. It's perfect."

"That's good. You want some cocaine?" she asked. Her attention span had run out. She didn't need to understand my work. It was for the best this way.

"You got a coke connection?"

"No. I just wondered. I could call Carlos and Norberto but I don't know if they're in the country."

"Don't ever call anyone from Hawaii. I told you that. That's how we'll get caught."

"Alright..."

One of the male waiters walked past, copped a long stare at my girl. I felt a small tinge of anger toward him. It was a huge change for me. I hadn't felt feelings like this before. I may have actually become attached to someone.

Something had changed when we left the island together. I was no longer the same man who would share women with Terry and sleep with eight girls a week. The perverse lifestyle had perverted me backward, toward this strange and animalist survival monogamy. I'd instinctively sought out the hardest woman, the one who could cut a man's throat and laugh, the one who could blow more lines than Carlos Enrique and still get up in time to make breakfast.

I finished with my napkin and the young man removed my plate. The waitress returned, slapped a bill on the table kindly and asked if there would be anything else.

"Another bottle of that Cab," I said.

"A whole nother bottle?" She seemed confused.

"I'm a big guy. It takes twice the juice to put me under."

"I can't serve you a third bottle—"

I flipped her a bill.

"Thank you. I'm sorry for being a stickler but it's my job. I've got a kid, college loans, busted car..."

"Don't worry about it," I said.

She brought the bottle, uncorked it, began pouring me a glass.

"I'll take it straight." I said, trying to puzzle her a bit.

"Excuse me?"

"Lemme see that." I took the bottle—by this time the old lady at the table beside us had looked over to investigate—put it to my lips, tilted it backward and took a third of the thing in one pull.

"Om..." She stood there looking around to see if anyone noticed. I nodded at her and she returned to the kitchen. We left a couple hundred on the table and walked out. The street was alive and we moved across and through traffic calmly, disappearing into our strange world, into dark and serious places that the young college waitress would never know.

*   *   *

Abandon the house and get the hell out of dodge before the place got too hot. That was the plan.

We were on month two of a projected four—the fourth month anniversary being Labor Day weekend. That great holiday would be our cue to get out of town before the pigs caught a whiff of the already stinking barbeque.

I was wrapping cash in aluminum in case of an emergency flight. I stuffed the bricks haphazardly beneath my desk. It was shaping up to be another long night at the warehouse and I was high as gas on Black Beauties. I'd finally found some speed...

Shipments were coming in around the clock and I had a team of about seven semis bringing in merchandise from all sorts of distributors. These companies were often fence wholesalers who were looking to unload it for cheap. Sometimes I would also acquire merchandise through companies that I was ripping off with bad checks from false identities.

My warehouse manager approached. "So, Dave, whaddya think about all those golf clubs, man? Where should we stack 'em?"

"Your call," I said, moving through the warehouse with a clipboard and taking inventory. I had a big sale coming tomorrow, an auction on the premises, and organization was key if I wanted to make a respectable profit.

"But Dave, we're running out of room in that corner." He turned, pointed, stumbled over something and almost went down.

"Oh yeah? No room?"

"Yeah."

"Well, what do you want ME to do, Cupcake? Hold your hand?"

"Jeez, Dave, I'm just trying—"

"Shut up, Ferris. Just shut up for a minute." I was counting.

He interrupted me again. "Should I try and get the boys to stack 'em on—"

"SHUT UP DAMMIT FERRIS!" I turned to him, slapped the clipboard in his hand. "YOU COUNT THIS SHIT!" I walked toward boxes in the back right corner. Most of it was shotguns and refrigerators.

"Hey, buddy," I said, talking to one of my employees.

"Yeah, Dave?"

"See all these golf clubs?"

"Yeah?"

"Well, first off, find out if anyone here plays golf and if they do tell 'em to take a set on me. And if they don't play I'm not giving 'em out for resale. Make sure you clarify that."

"O.K."

"Alright, then, after you give a set or two away, I want you to get Ferris to help you restack all this stuff at the front of the warehouse. Golf clubs are going to be a good item on auction tomorrow and we need them up front."

"O.K."

"Can you pull an all-nighter?"

"Om..." He scratched his head, dragged on a smashed and bent Marlboro.

"There's something in it for you," I said.

"Like how much, Dave? I already been here for 14 hours."

"You been dead on your feet the whole time. Go take a nap for an hour, get a coffee, some food, pop a Bennie or whatever you people do, and get back in here and let's make this thing work."

"I don't have any Bennies. Nobody does that stuff anymore."

"Here," I stretched out my hand. Ferris had been supplying me with the speed. They were tiny black pills, not the exact same as the Beauties I was used to but I called them that anyway. He called them Boosters, and we had no idea what they were except that they felt just like the Beauties and kept you up for 15 hours.

"What is it?"

"Just take it after the nap and get back in here."

I walked through the warehouse sliding boxes into rows, checking my list of prices, watching Ferris count products like a putz.

A beer came at me from the refrigerator. There was a monster in there, a supernatural force that shoved them at me like a fist punching up from the grave. And I drank them. Hell yes, I drank every last one of them and smashed the bottles in the dumpster out back. I'd wait until I had a six-pack of empties and I'd go out there and throw them one by one, from a distance like a three-pointer. Sometimes I missed but most of the times I made it. No one swept it up, either. The world was a worthless hole. Why not add to the pile?

*　　*　　*

At auctions we'd sell off 100k worth of TVs for 20k to the highest bidder. It was easy as taking candy from a baby—selling goods that I'd either stolen or gotten for near-free. The average price was 20 cents on the dollar and I made all the deals right at the warehouse, which was, as I have mentioned, attached to the back of my phony law office.

The buyers were everywhere. All I had to do was spread the word to a few guys with connections and before I knew it there was a fleet of Benzs and Caddies out back with a bunch of shyster drivers carrying briefcases of cash on their shoulders and .38s in their belts.

I swear that 80 percent of those old codgers in Southern Florida, especially the ones in Miami, had their hands a mile deep in criminal mud.

"We're supposed to be starting in an hour!" I yelled onto the warehouse floor. It was dawn and Ferris was still counting, still sorting and snorting and drinking and smoking. All that pot he smoked didn't help his math skills. He'd convinced me that taking a hit would mellow me out. I took one, a long one, and it didn't do anything but lose me an hour. Yes, for a solid hour of unthinkable agony I had stared into my wall, which had morphed into an undulating body of dark and rippling evil.

I laid my head down on the desk and tried to sleep off the buzz. Thanks a lot, Ferris.

"Bunch of damn idiots," I said, rummaging around the desk for a starting bid list for Mossberg shotguns. "You guys can't even COUNT!" They couldn't hear me through the wall of my office.

Lauren had come to work because I'd forgotten to tell her to take the day off. I paced around the filing cabinets. I was a sight: sweaty, tired, in my day-old suit and tie. I was talking to myself loudly when she cracked the office door.

"You lose one retail price sheet and you might as well can 20 grand of sales! Might as well CAN IT! How the hell am I going to afford a funeral for Ferris if we can't even sell enough to—"

The door let out a tiny creak and Lauren, like a kitten, poked her nose though.

"Are you alright, Dave?" She was smiling, giggling over my antics. "Were you just in that warehouse?"

"No," I said. "I've never been back there before. Take the day off."

"What?"

"Take the day off, kid. Paid vacation. Get lost."

"What are you doing in the warehouse?"

"Seriously, Lauren, it's not up for discussion."

"I wanna know!" She came into the office, leaned on my desk playfully. "Are you selling drugs back there?" She smiled. I guess she got off on the bad-boy mojo. What was new?

"No, nothing like that." I came up with something. "It's my father's warehouse. He owns a trucking company."

"I hear your phone conversations, Dave. I know what's going on back here."

"Yeah, well... what can I say other than the truth? Just take the day off and I'll see you tomorrow."

"I can stay and answer the phones for you. I won't say anything about what I see... or hear."

"It's a Saturday, Lauren. Don't you have something to do?"

"Not today." She pushed her lips out and shrugged her shoulders.

"Don't you kayak or something? Isn't that right?"

"Sometimes."

"Here, how about you take a couple hundred bucks and you and some lucky Shmo can go on a kayaking trip. A two-day thing. Overnighter. Go for it." I peeled off some bills, handed them across the desk. She took them, laughed at me.

"You can't buy your way out of everything, Dave."

"Oh yeah?"

Before I knew what had happened she was across the desk, her lips against mine. She was a cunning little animal and she had youth on me. The speed and flexibility of the early, EARLY 20s female was mind-boggling. It reminded me of how my father used to move when he'd beat me, only Lauren was more graceful about it.

"Yeah, Dave. Money's not everything..."

She walked out, dead wrong but not old enough to realize it.

From the warehouse I could hear footsteps approaching my rear office door. Ferris yelled like the oil main was on fire, like hot gas was spitting up all over everyone: "Davey, we got a problem!" Ferris busted in, a fat joint in his mouth and a cigarette in his hand. "Some guy's here in a Rolls Royce says he wants a peek before auction." He was out of breath, like he'd just run the length of the whole building. "I told him NO but he's gone ahead and busted in the door shelling out bills to Ed and talking about how he's friends with you!"

Strange days in that old East Commercial Avenue office building. But the money was right. And so was the receptionist.

* * *

After a while I had such a steady stream of clients coming in to buy merchandise I began charging a flat fee and stepping back as a middle man. I'd procure the goods, all stolen at this point, and sell them like a fence at what we in the business called "cost," which was a slightly inflated price from what I'd bought them for.

In exchange for my low prices, my buyers paid me a fee. It was similar to Service Merchandise only illegal and run by a bunch of alcoholic drug-heads. So, really, not much different from Service Merchandise.

*   *   *

The end of my projected four-month stay had arrived and Carrie was restless.

"We have enough money, Jay. Let's just get the hell out of here TONIGHT."

"Call me Dave, please. I don't want you to slip in public." We circled each other drunkenly around the kitchen at 10:40 p.m. It was a Thursday night in Ft. Lauderdale and all across America Budweiser sales were up. Everyone was dutifully drinking for an early Labor Day weekend, my old lady and me included.

"Three more days, baby. Three more days…" I gritted my teeth, took a seat at the kitchen bar.

"I'm going to miss this house," she said.

"Hell if I am."

"Why are you such a downer?"

"You're the one who started the argument."

"Oh you just shut up!" She screamed. She cut out a line of powder on the black marble countertop.

"You know the first thing I thought when I saw you sitting across that bar, Carrie?" I asked her. She puffed about my insistence on sticking to the name changes.

Her brown eyes looked up from the mound. I could see the reflection of the cocaine in her pupils: the white mountain against the black rock. She used a kitchen knife to spread it and the blade shined in her eyes like a lighthouse through a storm.

"What did you think, DAVE?"

"I thought, 'There's the kind of girl who'll cut your throat and laugh about it.'"

"Would you stop telling me that? You bring it up almost every day."

"I do not."

"What does it even MEAN?"

"I was drunk and had just gotten nailed in the face by a Samoan gangster. I don't know what it means, it's just what I thought." I held my arms out in surrender. "All I know is that you're the sexiest, most beautiful woman I've ever seen."

"You mean that, Jay? Dave... sorry."

"Yeah, I do." I took a drag off of a bottle of tequila and grabbed a satchel of money from beneath one of the couch cushions. "And what's more, you're totally right."

"About what?"

"About getting out of here before it's too late."

"Where are we going?"

"I'm sending you ahead to Chicago. You're going to go up there and get us a place, get things set up, find some coke or something, and I'll be up there after I close everything this weekend."

"You're leaving me, aren't you?" She burst into tears, emotional from the booze and drugs. It was uncharacteristic of her.

"No! Hell no! I just told you how I felt! Relax."

"You never said you were in love with me."

"Well, I..." What was "love" anyway? Who knew?

"It's alright, baby..." She leaned against me, sobbing hysterically. The cool moon peered through the skylights and snickered at me. The water from the earlier rainstorm was leaking in through the roof. I looked up at it, amazed, transfixed, taken aback, in shock and dismay as it trickled down the wall. It pooled on the floor slowly, brown and disgusting, like something had taken a dump up there.

That damn Damian Scott had sold me a lemon.

*　　*　　*

The girl was gone to Chicago with a small cut of the cash and jewelry. She knew I was coming. All that crap about crying and wondering if I was done with her was an act to get attention. Women will pull that shit sometimes just to reaffirm themselves. Those actions are of a most outright depravity, sometimes insanity, and they often evoke more in the way of contempt than compassion from the male heart.

It was 10 a.m. and I was driving toward my office on East Commercial with a briefcase containing 350k. Labor Day weekend was drawing to a close, which meant that all the stingy companies that wouldn't sell to me without a verified P.O. address would not be able to clear the cashier's checks until the coming Tuesday. It gave me a cushion, a three-day weekend to get the hell out of town before they traced everything to Dave Hutton.

I was swinging by my office in the late-model Lincoln, prepared to pick up a final 10 grand and hit the road. I turned into the alleyway off of East Commercial and was headed up the stone path toward the loading bay.

"What the hell?" I stared over the wheel. The trucks were parked out back, just as if they were unloading, but there was no one to be seen. What's more, all of the doors were hanging open. I slowed down, surveyed what seemed to be a scene from an eerie horror movie.

"What's going on here?" I said to myself.

My Lincoln came to a virtual stop about 30 yards from the dock and the gravel crunched very distractingly beneath the tires. I checked the rearview and sure enough, rolling up behind me were two four-door Dodge Monacos. They were white police interceptor vehicles, no lights, and each was packed with agents.

I gunned it, pulled the briefcase close to me and reached inside, checking that my Smith and Wesson .38 Special was still equipped. I hit 50 by the time I exited the alleyway and made a right turn at that speed, sliding out and slamming into the opposite sidewalk. The oncoming traffic skidded, swerved, stopped, and the slow pickup of the Lincoln trucked me along at 45, 50, 55, 60... I braked hard for the second corner. This one was a left, a hard left, and the rear end slid out and smashed into a pole.

The car kept running, gradually gathering speed with something grinding against the rear wheels. I looked back there: the Monacos were up on me like wolves nipping at a moose's ass. I had the pedal to the floor but my boat just didn't have the juice. I figured that my only chance would be to beat them on foot, maybe fire a few hurried shots to keep them at bay and take off down some alleyway or into the woods.

I heard the helicopter close overhead and yanked another hard left, this time taking the turn with no breaks at about 60 mph. Needless to say, the Lincoln's grandpa tires collapsed and the washy suspension nearly caused me to flip. The car fishtailed all the way across the road, one of those Chryslers riding right beside me, and we slammed a cement block at a gas station parking lot.

I laid down in the front seat, realizing that the chase had finally come to an end. The work in Hawaii, the scams, the cocaine, the speed, Leslie, Jennifer (Carrie), all my efforts had been in vain. I should have stayed in my father's garage. Imagine: I'd still be cleaning up loose arms in the Kaiser Hospital.

I rested my head on the 350k and prepared to let out my final, bullet-riddled breaths. All this stuff… such hell… for nothing!

The car was surrounded by Gestapo, each gun-toting serviceman smashing a window, the windshield, opening the driver's side door and yanking me feet first by my ankles.

I let go of the .38, just loosened my grip and was jerked out onto the pavement—THUMP—where the saints of this great nation kicked the shit out of me, then bolted my hands and feet together—SNAP, ZIP, ARG—and transferred me to the back seat of a squad car—THWACK—where the muffled exaggerations of their first high-speed chase, tales which would echo over Thanksgiving tables for years to come, could already be heard through the tinted safety glass.

10

DIVIDENDS

1975

THEY TOOK ME TO A THREE-STORY BUILDING, TOTED ME INSIDE AND hurled me into a makeshift holding cell with a TV hanging from one corner and no windows. There was a wire-glass window, but it had been painted over. Luckily, several others before me had been smart enough to scratch tiny pock marks in the paint with their fingernails so that a prisoner could peer through the window without the pigs noticing.

I sat in there while the rest of the world drank beers and cuddled in bed. Men paced up and down the hallway and half the time I didn't get up to see who it was. After 15 hours, which must have put the time around 1 a.m., I heard some commotion and several of the grand prize winners came goose-stepping down the hallway. I got up to check it out, hearing sparse fragments of a secret conversation.

"So, what's the score?"

"Barton's guessing around 300 grand but I think he's full of shit."

"Whaddaya mean?"

"I think it's more."

"More than—" The door closed behind them. I kept my face pinned against the painted glass and cut out one of the holes just a little more so that I could see the entire picture without having to move my head.

They were in what appeared to be a boardroom, each of them leaning against a stainless steel table beneath a billiard lamp.

Two of the men argued, but I couldn't hear about what. All in all there were three studs around that table, one guy wearing a suit and two others in jeans with racing T-shirts.

One of the goons reached below and removed a bag. My bag. He set it up there and popped it open, revealing the mountain of cash. There was no more talking after that, just a good long stare.

I saw the mouth of the guy who appeared to be running the show, the one in the suit.

"We split it three ways," he said, holding his fingers up and making eye contact with each man. Then, just like that, he set to work stacking the bricks next to each other and sliding them toward each man.

Then there was the jewelry, which they could only guess at. They passed it around, one of them trying on rings or necklaces and the others just waiting for the signal to go home.

They stuffed the cash into separate canvas bags. Then they left, each man going home to his wife, girlfriend, dog, saying, "Look, I just got our groceries for the next 10 years!" Or, "I'm buying a season pass to NASCAR!" They'd undoubtedly use it for the dumbest shit and probably get caught.

Funny how one man's win can be another man's loss; how one man can make aces full while the other guy just fades away; how the end of one story has the potential to be the beginning of another.

This time, however, I didn't feel that I was going to start fresh. I was up the river and long gone. I wanted to kill myself. It made no difference anymore whether I lived or died. Dying was only a question of WHEN. They had the money now. They'd do me, bury me somewhere in the woods, destroy the reports, avoid the red tape.

There wouldn't be any bailing me out, no restitutions, no father to slide me the crutch. I went over to the television and unplugged it. The cord came out of the back after a few tugs and I secured it to the sprinkler pipe. I made a loop with the cord and stuck my neck through.

"Damn..." I said. "What a terrible view."

I took that last hard step off of the toilet bowl and into the darkness.

*　　*　　*

Of course, the attempted suicide failed on the first go-round. When I awoke I was in severe pain, no less infuriated about my situation, and returned to the toilet for Round II. The same cord was used, and I got up on the steel bowl and repeated the process once more.

This attempt was also unsuccessful. I kept waking up with my arms on the marble stall where I'd caught myself. But this "catching" action was happening post-blackout. The second time I woke up I had forgotten entirely where I was, why I was there, and knew nothing about my life for at least a minute or two. The brain had been deprived of oxygen for too long.

I went over and looked through the wire-glass. When I saw the table, most of the memories came back. I fell onto the cold cement floor, passed out from exhaustion.

*　　*　　*

Sleep was short-lived. I'd wrenched my neck when attempting the hangings. Any position for rest generated agonizing shots of pain.

I had the strange and very sickening feeling that there was no one in the building. Maybe I was being left for dead? Maybe they thought I'd already killed myself? Maybe there was someone coming to kill me?

I wished desperately that I had a painkiller, a sleeping pill, something to knock me out from the crick in my neck. I had nothing, however, and rotted for another gruesome period of dripping blood and unnerving daydreams.

Two guards arrived and did the old "cuffs on through the door" trick and virtually dragged me upstairs and into a small makeshift interrogation room.

"This isn't the police station," I said. They said nothing. "This isn't the jail, either."

"Yeah it is. Shut up," one of them said. He removed a tape recorder, began fumbling with the tapes. "You gonna cooperate with us or what?"

"I'll think about it."

"It can be easy or hard."

I actually laughed at him. "Get some new lines, Dickhead."

"Dickhead?" He kicked me, knocked over the chair I was cuffed to. "Who's a Dickhead now, Jack?" My face dropped and he smiled a giant and evil grin. "That's right, buddy. You never thought we'd figure it out, did you? You're Jack Alexander, from California. Am I right, buddy? Are you willing to cooperate now?"

"I'll cooperate. Sure thing. Gimme a shot of Jack Daniels." I had seen a bottle in the other room.

"If you cooperate, you got it. How about that?"

"You guys are assholes."

He picked me up from the floor, slammed the chair upright and batted me in the back of the head with his palm.

He pulled my hair. "You're graying, buddy. You're such a pretty boy. Aren't you a little young to be graying?"

"You're a bit young to be coming out of the closet—" He kicked me over again. It was nothing to write home about. I'd done far worse to myself with the television cord.

"You're a real character, huh?" he said.

"A character... yeah. Something like that."

"You think you're a badass, don't you?"

"Yeah."

He didn't know how to take it. He set me upright.

"You going to cooperate with us or are we going to have to continue this routine until you're bleeding?"

"I'm already bleeding, Cupcake. Besides, blood's my preferred breakfast drink, so uh…"

"This guy's a sicko, Dickie."

"Wait a second," I laughed. "One of you guys is named Dickie? DICKIE? What a queer name! I never understood guys named—" The chair went over again, really hard this time. It didn't feel any worse than before, only harder. He was very unimaginative when it came to beating me.

I let him pick me up again, set me at the table. Honestly, it was probably more work on him than it was worth.

"You ready to cooperate?"

"Yeah, Dickie… that last kick really pushed me over the edge. I'll say anything."

He lit a cigarette and looked at his partner. "This punk watches too many James Cagney movies."

The other guy laughed.

"You're talking to a guy who just tried to hang himself from the sprinkler pipe with electrical cord and you think kicking over his CHAIR is going to make him cry UNCLE?"

He dragged on the smoke, exhaled a blue plume at the naked light bulb.

"Don't I get a cigarette? What do you smoke, Dick?" He remained silent. "You a dick, Dickie? Are you guys detectives? Dicks? Or just dickheads?"

"Shut this guy UP, Frank." Frank, the other guy, the big silent type with one of my rings on, came over and dragged the chair into the hallway. They had this thing about involving the chair in the beatings. I didn't get it. Why not just punch me in the face? The gut? Stomp on my toes for sport?

Anyway, he chucked me down the staircase like a rag doll. Big old useless Frank: graduated high school in '58, got married to the sweetheart, took a job at the desk for the academy, three kids, big German shepherd with three legs who retired from the force to sit in his front yard and BARK, quiet neighborhood (save for the dog), slight steak gut, Coke-bottle glasses, .44 magnum, old growth mustache. I could see all of this very clearly as he slung me downward and I LAUGHED...tumbling, tumbling...LAUGHING...clanging, snapping, flipping...coughing, slowly dying.

When it was over all I could feel was my neck. The rest of my body, though a bit beaten up, still wasn't that bad off. They carried me back into the interrogation room. Again: more work for them than trouble on me.

"So... you ready to cooperate?"

"Go ahead. Give me the questions."

He flipped on the tape recorder.

"Deputy Frank Barnet and Detective Richard Garrison speaking. Questioning detainee 8342890." He looked up at me. "Will the suspect please state his name?"

I stared at him, a stone face my only weapon against the greatest enemy of my kind.

"State your name, sir."

"Donald Duck. QUACK! QUACK! QUACK! QUACK!" He really hit the chair that time. I could tell he'd been holding back on the earlier ones. This kick sent me headfirst into the wall. Damn, it was actually painful.

He set me back up. "We'll try this one more time."

He tried it again, went through the whole "Detective Dickhead Garrison and so-and-so" routine and I just stone-faced him, made him ask me twice, and just when he was about to give up and nail the chair I pulled the Donald Duck line again and he threw the tape reorder at the wall and stormed out.

Amateur. Total amateur. I had a feeling, right after this display of aggression, that those two hicks were going to murder me. It was a sickening feeling and it wouldn't subside. Worst of all, it seemed totally logical.

* * *

I was taken from that facility, which was NOT a jail, and transferred to Broward County Jail in the back of a squad car. The car stunk like cheap cigars, which the driver smoked continually throughout the trip.

"Nice scenery down through here," he said.

I didn't respond and it was silent for a few more minutes.

"Who gave you the tip-off?" I asked him. Having hardly spoken in the past few days, and with my neck injury compounding the problem my voice sounded thick like an old man's.

"You were hiring drivers for those trucks and paying 'em cash, right?" he asked. I knew how the game worked. I never answered a cop's questions, no matter how obvious. "So, anyway, one of those boys was eating dinner with his family and told his uncle, who was visiting, that he was working for this great company. He told him you were giving out TVs and paying 500 bucks a day... cash."

The car hummed along, the guy lit another cigar. A really nasty one. Naturally.

"So, yeah... you guessed it: The uncle was a cop. He called the local police, gave them the hint, and there you go. You got nailed."

I nodded my appreciation. Knowing how I got caught didn't change the facts, but it brought me the kind of closure that I would need for the next 30 years.

* * *

After booking me in at Broward they jerked me into a car and transferred me to Dade County Jail, where I expected to stay for upwards of six months to a year before they transferred me to a permanent institution.

I took a shower, bought the tiniest bit of commissary, and laid in the bunk thinking about Jen (Carrie, or whatever her name was at this point). The sounds were all there: familiar hums, vocabularies, metal on metal when guards opened doors or closed them. A loud mouth ran wild in the holding cell and there were always several that stayed quiet in the corner of the room like they weren't supposed to be there or maybe they were too good to be there. Or maybe they were scared.

The lights went out and everyone slept, even me.

At midnight they called me out of the cell. What was it? A visit? No...

They walked me down the hallway and put me in one of the interrogation rooms. A Catholic priest came in, sat down at the table beside me.

"Are you alright, son?"

"Yes," I said.

"The Lord is with you," he said, gesturing at me with strange grace and a motion of his arm over his chest. He stood, exited, and I was returned to my cell. What was the purpose of that visit? It must have been a joke on me. For a while I imagined that it was a dream, but then I was back asleep and had forgotten about it.

At 3 a.m. the lights came on and they called me over the PA system.

"Donald Duck," I'd never given up my real name, so they had no choice but to call me what I'd given them. "Please report to the window with your bedding and personal belongings." I stood up, still half asleep, and walked to the door of the cell. They escorted me down a long hallway, locked me in a TINY room with a window and a woman on the other side sorting papers.

"Mr. Duck?" she asked, not removing her eyes from the desk. She had tight curly hair, wrinkles around her eyes from frowning so much.

"Yes," I said, leaning my head toward the tiny holes in the bullet-proof glass.

"Sign these papers, please."

I took the papers through the tray, looked them over, signed them. They were release papers! Wow! There must have been a mistake... UNBELIEVABLE! Someone had screwed up and I was the lucky bastard that would take the walk.

I was handed my belongings: $1.68 cash and the suit from the day of my arrest. The shirt was the same one I'd worn when trying to hang myself. Blood clung to the collar.

There was a limo out front of the jail and the driver came over.

"Hello, sir."

"Yeah?"

"I'm your ride. Are you ready?"

"Hell yes."

"Where you headed?"

"To my house. I need my things. Then to the train station." I gave him my address.

"Got it."

I got in and he took me home.

Inside my house I gathered my things, which were eerily packed and waiting on the floor of the bedroom just as I had left them. I deliberated whether or not to disappear out the back door and make a run for it. I wondered the probability that these guys were going to whack me somewhere during this whole process. There was no way I was supposed to be free. There had either been a mistake or the driver was a hit man.

I got back into the limo. Apathy and fatigue had pressured me toward laziness.

"You need anything before we go to the train station?"

"Case of Miller Lite and some cash," I said, half joking. He stopped at the gas station, purchased the case of beer and handed me 200 dollars.

"Thanks," I said. "Who are you? More importantly, who hired you?"

"Don't worry about all that."

He put me out at the train station just as the sun was coming up. I made a phone call to Jennifer in Chicago.

"They let me out."

"What? Jay? Dave…"

"Yeah. It's Donald Duck now. They let me out. I'm coming. I'll be on the train." I told her my arrival time, my train number, all the info. "You got any money?"

"Just what you gave me."

"Pick me up at the station."

"How'd you get out?"

"I don't know, but I don't like it."

"What?"

"I got a feeling either they screwed up, which would be good, or there's somebody around here tailing me to see where I lead them. Maybe they want to whack me, I don't know."

"Whack you? Dave? Are you serious!" she screamed.

"I don't know. I gotta go. Pick me up on time."

"I will."

I boarded the train.

*   *   *

In Nashville I was startled by a strangely dressed woman. She took a seat beside me and pinched my leg. It was Jennifer—in disguise, of course.

"What's your plan, boss?" she asked. She had flown to Nashville and boarded the train just to ride with me. What a girl.

"We get to Chicago in the morning and check the airports. We stay away from your place and take a flight out of there as soon as we can."

"Where do you want to go?"

"That depends on the closest flight time. I still have a bad feeling about all this."

"Is there anyone suspicious on the train?"

"No, but then again, there doesn't need to be."

She looked around. Nothing: a bunch of old folks, families, business dweebs.

"We get to Chicago and make a run to O'Hare straight from the train station. No limos, none of that stuff. Nothing traceable. Then we're out of there and nobody in the world will have any idea where we are." We didn't have enough money to rent a jet. Flying commercial was risky, but there weren't any other options.

"You have a city in mind?"

"Not really."

"Come on, I know you've got to know SOME place we can go where you've got a connection established. We can't go back to Hawaii, though... can we?"

"No. Hell, they're probably still looking for me from the first score."

"Probably so..." she pressed tight against me. "I feel scared."

"It's fine," I said. It was unlike Jennifer to be afraid. Her saying this made me uneasy.

"You've always got a plan. Why don't you have one now?"

"Relax, were going to Denver. That's the plan"

"I feel like they're going to catch us."

"We'll be fine."

After a while she calmed down and the train clattered toward the city. I stared out the window silently and Jennifer slept. The trees and fields rolled past. There was a man far off, standing on one of the gravel roads in the middle of nowhere. I watched him and he stood there watching me, staring at the train, his hands on his hips and his black silhouette totally motionless. He was a couple hundred yards off but I could feel strange energy radiating from him. I wondered who he was, where he'd come from, why he was in the middle of that road watching trains.

I resolved to close my eyes. It had been a long day and the sun was hidden behind a bunch of gray clouds that seemed to cover the entire country. I kept imagining that at any second someone was going to put a bullet through my head. Maybe that would solve everything. Probably not, though.

11

DENVER

1975

WE DIDN'T HAVE A BOATLOAD OF MONEY AND SO FLYING PRIVATE WAS OUT of the question. I could feel the iron hammer above me, slicing silently through the atmosphere and preparing to do me in. Despite these feelings of hopelessness, I was not content to hide out in a gutter or on skid row. We followed our plan and flew commercial from Chicago to Denver on a late-night flight.

We'd been in Chicago for one grueling and sweaty day, during which I had made 100 phony business cards, purchased a straight-edge haircut, shaved my facial hair, and revamped my entire identity.

My game plan for Denver was simple: arrive in the city with a small wad of cash under the easily respectable title of W. Scott Anderson, CPA.

We got off the plane and immediately contacted a property rental agent. He would take us around town like a family, showing us all the properties and pitching our case to the rental agencies. It was a minor hassle dealing with these agents, as they were often overly concerned with your well-being and personal affairs. Either way, hiring an agent beat the hell out of having some crummy landlord go digging through my giant library of on-the-spot bullshit.

Our agent drove us around for most of the day. Finally, as the sun was going down on the Mile High City, we found an apartment that would be both convenient and somewhat discreet. The company renting the apartments seemed nice enough. They didn't ask too many questions, had a good front office, and there were a few maintenance trucks on the grounds.

I stood outside trying to decide if I was happy with the location. It was just another crummy apartment. Who gave a damn where it was?

*   *   *

There was money for a car, just enough, but I couldn't bring myself to blow it all on one shot like that. Money, to me, was sometimes more valuable than the stuff it could purchase. Sometimes it was more important for me to HAVE money than to use what money I had in order to achieve any sort of physical comfort. Other times, depending upon my mood, I'd slap a C-note down for a six-pack and leave without getting the change.

There would always be more jobs, more money, more everything. The world was an endless geyser of opportunity… if only you knew the right places to drill.

I rode the bus around town looking for employment. It was the same story at every place: "Hi, I'm Scott Anderson, I'd love to work for So-And-So…"

And the woman behind the desk would take my resume, my card, and smile at me like we'd been dating for six months. She'd look up at me at some point during all of it, and inform me, always very nonchalantly, that the company was issuing polygraph tests to all applicants.

On that note I'd usually excuse myself to the bathroom and walk out the front door. There was no sense trying to beat the polygraph tests. No. No sense in screwing yourself over and trashing your persona any more than you had to. There was nothing worse than letting the machines get you down.

I was in an overly expensive suit, hopping on and off the bus all day long and getting nowhere because someone had made a device that could tell the difference between a lie and the truth. The knives and hammers were encroaching on my position. I had to make something happen. Quick.

Getting a good job would depend on my ability to network outside of the conventional system, to become friends with someone who held a position of power and could sneak me into the game.

I stared out the window and the bus came to a stop. It was about a half mile from my house. Not a bad walk, but not a good one to take after a long day of job-hunting failures.

Behind the bus kiosk was a car dealership, a place called Northglenn Dodge. I walked inside. It was about 7:30 and there were a couple guys still working the floor. A tall guy, a cup of lukewarm coffee in his hand, came over inquisitively.

"What can I do for you today, sir?"

"Let me speak to the sales manager."

"Is he expecting you?"

"No, but he'll probably want to talk to me."

The guy went into a back room and I could hear bits and pieces of a conversation. I got a vibe that hit me just right. The other guy on the floor was pretty stocky, looked like he'd lifted weights at some point, and he sat over in the corner sipping the same coffee. They burned cigarettes indoors and from the looks of things ran a comparatively tight pirate ship.

The sales manager came out: large man, about my height, huge chest, tattoos appearing here and there through his white shirt, a bright red tie, a baseball bat in his hand.

"Frank Ostimer," he said, extending no hand to shake. "What can I do for you?" His booming voice filled the entire showroom. The other guy just walked away, totally unimpressed that this guy had come out of his office carrying a Louisville Slugger.

"I'm looking for a job."

"You sold cars before?"

"I used to work for Ralph's, in San Bernardino." People in the car business knew who Ralph Williams was. The truth of the matter, however, was that I had only worked for him a very short time and had used his name and other information I'd gathered from his company to rip off a bunch of other car dealerships. Dropping his name as a reference had been a big part of my notorious bank draft scams.

"You aren't bullshitting me are you?"

"No, I worked for Ralph. Call him up. Check it out."

"I'll do that."

"Be my guest."

He asked me if I wanted the job and I did, so he sent me out front to get a demo for my driver (a Dodge Dart, a real piece of crap) and told me to come in the following morning at 8 a.m. for the sales meeting.

*   *   *

Weeks went by and I moved along at Northglenn. I did alright, pulling in about six grand my first month and climbing with more experience.

Jennifer had changed her name to Linda Anderson. I'd coached her through the classic "epileptic ID card" process, a scheme that tricked the DMV every time.

She got a job under this new alias working in the accounting department of a small bank. I wasn't like some guys who complained if their woman got a job. No, that wasn't me. If my girl wanted to work, more power to her. That may have been one of the reasons she and I got along so well. Linda (Jen) was just like me in the respect that she couldn't sit around while the world punched her in the face.

One weekend we decided to take a trip up to Aspen. We took my new car, a Charger SE, up there and got a room at a resort. We blew some money on booze, skiing, sightseeing, that sort of thing.

We were eating lunch in Aspen that Saturday, at the Hotel Jerome, when I recognized two men in their mid-20s coming through the door. Something struck me as familiar, but right off the bat I couldn't place them. I froze, debating whether they were men I'd screwed over or whether they were friends.

My mind drew a blank, was shocked for a few instants, and then I realized who we'd run into. It was Carlos and Norberto.

I remembered that Jennifer had once told me about their house in Aspen. They came over after a few minutes and took a seat at our booth.

"How's it been going, Jay?" Norberto asked.

"Uh, well…" I said, trying to keep my voice down. "The name's Scott Anderson." I flicked him a business card. He smiled, got a chuckle out of it.

"Oh, oh… I'm sorry. Right… Scott." He laughed a bit more.

"How are you doing these days?" I asked.

"I'm doing alright." The waitress came over and he and Carlos ordered lunch.

"So, you guys living in Aspen or what?" he asked.

Jen told them about our situation.

"Two regular home-builders." Everyone laughed. It was, after all, pretty ridiculous.

"We're looking at getting a house soon," I said.

"How long you been in town? Since you left...?"

"No. Hell no. I've been busted since then, lost everything I had."

"Damn, sorry. How'd you get out?"

"Corruption saves a guy sometimes."

"Bad cops?"

"All they wanted was the dough," I said.

"Wow." Norberto stared into the table. I got the feeling he was imagining his own demise. Criminals did that sometimes; hell, everybody did it, at least to some extent.

Carlos leaned in close and spoke. "We can set you guys up with anything you want. This is OUR show, you know? We basically run this town."

"Thanks," I said. "We really appreciate it." I contemplated taking him up on the offer.

"In fact, if you guys wanna come back to our house we can work something out right now."

I looked at Jen, Linda, my faux-wife, whoever that beautiful woman was, whatever we were. With so many names it was hard to remember who you were in love with. When I looked at one woman I saw two people. It was very awkward for the mind to comprehend those things.

We decided to follow them to their place and somehow the Charger made it through the snow and up the mountain. We were drinking beer on the drive and by the time we got there I was pretty well on my way. Norberto straightened me out as soon as we walked in the door. It was the first coke I'd had in over a month. It was a real long, thick, monster line that ran a good six inches across his coffee table.

He explained, over a few beers, about how a business associate of his wasn't able to find a secure location for the storage of his funds. He kept saying things like: "It's good to have a familiar face in town now." And, "I'm glad you've decided to be part of the team."

Sure, I thought. I was glad to be part of the team. But, then again, what could I offer them? What could I possibly help them with that they couldn't do themselves?

Carlos explained that their financial security methods consisted of burying money underground on the other side of Aspen Mountain, at some guy's vista opposite the ski slopes. There was some problem arising from that, but he wouldn't discuss it at the table.

"Well, I'm thinking about getting a house, if that would help," I said. I didn't understand what they needed, but felt as though I should offer anything I had.

"That would work, Scott." I think he kept saying my name to make sure that it stuck with him. We took a few more lines and drank a few more beers.

When we left, we were carrying a few grand extra and a half-key of the best cocaine to hit Denver since Carlos himself had gone down there and delivered it.

* * *

Linda made trips into the mountains for more and more work. She was doing the majority of our drug sales and I was progressing at Northglenn while simultaneously devising several detailed scams. Things were moving along like always.

I went to the real estate agent and inquired about purchasing a house. My tactic was to seem slightly uninterested, as though I had been browsing the market for years, so he wouldn't pick up on my urgency and connect it to some sort of criminal motive.

After a few weeks of casually examining the market, Linda and I were in the furniture stores buying items for our new house on the outskirts of Denver.

* * *

Carlos and Norberto stopped by at 10 p.m. and unloaded the contents of their truck into my basement. Both carried what appeared to be three or four armfuls of groceries, and at first I wondered what was going on.

"They're bringing in money," said Linda, rushing down the porch steps to lend a hand. "I forgot to tell you."

"Wow," I said, my jaw gaping at the sight of two grown men hauling grocery bags full of cash through my front door.

"You've got a basement we can use, Scott?" Carlos smiled. He handed me a box of Dominican Republic cigars.

"Yeah."

"Well, we're going to fill it," he laughed. They carried the bags downstairs, walking all the way to the farthest corner like a man would stack hay in a barn that he intended to fill.

"Nice truck out there," I said. I had sold it to him.

"Yeah."

"How much is in one of those bags?" I asked.

"It varies." He looked at Norberto.

"It depends on the denomination."

Carlos studied the cash, trying to remember his figures. "Well, if it's U.S currency, some bags are all 20s and at 10 lbs..." he bit his lip, mulling over the figures. "A bag of 20s is about 90 grand. Some bags are 50s. 10lbs of 50s is about 225 grand. Most of these, however, are 100s. 10 lbs of 100s is about $450K."

"Yup, that's it," Norberto agreed.

"Damn," I said.

"There's more to come," Carlos said, carefully surveying the basement.

"How much more?"

"That depends on how long winter lasts. You see, we usually bury this in the mountains at Woody's place. Woody's property is great because you can't get there except by skis or snowshoes in the winter. Problem is, around this time it gets too cold. When it's this cold and the ground freezes, we can't dig. That means we have to find another place to stash the dough."

"You can't thaw the ground out?"

"I mean, sure, in theory, but there's no way to do that without some kind of supply of hot water. And that would be stupid anyway because then it would just freeze harder on top of all the money."

"Right..."

"The best thing we got is a backhoe tractor, and even that thing can't get its claw through the ground when it's like this."

"Damn..." I looked at all the money; probably around a million bucks in the corner of my basement. It was a hell of a stash.

*   *   *

Gas prices shot through the roof and the buyer's market for new automobiles sank like a lead weight.

Norberto came into Northglenn Dodge one evening and purchased several 4x4 trucks. His employees needed transportation that could compete with the four-wheel-drive Saabs the Aspen police and DEA were driving.

The powers that be were engaged in what was called OPERATION SNOW STORM. The plan was to tear out the cocaine heart of Colorado (Carlos, Norberto, Woody, a guy named David, and several others) and leave the body to die.

According to Norberto, it was wild territory up there. Off-road vehicles were an undeniable necessity if you wanted to have an edge over law enforcement.

"I'll be by your place later this week," he said, shaking my hand as his drivers started their trucks and headed for the mountains. "It'll be Carlos and I. Wednesday at 8 p.m." He raised his eyebrows. "We got a truckload."

"What?" I was surprised. I'd never seen a truckload of cash before. Actually, I don't think I'd HEARD of a truckload of cash before.

"Yeah. Be home and be ready to help carry."

"Hey, Norb…"

"What is it?" He turned from the door.

"You think I can get a small loan, man? I've got some bills pending and some investment ideas."

"Take whatever you want. I don't care. Just be there Wednesday at 8."

"I will. Wednesday at 8."

"Tell Jen I said hi."

"I will." Why couldn't anyone understand the phony name thing? It was so totally necessary for my safety and yet, somehow, no one seemed to remember or care.

The owner of Northglenn came stomping through the door at the same time that Norberto exited. My manager, Frank Ostimer, the guy with the tattoos and baseball bat who had hired me, was in his office ranting about the crashing auto market.

"Frank! Frank! Get out here and tell me what the hell is going on!" He boomed into my boss's office.

"Mr. Herron, how's it going?" I saw Frank extend his hand and Herron didn't take it. He gave him the long stare, put one hand on his hip, and leaned backward as if to gesture at the showroom.

"What's the problem with this dealership?" he asked.

"Problem? Nothing. What do you mean?" Ostimer was confused, raised his large arms in question.

Sales had gone down over the past few weeks and the month wasn't on a path to make the numbers. Herron was pissed, but it wasn't our fault. Per capita, we were selling more cars than anyone in town. The mooches just weren't coming in.

Then, for some unexplainably stupid reason, I joined the conversation and got myself into a world of shit. Herron wanted to fire me on the spot for insubordination.

Frank walked me outside. "Take it easy, Scott," he said. "You got a good job here. Just stay cool."

"What do you mean by that? You think I can't get a job somewhere else?"

"I know your type," Frank said. He smiled. "I knew it from the way you stared at my jail tattoos and I knew it from how you got off the BUS wearing a thousand-dollar suit."

I gave him a good stare. Yeah, he had my number. There was no denying any of it.

"Don't talk to the boss like that, Scott. Not that I disagree, but it just makes it harder for everybody else."

"That guy's a jackass. That's all. Some people need to hear it. That guy needed to hear it and I know he wasn't going to hear it from anybody else but me." I looked around the lot. "I'm taking the day off."

"Take it easy, man."

"You too, Frank."

*   *   *

I spent a few hours in the basement organizing what little stuff I had accumulated down there. The place was damp and dark, and the cash made the whole room smell like money. I went over to the bags and flipped through some of the bills. What was to keep me from grabbing all the dough and taking off right then? Well, nothing I guess. But I didn't do it.

I held up one of the bags and felt the weight. It was a guy's retirement right there. A few cars, a down payment on a house, a boat, any number of expensive things were just sitting in the mildewing grocery bags. There were men in the world who would kill for the money I was holding, many more who would never see anything close to it.

I began to think out loud. "I wonder if this is it? My big score? If they put enough money down here it might eventually be worth it to buy a truck, load it up, leave Linda, and head for the border." I saw myself behind the wheel of the Charger, burning south while the rest of the world rode their desks and keyboards.

But then again, there was no way I could do it. I couldn't leave Linda. She'd stuck with me through the Fort Lauderdale episode. She'd met me on the train and held me up when the only thing I owned was the torn up suit on my back. She was a solid girl, and what's more, she trusted me. I wouldn't leave her like that... not for some lousy drug money.

Like I said, you can always find more money. On that note, I began to look for another job.

*   *   *

My recent employment history in the city of Denver made it easier for me to find work. Within a week I was a salesman at Frontier Chevrolet. I'd see Frank Ostimer every now and then driving around town. I'd be driving my new Corvette and he'd wave. I'd wave back. That was about it.

I began to get very comfortable and was putting a good bit of money into the continued furnishing of our new home. Linda got comfortable too, so comfortable that one night when I came home late from the dealership she was at the neighbor's house having drinks. I didn't go over there, just read her note and counted a stack of cash that she'd left on the counter.

I sat there and flipped through a magazine, stared at the wall, listened to sports radio.

Well, what the hell, what could it hurt to go over to the neighbor's for a beer? Linda was doing a good job selling blow, I was doing a good job at the Chevy dealership, the economy was back on track from its little stumble. Things were going alright. What sort of trouble could I get into over a few beers with the neighbors?

I knocked on the door. "Scott Anderson," I said, shaking the man's hand.

"Nice to meet you, Scott. Name's Karl Kruger, come in." He ushered me in, an older guy, friendly looking and probably retired. "My wife's in here. She loves having people over. She'll be glad you came."

"Hey Scott!" Linda yelled, a few drinks had loosened her up. Perhaps a few too many but who the hell was I to say? "Scotty, this is Hillary Kruger." Linda introduced us. I shook Karl's wife's hand and sat down on the couch.

His pad was admirable. There were jazz albums all over the walls and a few shots of him playing guitar in what appeared to be fairly notable groups. There was a really good one of he and Ella Fitzgerald having drinks at some bar. The photo was signed, "Ella."

Karl had his act together and right off I liked him for it.

"Music's your thing, eh?" I said.

"It's what I do, yeah." He and I walked out back for a cigarette. He cracked me a beer and passed me a book of matches. He smoked Camels. I didn't love a Camel, but I smoked it anyway.

I could sense that Karl may have at one point been a criminal of some kind. Maybe it was something minor like pot, or maybe it was the whole counterculture musician vibe; either way, I couldn't really figure him out.

We made conversation about a few things; mostly he wanted to talk about music, but we weren't into the same stuff.

"I was in San Francisco last weekend," he said.

"How was that?"

"Good. Saw the Dead at Winterland with my son. That was pretty awesome."

"Yeah."

That sort of thing went on and on. I made up some stories about normal person activities like watering the lawn, paying off a car, drinking three beers on the weekend, my thoughts on having kids, whatever seemed to strike the "Average Joe" chord.

We smoked and drank for most of the night. Linda and I left later than I expected.

"If you need anything, Scott, just let me know." Karl and I shook hands heartily and I walked loosely down the old brick steps and toward my house. Linda was under my arm, drunker than I'd seen her in a long time. They were good people, Karl and Hillary Kruger, living in the age of Gerald Ford and doing well.

*   *   *

When I got home from work the next afternoon Jennifer was on the couch crying. Yeah, yeah... I knew what she was crying about... I'd seen the van but I'd tried to ignore it; pass it off as the cable guy or something.

But, no, the cable guy didn't drive a blank white panel van with an antenna on top and government tags.

I grabbed a pen and paper and began writing:

It's alright. Relax and play it cool.
DON'T TALK, whatever you do...
Did they come in? Did they
WIRE the place?

She read it and responded on the notepad:

I sold an OZ to a
DEA agent. I'm sorry.

I pointed feverishly at my other questions. She nodded. They'd been in the house, they'd probably wired everything. It was a trap and they were aiming to get ME, not her.

Did they check the basement???

She shook her head: NO. Great. At least we still had the cash stronghold... for now.

I turned on the stereo, set it at a low volume, just as I would have done any other day, and tried to make it annoying for the guys in the van by clattering a bunch of dishes around and preparing steak on the grill.

Karl was outside, too, and he came over. We talked about nothing really, which was good considering the house was tapped. Any non-criminal that I was friends with made me look less like a target. Not that I was fooling anybody by running my mouth about jazz music, especially Karl, but it could temporarily make them think twice about raiding my home without sufficient evidence.

"We should do dinner some time, Scott," Karl said. "You know, you guys come over and hang out like we did the other night."

"I'm game," I said.

"I'll talk to Hillary and see what day will work for her. I'd love to hear some more about Kansas." I almost laughed out loud. I had forgotten that I'd told him we were from Kansas. Good, his comment might throw the pigs off a bit...

"Yeah, Karl, that sounds good. We'll talk about Kansas. Anything you want to know."

"Alright, I gotta head on." The old guy walked away laughing about a grasshopper that had landed on his shirtsleeve. He laughed just to laugh. He was the frugal type, a man that derived pleasure from the trees and the noise of the world rather than the cash in his bank account.

His exaggerated motion when the bug landed on him made me chuckle, which probably made the guys in the van laugh, which probably made the guys in the Fed laugh, and the whole world started laughing at the regular absurdity of all this crazy shit. What was the point! Why was I running? Why were they chasing! WHO WAS I? A deranged scream, beyond anything manmade or physically possible, tore through my mind like a jet engine.

I flipped that porterhouse steak once, then twice. Tweedle-dee-dee, tweedle-dee-dum... It was time to leave town. I'd give it a week, tops, and then I'd be gone.

* * *

If the DEA or whoever wanted to sit out in the driveway and listen to Linda and I run our mouths about baseball games and Led Zeppelin, that was just fine. It was good, in fact, because it meant that they didn't have enough evidence to come busting through the door and nail me. I felt safe with that van out there, just so long as I didn't make a wrong move.

Someone in the Bureau had no doubt begun putting together a file on me suggesting that I was the nationally wanted fugitive "Jack Alexander." One of the cops, I think it was Dickhead from Fort Lauderdale, had mentioned something about "The Interstate Criminal" from San Francisco, Hawaii, Atlanta, and San Diego. The problem was that I didn't look the same anymore (compliments of tricky shaving and hair dye) and they probably had no picture to go on other than the one they took when I was arrested three years ago in my apartment in La Jolla.

Their tactic, I imagined, was to connect me to the local cocaine distribution network and see if I would unwittingly lead them to Carlos and Norberto. They assumed, also, that Linda would cooperate with them in order to save her own ass. I knew that she wouldn't leave me hanging.

A few days later I purchased a brand new Dodge Charger SE, one of the nicest models that Northglenn carried, with a bad check. I hated Mr. Herron, the owner, and so figured I'd stick one to him under a false identity. I impersonated a local dealer over the phone and had a driver pick up the car so that no one would connect me to the heist.

I drove the new Charger to a field a quarter mile from my house where I parked it and walked through the woods all the way to Karl's fence, through his backyard, and into my own house. I sat down at the counter and scribbled notes to Linda:

The car's out back.
We eat at the Kruger's tonight and
climb over the fence after dinner.
They won't realize we're gone until
some time tomorrow.

She rubbed her fingers together as if to say: "What about money?"

Grab what we can take.
Nothing too noticeable.
20 grand, maybe more...
I'm going to try and sneak

New shred of paper:

15 pounds of 100s into the woods
up on the hill and bury it
along with the scales and all
the equipment.

I slapped the paper against the wall as hard as I could, hoping to vibrate the microphones in the windows and send one of the prying agents onto his ass.

*   *   *

I wrapped the cash in aluminum, 22 grand in 20s, 50s and 100s, and stuffed the bricks into a briefcase which contained a few clothing items and various valuables I planned to take on the run.

In the living room Linda was watching a Western. Three men on horseback were talking while two others rode off into the sunset. I watched it for a few seconds, imagining that I was there. Linda and I were the two riding off into the desert. In reality, it wasn't that far from the truth.

I swallowed a big gulp of vodka and pulled her off of the couch. The TV continued to play and I opened the back door and with discrete movements carried the briefcase across the yard and positioned it beside Karl's fence. We would climb this fence as part of our escape.

All that money in the basement, a fully furnished home, the new TVs and stereos, the wardrobe, my new grill, the dining set, all of it was gone because of one wrong move.

"Karl, how's it going?" He shook my hand somberly. I'd spoken with him about the plan. I hadn't told him the full story, but he knew why we had to leave. He and Hillary had agreed to help us make the escape.

"Sit down, sit down and eat," he said. We ate and had a few drinks. Karl explained modern jazz and told stories about how he'd played with some of the greatest musicians of all time.

And then, just like that, we were gone.

"You think that Bonnie and Clyde ever did anything like this?" Linda asked, taking my hand and pulling herself over the fence.

"All the time. Probably with loaded weapons and shooting at the cops."

"You think?"

"I mean, yeah. That's what they did for a living, right?"

"They robbed banks, didn't they?"

"We rob banks, just in an indirect way—Linda!" I grabbed her just in time to save her from falling into a creek.

"I guess you don't really need to call me 'Linda' anymore."

It seemed like the end of a great holiday. For a while, a very brief while, I'd felt like a normal guy. And honestly, the normalcy had been very enjoyable. I was going to miss having friends like Karl.

"I brought some coke," she said. I'd told her to leave it but what the hell did it matter? If we got caught, we got caught. If we needed to catch a flight, we'd ditch the coke. If we didn't get on any planes we could blow lines until we got somewhere else.

We found the car without a flashlight and started her up when there was no sign of traffic. I tore off into the night, merged onto the Interstate, took a hard line from Jen's tooter and off we rode, a couple of outlaws sticking to their guns and making a hard run into the Promised Land.

12

Houston

1975

I PARKED THE CHARGER IN A LOT SOMEWHERE IN SALT LAKE CITY, UTAH, and we boarded a train for the Lone Star State.

Why Houston? Because I couldn't think of another place where the Feds would be sleeping on the job. I also figured that I'd always been spotted heading north. Every train I'd taken, every Interstate, had always been northbound. I recalled these instances, trying to keep an accurate mental record of my moves: I had escaped from Fort Lauderdale and gone north to Chicago, then flown south under the radar to Denver. I was now escaping from Denver to the northwest, to Salt Lake, and then from here I was heading southeast to Texas.

Crisscrossing seemed like a good idea, and to a degree it was my momentary indecisiveness that made our moves so difficult for Johnny Lawman to predict.

The train grinded into the station and I was jarred from half sleep, remembering only a fragment of a prison dream. There we were: Houston. I'd been there once or twice, enough to get the lay of the town.

We didn't have much money, but something in the heavy Texas air made me feel like a king, like I already owned the place.

"Jen, let's go." I gently pulled her from the seat and we exited into the terminal. She leaned against me, wrapping her arm around my waist and walking with her eyes half shut.

Carrying only two small bags of luggage, we made our way to an expensive bar a block away from the station. I took a tall chair, chewing on the complementary nuts like dinner. I ordered a steak, a beer, and began flipping through my mental Rolodex for a list of potential contacts.

Oh well… nobody up there worth dialing.

I noticed that Jen was returning to "normal" from her three-day cocaine high. It had kept her going for the entire run, but the physical withdrawal was beginning to take a visible toll.

"You think you can eat something, babe?" I asked.

She didn't respond, just browsed the drink menu complacently.

"We're out of drugs, Jay," she said. As though I hadn't thought that… Being without drugs was a fundamental problem, a vastly incomprehensible culture shock for two people who were otherwise heavy users.

I felt that the situation was beginning to take a dreaded, but expected, turn for the worst. I was tired. When I got tired I stalled. I was stalling right then, sitting at the bar and brooding about life rather than making a move. The sun was setting and every moment that I wasn't making money the wallet came closer to the big ZERO.

"Double shot," I said to the bartender. "Vodka." I slapped a C-note on the counter and grimaced at the cramp in my right leg. Damn train.

In the droplets of sweat from the stagnant bar air I could sense my power draining and my strength fading even more rapidly than expected. I knew that I was missing something, but couldn't figure out what it was. I chewed on the nuts, downed the double shot, and chased everything with beer. I lit a square from a pack that I bought at the bar machine and pulled the plate of steak toward me.

Jen racked up an unnerving martini tab and eventually became so drunk that her head fell into her arms. No one in the bar seemed to give a damn.

I sat there and ate my meal stoically, chewing with strength, like a slow and deliberate lion. I stared at my reflection in the mirror behind the bar wondering who I had become and what I planned on doing about it.

A definable goal presented itself: I needed a quick quarter million. That's it. That was step one: pinpointing a definable figure. 250k would definitely get me out of this slump. The only question: How the hell was I going to pull it off this time?

*　　*　　*

The bartender gave me some lip because I kept asking to use the telephone, but his foul mood did nothing to stop me. People like him were merely unnoticeable speed bumps littered along the road to success. I gave him a good tip and we got the hell out of there before I did something out of line.

The agent took us around town and showed us the apartments. It was the same routine everywhere I went. I couldn't help but imagine how things would end up. Every home we saw I would wonder something like, "How would I escape if the pigs busted down the front door?" Or, "How would I fare when rocketing down these wet streets in a drunken rage? Would I be driving a stolen vehicle, the gleaming fangs of the local cops nipping at my ass? Or, would I be caught in a shootout? Killed? Maimed? Left for dead? Drowned in the Gulf?"

Who knew what the world held for a man like me.

"I like this place," I said, standing in the living room of the apartment.

"Yes, Westheimer is certainly one of the best streets in town," my agent read from his notebook. What an unimaginative fool.

"I think I'll take it."

"Wouldn't you like to know the rent?"

"Yeah, sure. But, I'll still take it." People...

*　　*　　*

I went across the street to the Service Merchandise store and purchased a very large television. I carried it back to my apartment through the pouring rain and came close to dropping the machine once or twice because the box was so slippery. An angry dog barked loudly at the storm. Great, I'm sure I'll be listening to his bark day in and day out.

I was dripping like a dishrag, peeling the wet cardboard off of the television while the woman pleaded with me.

"But, Jay, where are we going to SLEEP?"

The cold hardwood floors stared up at us.

"First off, don't call me 'Jay' anymore. Ever. Not even in the house. Not ever." I took off my jacket, hung it out to dry on a door knob.

"I can't even remember what your name IS this week," she pouted.

"Look, babe, if you got a problem with the lifestyle, I'd suggest just getting the hell out of here because it's not going to change unless they cart me into the pen or some wiseass shoots me."

"I'm just nervous, Matt."

"That's more like it." She came over and gave me a big hug. Lightning flashed outside. The half-cracked blinds created strange patterns all over the blank floors and walls of the apartment. "Just have a few more drinks, baby. I'll be back."

I went out into the rain for a second time. On foot. I grabbed a cart full of blankets and pillows from the Service Merchandise store. For dinner, I purchased a can of bean dip and a bag of tortilla chips from the gas station.

I went back to the apartment and Jen was watching some sitcom or another. We shared the beans and chips, spread the blankets on the floor, and after a half hour we were both asleep.

*   *   *

I took the bus around town looking for jobs but, as I had suspected, virtually ALL employers were requiring that applicants pass a polygraph test. The car dealerships, office machine jobs, anything and everything, were requiring that the applicant be an honest citizen. It was horseshit and I knew I'd find a way around it... but when?

By 6:30 p.m. I was still empty-handed and riding the bus back to Westheimer. I felt the same as I had on the train ride: I was missing something. Had I left something behind? (Other than Carlos' and Norberto's millions?) No, I hadn't left anything. It was security that I missed. I had felt, for the first time in my life, what it was like to have a home, neighbors, a job, a good lady keeping me focused, the stuff most people take for granted.

Sure, we'd been high on coke all the time and, sure, I was an alcoholic; but through and through we had been as honest as I'd ever been before. Something about leaving Denver bothered me, and I knew that one day I'd have to go back.

When I got off the bus it was dark. I was 10 miles from my apartment, which had happened because of my inability to read the bus schedule in the failing light. I stood beneath an awning, reading the billboards and bullshit and waiting for the rain to pass. There was a dealership right up the hill, a giant place with a sign that read:

BARNEY'S BOATS
GOING OUT OF BUSINESS SALE

I studied the building for few minutes, hoping that maybe the storm would ease up. A few minutes turned into an hour, and when I next checked my watch it was 9 p.m. The bus drivers had long ago abandoned their routes for the liquor store. I was on my own.

I ran through the rain toward the boat store, repeatedly telling myself that every second unemployed was a second closer to the guillotine.

"I'd like to speak to the manager."

"Is he expecting you?"

"Don't worry about it."

I walked on back there, sopping wet from the rain. I rounded a corner into a bright hallway and became frightened by the prospect of taking a job at a closing boat store.

The hallway smelled like cigar smoke and sweat. I tapped on the office door. Behind the desk was a larger man with deeply resigned eyes and a poorly trimmed beard. He had a giant Cuban cigar in his mouth, an Upham's cigar, which immediately swayed me to the belief that he and I would get along. He set down his Playboy magazine and extended his right arm.

I introduced myself as Matt Reynolds.

"Dennis Miller. General Manager. You want to sell me a boat, buy a boat, or are you stupid enough to come in here looking for a job dressed like some pimp?" I guess he was referring to my suit. It was more of a business suit than a pimp suit, but I don't think he gave a damn. To Dennis Miller, a suit was a suit, and all he knew was that he didn't own a single one.

I told him that I was looking for a job.

"You sell boats, Mr. Reynolds?"

I spun him the whole tangled ball of yarn: I had grown up on boats, owned boats for years, sold hundreds, if not thousands, of boats, father was a Navy man, etc. It was all BS, but it seemed to get me somewhere because he pushed the Playboy magazine into a drawer and led me to the showroom.

"Nice ring," he said. It was my pinky ring, the one I'd gotten after doing that favor for the cons in Vacaville. I made a very subtle comment about the Orange County Hell's Angels colors tattooed on his right arm. With a shit-eating grin he cocked his head at me and patted a thick hand on my back.

"Alright, Reynolds, you're hired." He laughed. I laughed too. "By the way, Matt, I didn't see you drive in?" He still had that jailhouse smile. He knew what was going on. Well, maybe not totally, but he knew that I wasn't a man of the conventional world.

"That's right. I have no car as of the moment."

"Well, that just won't do," he said jokingly, tossing me a set of keys. "Tomorrow morning, 8 a.m., this showroom. Sales meeting. Be here or I'll send my goons after you." He laughed and headed for his office. "That VW's a mess, but it runs fine and it's better than taking the damn BUS to work."

Hell yeah it was.

*   *   *

I made friends with Bass Williams, a really young salesman, probably about 21 years old, who had been a boat guy all his life. He taught me the ins and outs of boats and after just two weeks I'd raked $7,600 in commissions.

He took me down to his buddy's shop and I rented a Monte Carlo. I didn't have a credit card, so renting a car was difficult. The Beetle would have worked just fine, except that it was missing first gear and reverse, which meant that my life, already muddled by booze, was further complicated by "planning ahead" at every parking location.

Bass and I were outside work one afternoon, each about to take a long lunch break, when he told me about some crazy guy who was building boats out in Addicks.

"Well, I'll tell you a secret but you gotta take it to the grave." He didn't give me time to promise. "A buddy of mine, guy named Carl, stole a boat mold from Southwind." Southwind was a company based in California that made jet racing boats. Jet racing boats were basically the hottest items in the market. Hell, even I had heard of them.

"Yeah, go on," I said. We walked to my Monte Carlo, got in, headed for some restaurant.

"He's building them down there by the Reservoir, just off the Katy Freeway." Bass and I lit cigarettes and cracked the windows. "It's about 15 miles away. You wanna grab a burger and drive up there and check it out?"

"Where's the production facility?"

"I just told you."

"I mean WHERE—in a house, in a factory, the Marianas Trench…?"

"It's in a barn. At a ranch. You'll see."

"I wonder if we could sell these phony racing boats to the customers at Barney's?"

He mulled it over for a second, took a drag on his cigarette. "I guess anything's possible…"

*　　*　　*

There was a large old ranch house that had burnt to the ground and behind it was a barn of even greater size. We drove through a gate, passed some fields, and parked outside the barn. We went in and I met Carl Bunyan and his father, Paul.

We told them about our position in the boat market: We could sell their knock-off Southwinds like fresh bread. The guys looked at us like we each had two heads.

"We haven't even started MAKING the boats yet," they argued.

"That doesn't mean we can't start selling them," I said. They snickered, implying that I was ignorant. Who gave a damn what they thought? My plan would work. Those old farts just didn't have any imagination. We left the ranch and I went and had some business cards printed up. Bass and I called our new company Gulf Coast Ski and Marine.

Later that evening I told Jen about the Gulf Coast operation. I asked if she'd be interested in helping me keep records. She had a background in accounting and agreed to do whatever she could.

She hadn't been doing much of anything for as long as I could remember. Most of the time she just sat on the couch watching television. Her determination to succeed had dried up after the Denver fiasco.

In addition to laying around all day and sucking up monetary resources by buying useless furniture, Jen had gotten a cat. She named it Sugar and it was the meanest damn cat that had ever walked the face of the Earth. I hated it, often thought of taking it to the pound, but Jen loved it.

"It says something when a guy's wife loves an animal THAT mean," I used to joke. Jen would throw a ball of fabric across the room and the cat would attack it like an evil beast. It never gave up, either, just sat on the floor killing the little rags until they were torn to nothing.

*   *   *

It was a Saturday afternoon and my feet were tired from working the floor. We were making good money that day, and I almost let the last customer slip. When I saw him coming in I was headed for a cigarette but something caught me, held me, kept me in the game. It must have been his averted gaze, the way he seemed to look over his shoulder like he'd just robbed a bank. He probably had, come to think of it....

Rather than me approaching him, he came up to me.

"You guys sell jet boats here?"

"Well," I said, reaching for a business card. I couldn't believe it. "I represent a manufacturer of Southwind jet boats—knockoffs, mind you, but they're just as fast and reliable as the real deal." I cleared my throat. "And what's more, they're half the price."

He stared at the card somewhat disapprovingly, giving me the impression that he was disgusted.

"It's 10 grand, cash, and we have the thing on a trailer for you. It takes two weeks. No problem. No sweat."

"Only 10 grand? And the thing really works?"

"If not, you know where to find us." I pointed to Barney's Dealership. Little did Old Barney know...

"You have cash?" I asked, trying to put him on the defensive.

He flashed me a wad; a huge stack of 100s. I love a qualified buyer.

"Your operation sounds like bullshit," he said.

"Meet us out there. See the factory. Check it out for yourself."

"I'll do that."

I told him to come out to the ranch at 10 p.m. that evening and we'd give him a tour of the facility, show him some models. He could make the choice for himself.

Bass came up to me a few hours later, told me a similar story. His guy was meeting us at 11 p.m. Perfect. We'd only been in business two days and already things were taking off.

I called Carl Bunyan, the guy with the mold, and told him to meet us out at the Ranch at 9:45. For some reason or another he couldn't make it, told me he'd leave the key to the barn and the gate under a rock.

*   *   *

We got there at quarter til 10. There was no key under the rock. Maybe Carl had forgotten, maybe he'd decided not to trust us. Probably the latter.

Bass and I were standing there, right in front of the gate, hands on our hips, when the late model Corvette arrived.

It was my buyer. "What's going on here?" he asked. I sensed distrust in his tone.

"We forgot the key, man. Sorry. No big deal."

I climbed the fence. Luckily I kept a flashlight in the Monte Carlo. I went over to the barn and stuck the light into one of the windows. I could see the boat mold in there.

"What color boat do you want, Mr. Hale?"

"Blue with Silver pen stripes."

"Well, HOT DAMN!" I said, manufacturing a huge smile and laughing at my absurd acting skills. "It's YOUR boat in the mold right now!"

"No way?" He seemed shocked, excited, all the right things.

"Yeah!" I climbed back over the chain-link fence. "We can usually deliver in about two weeks. We take a deposit of $5,000 and will collect the rest on delivery."

"I'm not so sure…"

"It's the only way, Mr. Hale. This isn't exactly Barney's Boats. You gotta show us you're interested before we go blowing our materials on your stuff."

"I thought you said it was MY boat in the mold?"

"Yeah, sure, if you decide to BUY the thing. If not, I can go ahead and take it to—"

"Alright… alright…" He peeled off five grand and I signed one of my newly "updated" Gulf Coast Ski & Marine sales receipts.

An hour later the next customer came rolling through the field. The moon hung low and bright, almost like a spotlight on us, and I felt wild, reckless, daring, like an ancient warrior, an ancient salesman, if there was such a thing.

Bass and I repeated the same process on the next customer.

"Well, HOT DAMN! That's YOUR boat in the mold right now!" And the guy gave us five grand and signed the sales receipt. We'd deliver in two weeks, trailer included, and you'll be happy, we guarantee it…

*   *   *

I took the 10 grand and went on down to Houston Cadillac and put a down payment on a brand new four-door Seville, black, fully loaded. I had reversed custom wire wheels installed on it the next day.

I returned the rental car and thanked Bass's buddy for trusting me to make the payments in cash. I took the Cadillac to work the next day, Monday, and Bass and I discussed our plans for Gulf Coast Ski and Marine.

"We gotta get our own location," I said.

"You sure, man?"

"Trust me. I do stuff like this all the time. We need a location that's very public, where we can sell boats to impulse buyers as well as guys who are in the market."

"There's a place about a quarter mile from here," he said, thumbing through a book of contacts on his desk. "It used to be the Anthony Pool Company's location. They went out of business a while back."

"And it's still up for rent?"

"As far as I know."

"Is it a good place to sell boats?"

"Hell yeah. Great place," Bass said, dialing a number and pinning the telephone against his ear. "Hi, it's Bass Williams, with Gulf Coast Ski and Marine... Yeah, hi... looking for a property for our shop and saw... yeah... sure... 6 p.m. sounds good." He nodded to me in question. I nodded back. "See you there."

He hung up and we went back onto the floor and sold some boats for Dennis Miller. In two weeks we were gone, a quarter mile down the street, where we opened our first Gulf Coast Boat Store.

*　　*　　*

The old pool dealership was a good place for us. There were several large buildings equipped with clean showroom spaces, demo pools, hot tubs, and powerful lighting arrangements around palm trees. In addition to being in a prime location, the property had an older metal structure on the grounds. We soon realized that the 50x100-foot shed was a perfect place for a mechanic's shop.

The first thing we did, besides furnishing the place and stocking it with Southwind knockoffs, was put in a giant hanging wench so we could pull out engines and replace them without having to outsource to an outside mechanic. We needed to keep the operation as inclusive as possible. The less attention we got from the industry, the better. I knew that the Feds had my number; they just didn't know which state to dial it in.

The orders kept coming even though our new location wasn't open yet. Each client, usually referred by a friend who had bought from us, had no problem leaving us a deposit of five grand until his boat could be painted and delivered.

I sent Bass to California with a bunch of cash to purchase a trailer-load of rare authentic jet boats that we could use to supplement our in-store inventory.

I sent Bass because I was very busy advertising our grand opening, which would be in exactly one week. I knew that it would draw a crowd, and that the rare boats would be the items that would get the most attention from the affluent customers.

When Bass got back I realized that we needed more than just one truckload.

I called a wholesaler in California and ordered three more shipments, paying the drivers on delivery with company checks and hoping that on Monday, when our location opened, we'd be able to sell enough boats to get the money in the bank before those checks were cleared in California. It was a wobbly rope to walk, but so far we'd been balancing pretty well.

*   *   *

The grand opening of The Boat Store was something out of a movie. Jen was there, whom I now called Allison, and she was entertaining our special guests and running her mouth about how excited she was that, "Finally, my husband was able to complete his dream of opening his own boat store..." Blah-blah-blah... it was all fiction but everybody ate it up.

There were cameras from the local news stations. The mayor came, Red Adair showed up at one point, and Danny Pastorini of the Houston Oilers. Danny had just gotten off of the set doing a B-movie for some unheard-of producer. The film was titled "Weed: The Florida Connection" and I hadn't heard much about it but he seemed to think it was pretty good.

I was interested in Dan not because of his film or football career, but because he was the respected driver of all sorts of racing vehicles. Boats, dragsters, roadsters, whatever you gave him he could drive it. He was also married to a movie actress and always had very select and scantily clad woman along with him.

Sure not to disappoint anyone on such a special occasion, Dan had brought Marcia Sleeper as his date to our grand opening. She was wearing an open-to-the-navel aluminum foil jump suit. It was totally outrageous. She was the owner of After Dark, one of Houston's hottest nightclubs, which we often frequented to make deals. I did my best to make a memorable interaction with her.

We talked for a few minutes, and I mentioned to Dan that I'd been thinking about becoming directly involved with the racing scene. He told me to call him if I did and that maybe he could help.

I shook hands with some other guys out there, made a bunch of deals, sold most of the boats we'd ordered from California, and retired to my office at 10 p.m. where Bass and I counted cash from down payments. We drank heavily and laughed about the most frivolous stuff.

"You know, man, we need another location," I said.

"It's only Day One, man. Let's see how this thing goes before we make any sudden moves."

"Eh, yeah… maybe. But I'm telling you, man, we need to follow the high-performance market. That's where the money is."

"I like the matching car/trailer thing." We were selling boats with matching Corvette's or Cadillac's to pull them. The paint on the boats had been done to match the exact tint of the car. At 50k a pop, the unique duos became a best-seller overnight.

"You ever think about sponsoring a racing boat?" I asked.

"I thought about it, yeah. It's expensive." He took a swig from the bottle and kept counting. "I just wonder if it's worth the advertising. I mean, do we really need it?"

"I think it'd be a good idea."

"Yeah, I guess we could do some research."

"Let's just get a few booths at the races, anyway. Just sell beer and T-shirts and stuff like that. It'll be fun."

"True. Let's just think about it for a while and see what we come up with." He kept counting.

"At least I have a top-notch CPA and an attorney," I said. "We won't draw any attention from the outside about taxes or anything. And because we're running a good-looking operation, no one's going to find out about the mold."

"I hope nobody finds out about that damn mold. That would be the end of us."

"Think about it: Other than the mold, what about Gulf Coast is illegal?" I laughed. "Hell, Bass, the only thing we've got to worry about is how long the market will last! That's why we gotta expand it as fast as possible, make hay while the sun shines."

"I guess you're right."

"Hell yeah I'm right. I been in this game a long time and if there's one thing I've learned…"

*   *   *

Allison was laughing excitedly, swinging a newspaper at me while I was brushing my teeth.

"Look, Matt—put the brush down for a second—you'll never believe it! You'll never believe it!" She slapped the newspaper on the bathroom counter and there it was: Allison, Bass, Dan Pastorini, and Red Adair; all of them standing in front of an Anthony Jet-Racer boat with the Mayor and I smiling happily in the cockpit.

I doubled over with excited laughter, the toothpaste foaming wildly from my lips. Gulf Coast Ski and Marine had made the front page. What a riot.

*   *   *

We sponsored two boats at virtually every major race. We rented some vendor spots, sold beer and T-shirts, kept our business rolling, and gained notoriety among the racing community.

Instead of buying a house like Allison wanted to, we rented a nicer apartment in the Westheimer community. I was trying to build as much cash reserve as possible rather than blow all of the money on a golf course membership and three stories of furniture.

I had learned several things from the last run. Chief among my new principles was the understanding that a criminal must build assets in cash, not property. If I ever had to run from Houston, which I hoped wouldn't happen for a long time, I would like to run with a trunk full of loot rather than a lousy 22 grand.

Allison seemed to understand this, but insisted on pouring money into certain "important" home furnishings. I didn't complain, just so long as I didn't have to fill a full-size house.

*   *   *

I was sitting out there one day, out in front of The Boat Store, watching an old guy browse the selection. He had made it clear to me that he just wanted to LOOK. Apparently he didn't have his hearing aid in, so talking to him did no good anyway.

He ran his fingers across the paint and stared into one glossy finish after another. I doubted the guy had enough money to afford a boat. More than likely he was retired, just kicking by on whatever afternoon this happened to be and looking, touching, imagining, but never able to do anything about it.

I waited. Fifteen minutes passed. I smoked a cigarette and continued to study him. He remained oblivious.

I felt someone behind me. "The Cadillac is ready to be picked up," Bass said.

"Good…" I had forked over a good bit of cash to have one of my Cadillac Fleetwoods turned into a makeshift ambulance. I planned on using it at the boat races in case of accidents, which were fairly common. The Caddy Ambulance was more of a joke than a practical device, but I ended up using it more times than I'd originally imagined.

"How about Pastorini? Has he called you back about driving for us?" I asked, still watching that old man cruise the lot in his khakis and khaki jacket.

"No dice."

"Damn."

"His insurance won't cover it or something. I don't understand."

"You talk to Avery?" Avery was our other possible driver.

"Yeah, I talked to him."

"And?"

"He'll do it."

"Good, then we got a driver. Now, Bass, all we need is to invest in some more engines."

"How much are those things? You're looking at the Keith Black Chryslers, right?"

"Yeah, but I don't have the blue book on me. I'd say they're in the neighborhood of $17,000 to $17,500 apiece."

"Damn, 18 grand for a hunk of metal…"

"Yeah, and those boats will melt an engine in a single pass."

"Expensive sport we're getting into, Matt." He lit a cigarette, stared off into the lot. "What's Pops over there looking at?"

"Nothing. He's not going to buy a damn thing."

We watched him, each of us smoking our cigarettes and waiting for something to happen; a sale, a car accident, a bomb, a meteor, the Stock Market crash, ANYTHING to wake me from the trance.

We had a driver. We had a shot.

*   *   *

Our racing entourage was a quite a sight: three Cowboy Cadillacs (Eldorado models with horns on the hood and custom paint jobs that matched their boats and trailers), two custom Dually Chevy's towing giant enclosed trailers for the mechanic's gear and the extra Keith Black Chrysler engines (which turned out to be near 18 grand BEFORE adding the carburetor and blower) and, finally, my Cadillac Fleetwood-turned-ambulance, which I insisted on driving to all of the events.

We cruised all over the shoreline, building our store's reputation through Avery's ability on the water. After several months of racing, Bass and I opened another location at The Galleria in Houston, right next to Neiman-Marcus. They even photographed one of our Cowboy Cadillac's for their Christmas catalogue. In addition to this location, three new stores were set to open in Dallas in less than two months. I got the secure and comfortable feeling that I had finally found something that wouldn't be shut down by the Feds.

The mysteriousness of my identity eluded even key elected officials, who in some cases were regular customers. I felt like we'd pulled off the ultimate under-the-radar scam, the perfect score that would bear fruit for decades to come.

I had my arm out the window of my Cadillac, a boat in tow. Allison sat beside me in the front seat. She leaned over and began sharing her opinion about moving into a new house.

Was it time to do that? It was hard to say. I sure as hell had the money.

"Well, honey, maybe we should stick it out in the apartment for a little longer before we dump a big wad on furnishing a new place. Just think about all the trimmings that goes along with it. We'd have to falsify documents, procure another round of fake IDs, meet the neighbors...."

"Please?"

"No, I can't do it. Not now," I said.

"But, Jay, come on."

"Would you quit calling me JAY?"

She apologized, citing the long weekend as her excuse. She was right, it had been hell out there at the river races; but, in the end, it was worth it when the sales calls came. "Look, Ally, just stay in the apartment for a little bit longer. All I gotta do is open those Dallas stores, then I'll have so much money that we won't have to worry about anything. We can move to France, for all I care." I lit a cigarette and imagined the plan. "I want to take Dallas, babe, and then we'll get on with our lives."

"TAKE Dallas…? Matt, you're getting ahead of yourself. Why do you have to push it every time?"

"If you don't push it, it pushes you."

"Yeah, well…"

I pulled into the Gulf Coast Boat Store and left her in the car. It was a Sunday, but I knew I had to check my messages. We'd left halfway through the day on Friday for the race and I was sure that someone had called between 12 and 5.

I clicked my answering machine.

"11 New Messages." Damn it. "First New Message: Mr. Reynolds, this is Taylor Dyer with Pincer Racing, I was wondering why the hell you thought it was alright to try and STEAL my advertising spot on— Message Deleted. Next Message: Matt, hey, it's Frank Wilson calling about Aardvark's position poll, I've got good news for the Saturday race— Message Deleted. Next Message: Hey, honey, it's Allison, are you coming home to pick me up or— Message Deleted."

11 messages… give me a break. I looked out to the mechanic's shop from my office window and could see Bass and Phil out there removing one of the destroyed engines from a trailer, nearly smashing it through a wall. Jockeying the answering machine with my left hand, I muttered to myself, "This place is right out of a damn comic strip." I heard my voice through the phone. It sounded like it was someone else talking.

"Next Message: Mr. Reynolds, this is Bill Eanus with the… uh… Service. I am calling to request a meeting about your company, 'Gulf Coast Ski and Marine,' and various other enterprises that have sprung from that company in the past six months. I have records showing that you have failed to file for— Message Deleted. Damn. Next Message: Mr. Reynolds, Herb Mason, Internal Revenue Service, just wanted to ask you a few questions about your Social Security Num— I slammed the phone, went out to the car, lit a cigar, leaned back, exhaled, turned off the radio, and felt the tiny droplets of sweat accumulate on my brow.

"They are trying to figure out who I am, Ally. It's over."

"What the HELL are you talking about, Jay?"

"Can you keep it DOWN with that 'Jay' shit? Please? I can't DEAL with that. I got a cover going on here. Don't screw me up! Especially not now."

"What's the problem?"

"I got 11 messages, most of which are from you or the IRS."

"ELEVEN MESSAGES FROM THE—"

"HEY, what'd I say about blowing our cover? Huh?"

"How can this be happening to us?" she said, tears already streaming down her face.

"It's simple." I said, dragging on the cigar. "You sell knockoff jet boats for long enough and someone starts to notice that you're paying thousands of bucks into an account with a fake Social Security Number. It's simple if you think about it from their end."

"Where are we going to go?"

"Leave that to me." I took a moment to think. There was no way out of this one. "It's over, Ally. Flat out. The Feds will be here Monday, gats drawn. I guarantee it. They've probably already figured out that it's ME. They just don't want to interrupt their afternoon picnics for a bloody manhunt."

I went out back and found Bass, who was still trying to remove the giant Chrysler engine from the trailer.

I gave him a hard look, motioned that he come speak with me. He told the mechanics to continue without him, jogged over. I told him the same thing that I'd told Allison and he couldn't believe it. The axe had fallen. Good riddance, Texas.

*   *   *

It was 8 a.m. and finally, after an all-night scramble, we had the place cleaned out and virtually free of incriminating documents.

After shredding most of our records, which hadn't been necessary, we left the boat store and went to the bank, where we withdrew all of the money from our business, save for that which was necessary to finish paying out the bills.

We made out a month of extra paychecks to all 67 employees and attached a note to each envelope of checks explaining why we had to leave the business and how sorry we were. Maybe someone could pick up the pieces of Gulf Coast? But, more than likely the Feds would snatch everything and sell it to make up for the non-filed returns.

The good thing about Gulf Coast Ski and Marine was that we had made all of our deposits legitimately. The only shady spot was that I had paid the Social Security tax into someone else's account. I couldn't use mine, obviously, since I was a fugitive. This meant that the government wouldn't care too much about Bass's role in all of this. They were more interested in nailing a fugitive than nailing some poor schmuck who had legally paid all of his debts.

I slid the briefcase of cash into the trunk of my Cowboy Cadillac and gave Bass Williams a good handshake.

"It's been good," he said. "We made a helluva run at this one."

"We came out alright," I said, gesturing at the trunk of my car, which now contained $350,000. His briefcase, containing a significantly smaller amount, was in his right hand. He shook it, looked up into the sky, and began to walk away.

"They shouldn't be on you too hard about this one, Bass. They gotta shut down the store because of the false account, but I don't think they'll take anybody else to jail. It's me they're after."

"What are your plans?" he said, turning to face me while stepping backward across the lot.

"None of your damn business." We laughed. He turned and disappeared into his Corvette and I merged onto the Interstate with nothing in my car but an unhappy woman and 350 big ones.

I grabbed a bottle of liquor from the floor and took a quick slug during a lull in traffic. I'd need every bit of that fifth if I was going to escape from this one.

The accelerator gave very little resistance beneath my foot and I looked over the steering wheel with quiet desperation as the highway, the fugitive's main artery, rolled swiftly beneath me. The blacktop carried our getaway car toward the horizon, toward freedom, and it kept us fueled, safe, and on an even keel against a heartless world.

13

BOSTON

1977

JENNIFER AND I SPENT THE NEXT YEAR RENTING A CHALET AT A SKI RESORT in Stowe, Vermont. I had succeeded in avoiding capture yet again, but I knew that staying in one spot begged exposure.

For the sake of dramatics, I burnt-out down the icy roadway of Mansfield View Ski Resort, leaving our furniture and the majority of our accumulated possessions behind. Jen was fine with leaving everything to rot, except she was very attached to a portrait of me that our neighbor had painted on my birthday. I thought it was strange, somewhat creepy, but Jen loved it.

My car, a brand new Lincoln Mark IV, was chock full of liquor, money, cocaine, that giant painting, and four of our pets (including that horribly mean cat Jen had adopted right when we first moved to Houston). We were on the road again...

We arrived in Boston and after two nights in a hotel rented a house in Hingham Harbor. The house was owned by two very strange older folks who tried, on several occasions, to coerce us into attending one of their "swinger parties." I wasn't into crazy group sex anymore, and so after several months I interviewed for the job of National Sales Manager for a company called Micom.Once I secured this job it would be necessary for me to move closer to downtown, and thus away from the swingers.

The Micom branch in Boston, one of several divisional branches in the state of Massachusetts, was run by a despicable jackass named Bill Fallie. He was so horrible in interviews—telling me stories about how many times he'd cheated on his wife, how he'd hired a woman as a sales representative just to get what he wanted, how his sole motivation in handing out Christmas bonuses was so he'd have money for call girls, etc.—that I nearly abandoned the idea of working for him.

It wasn't his womanizing that bothered me; no, I could relate to that part of his life. It was the fact that he did all of this stuff despite his being married with children. I figured that if a guy was to have kids it was about time he cut out all the sleeping around. I couldn't see ruining a child's life with a messy divorce over two hours with a drugged-out call girl. It just didn't make sense. Then again, neither did most things.

Jen and I relocated to an apartment on Beacon Street and I took the damn job at Micom.

*　　*　　*

Jen and I arrived at Jason's Nightclub on Friday night. As always, we walked past the line and I passed a C-Note to Rick at the door. We slid inside to our roped-off table high up in the corner of the disco lounge. The table looked out over the dance floor, to the 50-foot saltwater tropical fish tank that backed the front bar. I surveyed the scene, lit a cigar, and we settled in for our usual drinks and dinner.

I noticed that there was a man on the other side of the club, a tall black guy, totally surrounded by people. He was signing autographs, laughing, kissing girls. I didn't pay much attention, just worked on the drink and a cigar.

Jen was high on something and didn't seem to hear me when I asked her what she wanted for dinner.

"How the hell do you plan on functioning if you can't even TALK when you're high on that shit?"

"Just shut up," she said.

"Order something or I'm leaving and going—"

"It's Sugar Riley!" A woman's shrill voice interrupted me.

"From the Celtics?" another asked.

"Yeah!"

"Oh my god!" They screamed.

It was grating my nerves. I still had no idea who Sugar Riley was. I guess I had never been much of a basketball fan. Sugar looked over at my table, gave Jen the eye. She smiled back at him. It was her way of getting under my skin.

About an hour later, when I came back from taking a piss, my seat was taken. Jen was running her mouth, laughing, beaming at this guy like I hadn't seen her do in quite some time. Shug just kept smiling and holding his arm around her shoulders. The man wasn't a stranger to good times with women. He knew how to attract them, treat them, talk to them, and I could see that he was working his magic on my girl.

A round of drinks arrived right when I got back. Shug tipped the waitress and flipped her a 100 for the tab.

I slid in beside them like it was no big deal. I wasn't the jealous type, right?

An extended hand reached out at me. "I'm Shug Riley," he said.

"Jeff." I gripped it tightly.

"Take your seat back, man," he said. Everyone giggled and laughed and Shug kept talking to some of the girls. They had begun swarming him en masse. I ripped a quick toot from my pocket to ward off the frustration.

The powder kicked in after a minute, thankfully, and Shug said: "You guys wanna come to my place, listen to some jams, and I'll cook you two some breakfast?"

"Yeah, man, sure."

We followed his Silver 450 Benz and wound up at a high-rise down by the Boston Garden. He had a cool place. It was almost as nice as mine and he had some good music on the stereo. We had copious rounds of drinks and cocaine. He and Jen made constant conversation while I stared into space and wondered about my future.

The hours passed, me on the edge of the couch nearly oblivious to what was happening in the room. My brain was literally frying from the coke. It was frenzied to the point where all I could was stare at Shug's album collection and chatter my teeth. Several hours later, when the sun rose, he made an unbelievable breakfast for us.

*   *   *

Climbing the front stairs to my place was always borderline impossible after work. My afternoon drunk had worn off almost entirely and the cold sweat poured, leaving me depressed, dehydrated, tired, and numb. My brain began to collapse on the landing and I tried the door. Locked. I fumbled for my key. Someone on the street blasted their horn and I spun around in fear. There had almost been an accident. I saw an expensive Mercedes parked on the curb a few spaces down from my Lincoln. I felt like I'd seen that car before...

The door swung open and I staggered in, reaching directly for the cupboard in the hallway where I kept my mini-bar. I removed a bottle of vodka, poured a glass at room temperature, and took it into the living room. I slid into my favorite chair and set the glass on the table beside me. There was a peculiar amount of cocaine on the end-table. I reached over and examined the bag, took a taste of the stuff.

"This isn't our stash," I said, concerned. Wait a second... why had the door been locked? I stood up, went into the kitchen, grabbed a hammer, and peered up the stairs. I heard voices and debated on running from the house to avoid being killed. The first thing I thought was that it was coke dealers. Hell, maybe Jen had racked up some unspeakable debt that she hadn't told me about. Maybe these guys were here to collect?

I listened really hard.

"Who's up there?" I yelled. Nothing. "Come out or I'm gonna start shooting!" A shadow cast itself on the wall and rippled past the bathroom door like a ghost. I shuddered and pinned myself against the wall, ready to dive backward in case of a gunfight. Sweat continued to drain like hot oil from my skin.

"Jeff, just relax!" It was Jen. The bastards were holding her captive! Probably torturing her! I charged up the stairs and into the bedroom. There she was: half naked and watching television.

"Is someone else up here?" I gripped the hammer tightly.

"No, it's the TV, Jeff. You need to get some sleep."

"What's with that coke down there? It's not the usual stuff."

"I got it last night at Jason's. Some guy just gave it to me."

I knew that she wasn't telling the truth. Something else was going on.

"If you ever cheat on me I swear I'll leave you. You won't even see it coming, but I'll leave you high and dry."

"Get some rest," she said exasperatedly.

*   *   *

Shug called one afternoon and asked if I wanted to watch football. I said sure and he came on over.

"I got traded to Golden State," he said.

"You're kidding."

"Nope."

"Celtics can't use you anymore?"

"Guess the other guys think I'm worth it. They gave up some good players for me."

"It's nice out there," I said.

"You ever been out there?" We walked into my bedroom. I always watched TV in my bed. I warned Shug about this and he said he didn't give a damn.

"I've known guys who watch football in stranger places than bed," he said. True enough.

"I've been out there a couple times, yeah."

"I'm glad to be getting out of Boston for a while. Too damn cold."

"I'll be glad to get out of here, too."

We turned on the TV. It was a Packers vs. Patriots game. Neither of us cared too much about either team.

"Hey, man... I been meaning to talk to you," said Shug.

"Yeah?"

"You remember the other day when Jen came over to bring me back those tapes?"

"Yeah?" I flipped through the channels, hoping that the Steelers vs. 49er's game had started. It hadn't.

"Well, she came in and we had some drinks, man..."

"Yeah, what's your point?"

"Well, she started coming onto me, man. I couldn't help myself. She just came onto me like THAT." He snapped his fingers. "She's good at what she does. Real good at it, you know?"

"I know."

"I'm sorry man."

"No, don't be. It was her fault, not yours." I wasn't the jealous type, but I HAD made a promise that if she ran around on me I'd leave her. I began to think about it and tried to figure out the best way to handle the situation. Jen and Barb, Shug's girlfriend, were out in the living room playing backgammon. I could hear them chatting.

"She came onto you, huh?" I wanted to make sure he was giving me the whole story.

"Yeah, for sure."

"You swear it?"

"I swear it, man."

"I been with this girl a long time," I said. "Don't lie to me. I can tell when a guy's lying to me."

"You think I'm lying?"

"I can't tell you that." I laughed. He was a bit nervous but kept himself in check. The game continued for another half hour and then, finally, the Steelers vs. 49er's came on.

"I know you're not lying, Shug. She's like that. I always knew she was like that right from the moment I met her."

"She's a little devil," he said.

"She'll cut your throat without thinking twice. Hell, back in Denver the DEA damn near convinced her to turn me in. I walked into the house one afternoon and she was crying her eyes out because she'd been thinking about sending me up the river."

"That's some heavy shit. Betrayal..." he spoke in a way that made me believe he'd experienced it himself.

"I never let on that I knew. I just pretended that she was crying because she'd gotten caught. I knew she was upset about whether or not to turn me in."

"And she didn't, huh?"

"She was a different girl back then. Times were different. I can't say what she would do now."

"You think she'd turn you in?"

"Like I said, I can't say for sure either way."

We watched the game. At 10 p.m. the four of us went out together. It was nice to sit in the bar and drink now that I finally knew the secret. Hell, Jen was still beautiful. There was no change in that. I still found her totally attractive. The worst part, the part that made me the angriest, was that she hadn't told me what she'd done. That's how I knew Shug was telling the truth about her coming onto him. I could see the way she casually flirted with him at our table, the way she touched his arm getting into the limo. She was a seductress. The world was calling me and I knew that soon we'd part.

*   *   *

I gradually lost the sense of paranoia and jealousy. I made the relationship seem normal and Jen assumed that all was going well. She had no idea that every night when I went out to do deals, which was four or more times a week, I was seeing a young lady named Stephanie Greenstein who worked with me at Micom. She was one of the girls Bill Fallie had hired on the sole premise that she was good in bed.

And she was.

The booze and cocaine compounded, hangovers multiplied to the point of unbearable extremity, and I found myself at 2 p.m. on the living room floor too tired to move.

At 4 p.m., the sunlight already waning at a steep angle through the blinds, Jen came in and woke me up.

"Have you quit your job at Micom?" she asked, stabbing me on the shoulder with her fingernails.

"No..."

"Well, why did they leave a message asking if you were still alive? It was a girl... she sounded like she knew you pretty well..." It was Stephanie.

"I haven't been going in."

"Have you been messing around with that girl? She sounded concerned for you, like she missed you." I gave no response, just closed my eyes again. "Are you alright, Jay?"

"Call me Jeff. I'm Jeff Taylor, damn it," I moaned.

She sighed, flustered, and exited the room in a flash.

*   *   *

My patience with Bill Fallie came crashing to the floor at a 9 a.m. sales meeting. We were in the conference room, all 12 of the Micom sales reps and me, listening to Bill as he exaggeratedly berated the weakest members of our team.

"You people can't keep your heads on straight! You're like a bunch of lost dogs! It's absurd. Ernst, you can't show up on time. And Jeff, you can sell more than anyone in this office but you can't show up but three days a week!" I was getting sick of his crap, but what really pushed me over the edge came next.

Bill addressed Stephanie. She was the only female salesperson in the room.

"And so what about you, honey? What's your damage? You couldn't sell a raw steak to a lion!" He laughed. No one else made a sound. I took a sip of coffee and thumbed through my planner, wondering how long I'd wait before I left the office to sell a truckload of stolen ammunition that was waiting for me on Ferris Street. A cigarette burned in the ashtray and I removed it for a drag.

"But seriously, Stephanie's easier to be with than a Japanese hooker and twice as dirty!" He continued, delving into several details that are better left unsaid. Stephanie stood, cast her folder into the center of the table, and exited the boardroom with a SLAM.

He continued to discuss her sexuality and the rest of us stared in disbelief. I squinted at him from across the room, wondering how I'd fix him up for this one. In my eyes, words like his were chargeable in the deepest and cruelest of ways.

The afternoon came. It was damn near time to leave Boston. I could feel the darkness rapidly approaching. I had yet to dodge it.

First thing on my agenda was to steal a few of Mr. Fallie's business checks and deposit slips. I went into his office for a talk about sales. Luckily, he left in a hurry for the restroom, told me to wait in his office. While he was gone I made my move. Sure enough, they were right where he always kept them. I removed the booklets and took three slips from each.

I very hurriedly snuck out the back door and headed into the city. I went to the ammunition truck, which was right where I expected it to be, made a call from a pay phone, and found my buyer waiting one block away.

He argued about the price because I didn't have a driver for the truck. I told him that I was sorry, that the whole thing had sprung up in such a hurry. He counted out the cash in the front seat of my rental car and we cruised around the block toward the goods. One of his goons followed us in a late-model Lincoln. I gave him 300 bucks off for having to hire his own driver. He wasn't very appreciative.

From there I went to the bank and withdrew a decent amount of cash from Bill Fallie's personal account. I removed his business checks from my wallet and illegally deposited funds from the Micom account into his savings account. This deposit would make it look like Bill had embezzled over 50 grand from the company. There was no doubt that someone at corporate would notice this and phone the authorities.

I also did my best to implicate Bill Fallie as the stolen ammunition salesman. This attempt, however, was fabricated on the spur of the moment and not quite as well done. I called the police and reported that I'd seen Fallie's vehicle on Ferris Street that afternoon engaging in what appeared to be a deal for a truckload of stolen goods. Sure, he'd have an alibi, but after they realized that he'd also been transferring funds during that same hour the judge would have less reason to trust him.

Either way, he'd be taken to jail for at least a week. If I was lucky, he'd get a conviction and end up in the pen for a few years.

*　　*　　*

I must have looked near-dead traipsing into the house at 3 p.m., but I still had business to take care of before I could leave. I fell onto the floor, breathed out a hard sigh.

"Is that all you do anymore? Why aren't you at work?" Jen asked. She was drinking some sort of blended beverage from a pint glass and I looked up at her with disgust. How could she have slept with one of my only friends? What a bitch...

"I do deals all the time. Where do you think we get all this money? Huh? Where do you think the money comes from?"

"I make plenty of money," she said, walking out of the living room. "All you ever do is lie on the floor drunk."

"Yeah, right..."

I peeled myself up, walked wearily down my front steps, got into the Lincoln, took it to a dealership on the edge of town.

I traded the Mark IV for a few bucks on a brand new Cadillac Eldorado.

I called Stephanie Greenstein from a payphone. After only a few dates Greenstein had confessed that she was in love with me. It didn't come as a surprise, but I wondered how serious she really was. The phone rang for four or five times. Finally she answered.

"Micom Incorporated, Stephanie Greenstein."

"It's Jeff Taylor. I'm leaving town."

"What? Why?"

"Are you coming?" I asked, a sense of urgency present in my voice.

"Well... Yes. What about your wife?"

"Long story. She's been cheating on me, I've been cheating on her with you... don't worry about it."

"Umm..."

"Meet me in 20 minutes outside your place. I'll pick you up. Bring whatever cash and jewelry you've got. We won't be coming back for a long time."

"What about my lease?"

"Forget the lease. I'll pay you for it. Just be on the sidewalk in half an hour."

"Alright..."

I took the Eldorado back to the apartment and luckily Jen had gone out to the store. I climbed those horrible steps—damn those steps—and stood in the foyer with a wad of checks, car titles, IDs, cash, you name it. I gathered the strongbox, my bullshit documents and financial records, my favorite shirts and pants and an extra pair of shoes. All of it fit, very cramped, into a giant duffle bag.

My bag slid tightly into the trunk. I had an ounce of cocaine in the console, just enough for a good run. I opened the bag and filled my tooter with powder. I swung by Stephanie's and we merged onto the highway without looking back.

I began talking to myself.

"Baltimore... Delaware... No. Neither of those. I gotta keep a bit farther south than that. Well, maybe not..." I passed a highway cop. All it would take was for one of those bastards to get suspicious of me—or if a taillight was out, a dangling fender—and the whole joyride would be over.

I thought about Washington, D.C. That sounded like a good plan. Maybe a bit south of the city? What better place to hide from the beast than right under its nose? I moved southward, planning to make the whole drive in one fell swoop.

I glanced in the rearview mirror as I changed lanes. I could see the Boston skyline, heavy clouds hanging over the city in the early evening. It got me in the gut to leave Jen after all we'd been through, after all she'd done for me. I imagined that right then, at that very moment when I saw the skyline, Jen had opened the front door and found the note.

Jennifer...

I remembered her face on the train just after I'd been released from Fort Lauderdale. Honest to god, to see that face in my mind... it hurt me deep. I felt horrible; but, then again, she'd turned on me. You can't forgive that. Not in this world and certainly not in these times. Everything is precious, every second counts, and for each time you flick your endless cigarettes out the window of the Cadillac and gripe about your girlfriend or the endlessness of the run, just remember that there are countless men in the yard doing pull-ups in the California sun, countless men welded into their cells beneath the Earth serving jacked-up sentences and being crushed beneath the heavy foot of the justice system.

Just remember all that, I told myself, whenever you think YOU got it bad.

14

JOHN PAYNE

1979

STEPHANIE AND I SAT AROUND MY NEW APARTMENT FOR A SOLID MONTH, give or take a few days, doing nothing but railing cocaine off my kitchen countertop and watching rerun television shows. The plan was to lie low, establish a new identity, maybe grab another job in sales.

John Payne had been a friend of mine at Micom. We'd gone out for beers once or twice, and I figured that I was far enough away that I could use his identity for a short time. I put together a resume with his information, schooling, diplomas, business experience, etc. John was currently unemployed, had quit Micom around the same time I had, and so if they did a search for his employment history it would look legit that he was in Alexandria searching for a new job. Even if he'd found a job, the paperwork would be so backed up that no one would realize I wasn't Payne until it was too late.

All in all, putting together the resume should have taken one afternoon. Instead, as I mentioned, I strung it out for a month. Meanwhile, I blew as much cash on booze, cocaine, and partying as I could. It was my way of staying normal, convincing myself that nothing had changed.

Like they say, "If it ain't broke, don't fix it."

*   *   *

Using an early version of a fake resume I applied at several companies. No one was taking the bait. Everybody was fully staffed and too busy to listen. My charm, wit, and good looks did nothing for me.

It was back to the drawing board. The assembly of several falsified "John Payne" resume packets had been executed during one week of back-to-back late-night kitchen sessions. I mailed the documents to a few companies. After mailing the packets I went around town to do quick follow-ups.

I went to two offices and had little luck. I ate a good lunch and called ahead to the General Manager of a company called Savin. He said he was anxious to meet me, which seemed about right since my resume was so overwhelmingly impressive. I wasted no time and drove right to his office.

I parked the Cadillac and walked inside. Their building was pretty nice and I could see myself fitting in very well. I told the receptionist my name was John Payne and that I had an appointment. I was there to see Mr. Walker.

The Savin Company sold the same copiers and word processors that I had been selling when I worked for Royal Business Machines, the job I had before meeting Stephanie at Micom.

The secretary took the phone on her shoulder, made a few quick punches with a skilled index finger, and asked me to have a seat. Mr. Walker would see me shortly.

I waited. It was very good that the man was anxious to speak with me on such short notice. He must have thoroughly reviewed the resume. Hell, I'm sure he liked it if he took the time to read all the small stuff.

I began to think: This job was my best chance to get back into the swing of things. I needed a break from the sleepless nights, endless bars, deals, and glowing television sets. I needed to get busy again, meet someone other than Stephanie. Don't get me wrong, she was a real sweet girl, but not what you'd call "my type." After dealing with Jen, I had thought it time to try a halfway-normal woman as my partner and had soon realized that they can be more trouble than they're worth.

The secretary's phone rang.

"Mr. Walker is ready to see you." She turned toward the door. "Go straight, make a right, last office at the end of the hallway." She had one of those giant fake smiles. I gave her one right back.

I knocked and he invited me right in, told me to take a seat. I shook his hand, introduced myself.

"So, you're John Payne?" He asked, seemingly surprised.

"Yes, sir. You liked my resume?"

"I love the resume." He reached into some papers, pulled out a copy. "I can see you're a trained killer, Mr. Payne. I'd love to hire you." He looked at me straight on. "I've got one small problem, though."

"What's that?"

"I roomed with John Payne at Yale."

"Oh yeah?" I laughed, pretended that I thought he was kidding.

"Yeah. I called him yesterday. He's still in Boston. He seems to think he knows who YOU are."

"I'm John Payne. You've got my resume. You're mistaken." I stayed cool, calm, collected.

"You don't understand. See, I ROOMED with John Payne at Yale. Class of '65."

"I'm John Payne."

"Listen, buddy: You're not John Payne. I've already called the FBI. We know who you really are. John already told me about you—said you walked away from your job with Micom and he quit shortly thereafter." He paused. "Funny thing how he remembered the Feds showing up right after you left. He said you're on the FBI's Most Wanted List." He looked at me disapprovingly. "The good guys are on the way, Jeff." He used my Boston name... He really HAD talked to John Payne.

Two other men came into the office. I suppose they were Walker's protection in case I tried to pull something crazy.

"Nice meeting you," I said. I stood up, noticed that he had a plain view of my license plate from the window of his office. He noticed that I noticed this, and nodded like he'd already given the plate number to the authorities; or, at least, he HAD the plate number and would give it to them when they arrived.

*   *   *

Going back to the apartment was out of the question. More than likely I'd be nabbed at the front door, before I could even BEGIN to hide the cash or take it with me. I'd chipped my stash down to about 150 grand anyway. It wasn't worth risking the rest of my life for 150 grand and the half pound of rock cocaine that I had hidden in the ceiling of the carport, which Stephanie didn't even know about.

That was the difference between me and the rest of the criminals. I was willing to walk away. Other guys I'd known, guys who were now in the pen, they'd call a moving truck at a time like this. It was stupidity. If you were smart, you could generally stay ahead of the law.

I drove from Mr. Walker's office directly to the airport and purchased a plane ticket under a fake name (not John Payne) to Chicago. The Windy City had always been a good staging ground for me. I left the Cadillac in the lot, tossed the keys into a trashcan, smoked three consecutive cigarettes like it was my job, and boarded the plane. I made sure not to look back on the city. Poor Stephanie... at least she could play dumb and they'd probably leave her alone.

It was rough to stomach the whole situation: I was out 150 large, missing all of my personal items, womanless, carrying only $79 cash after buying the ticket. I had one briefcase, a Porsche black leather business style carryon, which contained virtually nothing important. The whole John Payne idea had been a mess. The only thing worse would have been prison.

On the plane I got a pretty good heat on and felt several times that my sanity was slipping. I stared into the seat in front of me, contemplating the fabric for over an hour—how had it been assembled, who had sold it, why was it here?

Was there a chance that maybe the Feds hadn't raided my apartment? Was Walker bluffing me when he said he'd called the Bureau? Who the hell called the Bureau anyway? Didn't most people just call the local cops? He had been BLUFFING!

No. No, no, no... wishful thinking, but he had not been bluffing.

Adrenaline rose from deep within me and a bizarre force overtook my body. I had felt this feeling only once or twice before. I downed several more shots, but nothing seemed to suppress it. My hands shook and my stomach rocked uneasily in the turbulence. It was the flying that had unsettled me, right? No... it was the lack of food. No... wait! It was the lack of cocaine! That's what I was missing! Cocaine! I'd left ALL that rock!

"Please excuse me," I said, staring into the seat. "Reality is just... very slowly... setting in." The man next to me kept his head facing forward and pretended not to notice me.

I stood up, made for the bathroom. I scoured my pockets, turned my pants inside out, checked my socks. There was nothing. Of course there was nothing. I KNEW there was nothing, but I had to check for checking's sake. The plane rocked and the toilet made funny sounds. I listened to those sounds, wondering if they were contributing to my uneasiness. Hurling was not an option. I had no food in my stomach, just several ounces of vodka. The last thing I wanted to do was get rid of my only medicine into the little blue drain.

How about searching the bathroom for cash? Maybe my briefcase had—wait, maybe I hadn't brought it. Maybe the sink was... what? What the hell was I thinking? The lights in the bathroom ceased to glow. It was darkness that enveloped me; a type of darkness that I could feel as well as see. I stared into it and horrible images flashed before me. The plane rocked from side to side and the pilot made an announcement. I braced myself against the walls of the compartment. The lock mechanism slipped open and the door came ajar. I exited the bathroom and found that the light was slowly returning.

My seat was still open when I got back, which surprised me because I had imagined that it had been removed from the airplane. The old guy next to me seemed nervous as well. We exchanged a few words, made brief conversation, and I immediately realized that he was out of his mind, a lunatic, someone not worth speaking to even one bit! I opened a magazine and stared at the pictures and advertisements. I wondered who had placed them in the publication and for how much money. Could I get involved with advertising? Would that be the next route?

Where was my briefcase? On the plane? No... I'd left it, remember?

A debate raged within me about whether or not to flee the country on horseback with a rifle and find a beautiful Spanish woman. It was a realistic possibility to acquire a good horse in southern Arizona. Of course, I hadn't ridden a horse for 15 years. The last one I'd ridden was a strawberry roan in Northern California named Witch. What a horse! She wouldn't let anybody ride her but me. Maybe there was something to be said for that. Maybe not.

The Mexico dream vanished and was replaced by the desire to have about 50 million dollars and live in LA. This fantasy continued, haunted me as I remembered the awesome beach house in Malibu that I had rented so many summers ago.

My brain was racing. When it came time to disembark the aircraft I went out the passenger exit onto the gangway and down the stairs through the luggage area. I had to be cautious in case the Feds had managed to follow me.

I watched myself spend all 70-some-odd dollars at the Speakeasy, the bar at the hotel in the center of O'Hare. I bought drinks for me and this one lonely chick who was recently dumped. Maybe a few other people jumped on the tab. Who knows. I was drunk and didn't care.

"I've been dumped before," I said. "My girl cheated on me with an NBA player. I guess I dumped her, though... in the end."

My lady friend didn't respond. She was the simple type: drank beer, smoked Marlboros, watched the garbage on television for two hours every night and told stories of state college and cheap frat house keg parties. She talked a bit about the Who, the members of which I had met during a college drinking binge in Detroit at the Grande Ballroom. I told her this, very drunkenly, and she laughed at me. Damn it, it was the TRUTH! I asked her if she wanted another round and her laughing subsided.

By this time I was literally stretched across the bar, my lower half still positioned on the stool but my upper torso resting on the countertop. I was in a 3k suit but it looked like something out of a POW camp.

My wallet came out, unfolded itself, and was literally devoid of cash. This hadn't happened to me in quite some time, and the severe shock that enveloped my bloodstream was too much to fathom or describe. It overtook me, drove me away from the bar, away from that wretched money-hungry wench.

"That simple piece of trash," I mumbled, weaving down the flight terminal, which was all but empty. I headed toward the "Boarding Exit" sign.

Being broke didn't really bother me. Did it? I could always get more money, but it would be nice if I had enough money to get a room.

It was raining out there and a jet was revving its turbines. I made my way down a set of stairs, my drunken form swaying with the wind and blending well with the night. I had nothing, and therefore had become nobody—formless. Even the men directing the airlines, the guards, the baggage handlers, ignored me like a wisp of smoke.

There it was, my oasis: a screaming jet engine. The spinning blades beckoned me. The piercing voices tantalized my mind, unlocked it like shrieking keys. I walked on over there, intended to go right up to it and fling myself inside.

15

K C M F

1979

MUCH TO MY SURPRISE, AIRPORT SECURITY HAD TURNED ME OVER TO THE police after removing my drunken carcass from the tarmac. It was week two of rotting in one of Charles Street Jail's orientation cells. There was moss covering the floor, no mattress on a box spring, and a grotesque commode, the contents of which had long ago hardened into a brown cork-like plug. I was alone down there, deep within the iron heart of the dungeon sub-basement, with all the time in the world to think about how it would feel to be locked up for the rest of my life.

I was issued a metal bucket that was at least 100 years old. The guards filled it with water every morning, which I used to wash my face. After washing my face, the bucket sufficed as my toilet. I would have been out of there after day three, but I insisted on staying. The reason I prolonged my time in the tank was to make a personal protest to the out-right lie that the police had "lost" my Porsche briefcase.

Their effort was part of a half-hearted attempt to break my morale and force me into signing the extradition papers. They needed me to sign those papers in order to transfer me from Charles Street Jail in Boston to Adams County Jail in Colorado, where I was wanted on numerous charges. Just like any normal man, I did not want to travel without my luggage. Thus, information concerning the unfortunate misplacement did not sit well with me.

The black leather suitcase had been my only property in the entire world. It was important to every man in that jail that I retained my dignity and did not cave to the twisted and corrupt ways of law enforcement. I felt like I was an important part of the struggle between prisoner and guard. If one link of the prisoner chain snapped, the fight against corruption would be virtually useless.

*   *   *

I was a different man after those two weeks in the hole. The walls of the dungeon had become a part of me. The thickness of everything, the sheet metal and cold steel bars, made me realize how fragile I was. Sure, I put on the face of the toughest guy in the world, and I probably was, but no matter how hard I tried, I was still just a human. There were things out there much more powerful than me. I was beginning to see that.

"What kind of life am I living?" I asked myself. "What good is this? I'm in jail. I'm rotting in a shit can. This isn't productive. I'm not making any money doing this."

I'd stare at the ceiling for days at a time asking myself the same pointless questions I knew that I had to change, but change was hard for a guy like me. I could think about it all I wanted, but no change in my life had ever happened unless there had been a dire need for it. This need, like it or not, was usually created by the police.

"Hell, if I could have it my way I'd still be at Lacy's. I'd probably be an executive by now, still selling my own shit to the store and taking vodka breaks at 10 a.m." I laughed out loud. A guard approached the window, eyeing me suspiciously.

"Please, Mr. Anderson, just sign the extradition papers and you'll be out of this can. These are no conditions for a man to endure for two weeks."

I smirked at him.

"I'm not signing anything until I get my luggage. I got some sentimental items in there and if you don't find it I'll stay right here for the rest of my natural life."

"Mr. Anderson, no one wants to stay in this damn holding cell for-ever. You're going nuts as it is. I hear you in here talking to your self all the time. All you have to do is sign."

"Kill it, cupcake. I'm not giving in. If one link rips..."

"We know, Mr. Anderson, 'the whole chain would be useless.'" He rolled his eyes. "We're sorry we lost your stuff, but it's time you sign the papers and get on your way. You've got a trial in Adams County that you can't miss."

"There's no date set for that thing, genius. Don't bullshit me." I leaned up against the window and screamed at him. "I'LL STAY HERE FOR THE REST OF MY NATURAL..." He walked away dejectedly, hopelessly lost in the same mess only in a slightly different way.

It was good to frustrate the guards as much as possible. In the begin-ning, this would only lead to contempt and ill-treatment. In the end, however, it would coerce them into doing ANYTHING to get you out of their hair. I could feel that after another week my bag would be "found" beneath the booking officer's main desk.

Honestly, it didn't make much of a difference whether I got my bag back or not. It was the police's amorality, the principal of their evil deed, which led me to actively pursue uncooperative behavior.

*   *   *

Finally, in the third and most boring week of my orientation cell peri-od, my briefcase was located and displayed to me through the cell win-dow.

"Gimme the papers," I said. "Send me to Adams County. I don't give a damn anymore." Before I left Charles Street, while the papers were being processed, they moved me up to a regular tier. I was permitted to play in the football games that happened once a day in the yard.

The yard was all but 70 yards long and filled with about 900 guys. It made for a fairly narrow playing surface and the goal lines were the double razor wire fences on each end. Not seeing daylight for almost a month made it a little hard on my eyes, but I quickly secured a split end position on one of the teams. I had been so disheartened by the orienta-tion cell that just one hour a day to play football seemed like total free-dom.

The time passed quickly with all the excitement (anything was a thrill compared to the sub-basement), and after two weeks I was transported to Denver. Honestly, I had grown to enjoy the football games so much that I was sad to leave.

*   *   *

The Felony Tank at Adams County came pretty close to Dead Last in the "Lovely Jail Spots of 1979" list. It was small: about 30 feet wide by 80 feet long, containing anywhere from 30 to 50 men, and perpetually smelled like dung from bad plumbing. It was constructed of solid steel plating with at least 50 coats of paint over the walls.

There were no windows and about 10 vents blew freezing air around the clock. Some of us called it the Meat Cooler because it was always about 55 degrees and there were no blankets or beds. You just sat in there and froze, nothing to do but stare at the wall or talk crazy with cons.

At night, or whenever, we tried as best we could to get sleep. They issued us one sheet and a one-inch hard mattress for our bunk, which was merely a steel shelf welded onto the wall. With a full house, all those people coughing, talking, breathing, dumping, crying, it was borderline impossible to get any rest.

The idea to break me (this time) was to keep me in the Meat Cooler until, finally, after countless court appearances, I would make the wrong statement and give myself away as the "Interstate Criminal."

I knew I wouldn't cave. I think they knew it too.

*   *   *

It was my third sleepless night, probably around 1 a.m., when I found out about Meat Cooler entertainment.

As I lay in my bunk, one of the smaller guys tapped my shoulder and spoke. "Alright, when the guard comes by I need everybody to just jump up and make some noise. That includes YOU, buddy."

"What? Are you trying to scare him or something?" I asked. "That's the stupidest thing I've ever heard."

The man leaned in closer to me. "Listen, stop bitching. We're going to nail that guard with a stink bomb. When he comes by, as soon as you see my boy make the move, just jump up from your spot and make some noise."

"Why?"

"'Cause, man, that way he'll have no idea who did it."

"The cameras won't show it?" I asked.

"The cameras in here are fakes. It's all for show."

We waited, listening for the sound of the guard's footsteps. Several of the inmates chuckled in a corner as they prepared the dish of human feces. I couldn't wait for the guard to get what he deserved. I knew which guard it was, too. It was the same piece of worthless trash who had been cuffing me at 4 a.m. each morning and leading me to the basement of the court house.

The other plan to break me, one that was extremely common among institutions like Adams County, was to wake me up at 4 a.m. every day so that I'd lose my mind from lack of sleep. I was on trial five days a week and had to make statements that could make or break my case. Without good rest, they assumed that any normal man would cave to the pressures of the District Attorney. Problem was I wasn't a normal man. Lack of sleep had never stopped me before. I'd gone weeks on speed and booze and still gone on buying trips for Lacy's. And what's more, I'd never messed up ONCE!

The guard rounded the corner and one of the inmates leapt up and threw the turd-bomb at his face. I sat there in my bunk, still as a rock, as the other inmates screamed and carried on. I let out a good laugh when the guard lost his dinner. Hell, it may have been horrible, but he deserved every bit of it.

The ringleader of the turd throwing club came over to me a couple hours later, around 2 a.m., and put his hand around my neck.

"Hey, dummy, why didn't you get up when—"

I tore his arm away, punched him in the throat, followed him to the floor, and beat his face several times with my right fist. The sound of his skull thumping on the floor was like church bells. I stood over him, wiping the blood onto his jump suit, and felt the distured gaze of every man on my back.

"Anybody else tries anything, the same will happen to you. Mind your own business and don't worry what I do."

Several guards came in and carried his bloody carcass out for stitches. They didn't care who'd beaten him up. What's more, they probably knew. To the guards, it was one less guy to hurl human waste into their eyes. They'd be happy to cart him down to the hospital for the next three days and question him while he was drugged up.

* * *

The 4 a.m. wake-up routines continued. The waste throwing at guards by disgruntled inmates happened at least once a week. One time they threw in tear gas, but other than that they weren't able to do anything except make it colder, delay meals, leave high-beam lights on all night, etc. Occasionally someone would get the infamous "Elevator Ride." On the elevator there were no witnesses, so the guards could take turns beating a man with clubs. I'll never forget the time they took me on that thing...

In court, the District Attorney had begun playing a no-rules ball game. It all started when, during my second week of trial, the D.A. called Linda Taylor (formerly Linda Anderson, aka Jennifer), my supposed ex-wife, to the stand.

At first, I couldn't believe that he was serious. I turned to see if it was really Jen. A woman who looked nothing like her entered the courtroom and approached the stand. She took a seat and the D.A. addressed her.

"Ms. Taylor, how long had you and Scott Anderson been married before he disappeared?"

"About four years."

"And you met him where?"

"Hawaii."

"And what was he doing in Hawaii?"

"Dealing cocaine, stealing from companies, writing bad checks..." Her testimony was semi-accurate, enough to put a bit of fear into my bones. There was one thing I knew for sure: The D.A. had all the facts on me. His only problem was producing a REAL witness to seal the deal. Surely he'd never find Jen or anyone else I'd worked with. It was his plan to try faking the jury with phonies in hopes that one of them could stand up to the challenge.

Every day in court he brought a new witness I'd never seen before. Each time someone new took the stand it always came down to this: "Is Scott Anderson in the court room? If so, could you please point him out to the jury?" And then the poor lady would scour the courtroom, studying the faces of the men at my bench. The woman would have no idea what I looked like without a beard and long hair. My old scruffy mug shots were the only pictures the D.A. had been able to prep her with. The witnesses would shrug her shoulders every time.

"I don't recognize him," She'd say. "I don't know if he's in here. He must have changed his appearance."

The D.A. would turn away with anger as my lawyer objected to each witness's validity. Finally, after six months of this, six months of the judge not caring to stop the parading of false witnesses, I began to get nervous that the D.A.'s evil plan was going to work. It was apparent that the judge didn't give a damn about the legality. He didn't like me. He wanted me to be put away forever.

* * *

Six months passed in the Meat Cooler. No heat, no blankets, one shower a week at best, no bed, human waste everywhere, and court five days a week. I was on a very strict push-up regimen, and would do so many that I sometimes wondered if I'd lost the ability to feel pain. More than likely I had lost my sanity, but the guards never noticed a crazy person in a place like that.

It was a normal day at the end of my sixth month and I was doing squats with some giant black man on my shoulders. The guards came and buzzed the cell door.

"Scott Anderson?" One of the guards asked. I didn't quite hear him.

"KCMF! The guard wants you," said the guy to my right. KCMF, King Crazy Mother Fucker., had become my nickname in the Felony Tank. I'd earned this name because of how badly I'd beaten the inmate who had grabbed my throat. Also, people thought I was crazy because I wasn't afraid to share my story. This was uncommon in the world of prisoners. In most cases, men didn't know why they'd been arrested. Or, as was common, they claimed their imprisonment was a big mistake. I had nothing good coming in my life, so I figured I'd be honest about it.

I set the man down from my shoulders and walked over to the door. I removed the wet toilet paper from the speaker.

"What the hell are you people bothering me for?"

"Turn around. Put your hands through the door."

"Where am I going?" The wild side of my imagination had convinced me that I was on death row.

"You're done here. Time to go home."

"What?" It seemed impossible, like a hallucination. Besides, I didn't have a home to go to. People didn't understand how such simple comments could generate profound reactions within the minds of the lost.

The giant guard's lips—lips and face that had once been splattered with human waste—continued to open and close.

"You're out of here. The D.A. can't make a case against you. You don't remember court this morning?" I didn't remember anything. "Don't leave town. They are going to re-file. So, technically, you're not free, just on a tether."

I had no idea what had happened in court that morning, but it must have been good. Truth be told, I hadn't paid attention to the courtroom in weeks. The sleep deprivation had worked. Somehow, my subconscious had been able to stay on top of the game without personal interference.

I stuck my hands through the doors. I was pretty happy to get out. It had been tough. I could have taken more, but there was a point where any man began to lose himself inside the nightmare.

They handed me my briefcase and I donned the old suit. I'd been given a shower before court that day so didn't smell as terrible as would otherwise have been possible. I put on my socks, my old belt, found my cigar case, and headed into the jail parking lot. I called a cab from the pay phone outside Adam's County Jail and took a ride down to Northglenn Dodge.

*　　*　　*

I walked into the lot and Frank offered me a cigar. I took it, lit it, breathed it in.

"You still smell like crap," he said, looking me up and down. "You been back in jail, huh?"

"First time in a few years."

"Lose the suit. That thing looks terrible." We walked into his office and he cut me a check for $500.

"It's an advance," he said. "You got the job, just show up on Monday. Take the weekend to get yourself established. You can take that red Vette over there, just don't wreck it."

"No offense, Frank, but there's nothing else for me to do but work. Could you get me on the floor tomorrow?"

"You wanna start working on your first day out? Don't you wanna go to the bars or something? Did they reform you in there?"

"Look, man, all I'm saying is that I need money. I appreciate the advance, I really do, but I gotta get going." I felt an uncontrollable need to procure more and more wealth. Time had been cheated from me, I was back to square one, and if I didn't get started I'd never amount to anything.

"Chuck!" Frank yelled across the showroom to one of the salesmen. "You want to take tomorrow off?"

"Eh, yeah, sure. Why?"

"Scotty's back. He wants the floor."

"Hey, Scott, how's it going?" Chuck yelled. I waved back at him and nodded. "Yeah, Scott, go for it. I'll go down to the game or something."

Frank turned back to me and nodded. I followed him into his office.

"What do you keep getting locked up for, Scott? If you don't mind me asking?"

"It's a long story. I hit a city bus when I was drunk. Rear ended it. They locked me up for a while because I didn't want to pay the fines."

We were silent for a few moments, each of us smoking the cigars.

"You're so full of shit..." he said, laughing. "I'll see you in the morning."

* * *

My job at Northglenn went well. Small advances in capital facilitated my resurgence into the cocaine trade.

The idea was to keep my customer list relatively small. I didn't want to draw too much attention to myself for fear that OPERATION SNOW STORM was still under way and certain people may not be happy with how I'd left Denver last time. Also, I tried my best to keep my name secret from Carlos and Norberto for fear that they were once again involved with Jennifer and may have heard about how I'd abandoned her in Boston.

There were so many people after me, including the authorities, that I purchased a .45-caliber MAC-10 machine pistol and a .38 Special revolver. I kept the .38 in my car and the MAC in my bedroom. These guns, while providing ample security, reminded me of the nightmare I'd worked myself into.

"Who the hell am I?" I asked one day while waiting in line at the gun store. I had nine boxes of ammunition in my hands and a few holsters slung over my shoulder. I caught a glimpse of myself in a sunglasses mirror and didn't recognize my own face. I felt a twinge of fear, like something had gone wrong in my brain, and when I set the ammunition on the counter it toppled over onto the floor.

I was exhausted. There was no period of rest in Denver, never had been, and my mind and muscles trembled throughout. Over the next few weeks I delved deeper and deeper into cocaine and began selling stolen diamonds.

The diamond connection had suckered me in even though I'd told him that I wasn't interested. He had called me one evening and like a fool I'd entertained his conversation.

"So, Scott, look here, man… I got a train full of coal that I need you to check out."

"What?" I was drinking at my apartment, my television the only source of light in the living room. I had no idea what he was talking about. I originally assumed that by "coal" he meant cocaine.

"I got some stones, man. A few stones that you gotta check for me. I heard you're good in the biz." The guy was a trip. He dipped his hands in every business but knew less about crime than anyone I'd ever known. He was just a fat little rich boy with daddy's capital and a twisted ethics system.

"Alright, when you want me to look at it?" I still had no idea what he was talking about. I took a dreg from the beer, remained focused on the television.

"Come over right now if you want." I felt a pang of adrenaline whenever a person requested that I come somewhere for a meeting. The most innocent invitations had the potential to be robberies, setups, whack jobs…

Nonetheless, I needed to take any work I could get. If this guy needed my opinion on something and was willing to pay for it, I figured I'd better drive down there. I loaded the MAC into the car and drove across town. It turned out that my guy was being honest. He didn't know his head from his ass and someone had fronted him a satchel of rubies and diamonds on the cuff before leaving for prison.

"He told me that his connection would work through me now, you know, until he gets out of the pen," my friend told me. We were meeting in his basement and there was only one tiny light down there. We spread the stones on a mat of black felt. "He'll be locked up for five years. So, I guess I got us a connection for five years."

"Us? I got the connection, buddy. You don't know anything. Send all the merchandise to me and I'll cut you in on some of the loot for the tip."

"Bullshit," he said. I felt tension rise. The sweat on the tip of his nose dripped, very slowly, falling—SLAP—right on the surface of one of the diamonds.

"You're a sweaty mess. Get some sleep, lay off the coke, and I'll handle this." He put a hand up to stop me from leaving. I had gathered up the stones in the bag. "Trust me, buddy, you'll get yours. Just let me do my thing. I'm not in the business of screwing people over. I'm in the business of making money." I didn't really know what that meant, but it kept him away from me.

"I work with the guy who sold you your guns, Scott," he said. "And you know I got plenty of my own."

"Yeah. Quit with the hard talk. I'll have you some money by the end of next week and we'll be ready for another load. Tell your connection to bring as much as he can. We'll sell it all. No problem. This stuff beats cocaine hands down." In all honesty, stones didn't beat cocaine as far as profit was concerned. My true motive was that I wanted to make some personal necklaces in case I had to go on the run. An expensive personal necklace was like an insurance policy; it would always be around my neck and I could always sell it if I had to split town.

*   *   *

Over the course of about three months I shifted from working at Northglenn to becoming an independent car wholesaler. I would go out five days a week to buy cars at auction and resell them to local dealerships. My money situation, between wholesaling cars and selling coke and stones, began to see a noticeable increase.

One afternoon while lifting weights I met a very attractive young lady at the health club named Sheryl. Sheryl was a personal trainer and had a perfect physique. I had noticed her for weeks but figured I better not say anything for fear of blowing my cover. Finally, one day, she came up to me.

She had a body like a supermodel, great hair, deep tan, short shorts and a low cut shirt. We went on a few dates and she confessed that she'd fallen for me at first sight. I had a hunch that it may have had something to do with my necklace.

She was a bit overwhelming but I rode it out. There wasn't much else going on.

Then, very unexpectedly, the sand in the hourglass began to sink faster beneath my feet. I noticed strange things happening on the street in front of my apartment and realized, over the course of three days, that my home and usual business stops were under minor surveillance.

I stared at myself in my bathroom mirror at all hours giving verbal advice.

"It'll only be time, Scott, before they nail you to the wall." I paced the slippery tile. "That D.A. will produce a witness, maybe they'll even find Jen, and then you'll be screwed. You need to find a way to get more cash without anyone knowing."

I remembered the last time we'd been in Denver together, how the Feds had gotten to her and she'd almost rolled over on me. There was no reason for them to have let her go unless she told them who she was working with. What kind of a girlfriend was she? It became clearer and clearer how treacherous Jennifer could be if they put her on the stand.

"You gotta bail out of here, Scott," I said, pointing to myself with resolve. "You gotta bail out before things get too serious and they figure out a way to stick you. They can hold you in Adam's forever. They'll give you the 4 a.m. shifts and keep you on the bus for a decade if they want... It's no problem for those snakes."

I came up with a fast and easy plan. Step 1: Make a large and final cocaine purchase on the front—meaning, the dealer would give me the cocaine on the trust that I would pay him back after I sold it. This would give me a large profit margin once I stole it and left town. Step 2: Through my wholesaling contacts I would purchase an upper-level luxury car with a fake bank draft. Step 3: Try to procure a good amount of rare stones for the ride.

"Where do you wanna go?" I asked myself, pacing my bedroom and whispering. Sheryl was asleep in the bed, oblivious to my schemes. "Seattle would be the place... I can stay with Leslie from Hawaii. She lives in Seattle now. Maybe she's still a stewardess! Maybe she'll know a way to sell the coke? That's the game plan," I said. I took another line from the top of the television, which was playing a black-and-white World War II movie that I'd seen on that channel at least a dozen times that week.

*   *   *

I purchased a 6.9 liter Mercedes from a dealer who had screwed me over once or twice in the past. We had a minor beef over some lemons he'd sold me, but I kept him as an underground associate. Regardless of how bad his cars were, he bought a ton of stones from me. This made him extremely valuable. Besides, it was important to keep other criminals your friends. I could have made bad blood between us over the cars, but since I stayed cool and kept him on my side he was now very easy to manipulate.

After only a few lines I had him right where I wanted him. I haggled down from 50k to 45k and purchased the vehicle with a phony bank draft. It would probably get him caught, but I'd be gone so it wouldn't matter. He couldn't roll over on a man he didn't really know.

I laughed manically, immediately driving home to my apartment and preparing for a long run. Sheryl was at the gym and I had the apartment to myself. It felt similar to the time that I'd left Jen in Boston, how she'd gone to the store and I'd just packed up and headed south.

Well, maybe times were different now. Maybe she could come with me? No, absolutely not.

"Times are too tight to be paying for two people, man. Keep your cool. She was good while she lasted, now it's over. You need to move on and get away from all this." I grabbed a few of my personal belongings and stuffed them into my pockets.

I slid effortlessly into the leather interior, adjusting the seat, the radio, the heater, the ashtray, all the important things a man needs to spend a few days on the run. I'd burnt that city for the last time and I knew that I'd never come back as long as I lived. Not that it bothered me, but it was somewhat gut-wrenching to look down a familiar street and know that you'd never lay eyes on it again.

The car cruised down the block and I signaled for a right turn. A cop gave me a good stare and I winked through my sunglasses, a cigar protruding triumphantly from my beard. The little putz, 23 years old at best, cruised through the stop sign and over a hill. I chuckled at the bastard's blindness. It takes skill to stay out of jail. It also takes a little luck. No matter how stupid the police are, even a broken clock is right twice a day.

16

NIGHT RIDER

1980

I HAD ABOUT 10 GRAND CASH SHOVED INTO THE CRACK OF THE PASSENGER seat and a thousand bucks spending money in the glove box for gas, booze, smokes, nuts, water, all that shit.

I'd pulled some rough deals in Denver and I could sense that the Gestapo had finally caught on. I didn't give a damn either way. I was gone now.

The MAC-10 machine pistol was lodged securely beneath the passenger seat like an angry pit bull. A dozen 32-round mags were strewn all over the trunk along with my Smith and Wesson .38 revolver.

The Smith was the backup weapon, my strong-arm that was good for penetrating the doors of vehicles. Then again, I'd never use the thing unless I ran out of .45s for the MAC. And running out of .45s was a very unsettling possibility, considering that the full-auto could eat 32 rounds in just under two seconds.

I lit up a square, cracked the window, blared the tunes, and put the Benz through its gears. Night was coming on fast; the hardened p.m./a.m. shift of highway patrol would soon be on the prowl.

A fresh army of cops would be out looking for drunks, drug runners, and serial criminals like me. Like hell I wanted to get pinched on a night like this. By a guy like that. Hell no. Too nice of an evening to end up freezing to death in jail; then again, jail's not so bad when you're high as a hot air balloon on coke.

I had to bear in mind the magnitude of my situation: piloting a high-end Benz chocked full of weaponry, drugs, and cash. Such blatant disregard arouses deep contempt from the lawman, and it's possible that the offending individual might never make it to the Big House. The cops have been known to make guys like me disappear for stuff like this. Seriously.

*　　*　　*

My plan was to make it to Seattle in one piece. Get up there and take a load off. First things first: pitch the cocaine and the Black Beauties—about 200 of them—to a capable buyer. I'd put a high tax on everything for the quality, since it was great blow and the trip had cost me a few bucks.

Once the drugs started moving I'd be working with a decent bankroll and could get involved with something a little more lucrative, such as borrowing some more Learjets or tractor trailer loads of ammunition or televisions...maybe another round of diamonds from Denver.

I-25 was a grueling, cold, straight barrel of a gun. I rifled down it, leaving a trail of fire behind me like I'd just been hocked out of hell.

I kept on railing coke and smoking squares along with the occasional Antonio Y Cleopatra cigar. Every now and then I'd lose focus and swerve crazily. I'd check for pigs, but none were around. I was basically the only car on the road. I passed an old guy. He gave me the finger when I looked over and I contemplated brandishing the piece.

There was no sense risking the job over sending some geriatric jackass into Kingdom Come. I wasn't all out of luck just yet. Sure, all my chips were on the table, but the hand wasn't over. I planned on making some serious loot in the next few months.

*　　*　　*

About five hours in I took an early break and stopped at some hole-in-the-wall bar called Baby Amanda's or something. Hell if I knew what it said I was so blown. It was in Wyoming somewhere and the parking lot was filled with $500 slugs. My 50k Benz was like a nugget of gold in a sea of chicken shit. And believe me, most of the men driving those trucks were pansies.

I left the hardware in the car rather than try to shove it down my pants and go waddling in there like some stoned sheriff. There was no need for a piece anyway. I had a knife, and if someone wanted to start something I'd probably break off a bottle and get their throat with it rather than waste time pulling the blade. I'd heard men say that a sharp object is a better weapon than a gun. You can't miss with a bottle and you get to be right up on the guy when you're about to stick him (which was the way I'd rather do it anyway).

As I got closer to the door I noticed a bunch of white starbursts all over my black mink jacket and leather pants. No doubt it was all coke. Oh well, what the hell, who gives a damn anyway. I busted in there.

"What can I getcha baby?" The bartendress was all teeth with yellow, hollow, vacant cigarette eyes.

"Mezcal."

"You want that mixed with something?"

"Just give me that bottle of tequila on the shelf with the worm."

"Got into that stuff when I got stuck down in Qaxaco once...that's a long story for another time," she said. She turned toward the back of the bar.

"Gimme a Heineken too."

"Ain't got that."

"Whaddaya got then?" I muttered something unpleasant and indecipherable about the establishment.

She listed some cheap beers. I picked one.

*   *   *

Some putz off in the corner was hogging the jukebox and playing nothing but Beach Boys. The whole damned world had lost their senses of taste, decency, intelligence, courage, knowledge, anything that commanded respect—which, after all, is why I gave them none.

"Who's that jackass over there on the juke?" I asked Ms. Cigarette Eyes.

"That's Ed."

"He's a big boy, huh?"

"He ain't big as you."

"That doesn't always matter, lady."

I went on over there and looked down at him.

"Hey, Ed?"

"Yeah?" He looked up from the pool table. He was one of those old 40-something tattooed and gutted farts. Big old teeth and coke-bottle glasses with stains from wings and beer all down the front of a hand-me-down flannel from 1950 with the sleeves cut off. A real backwoods character with nothing but Budweiser and true-blue idiocy.

"This music is for faggots, Ed."

"What are you trying to say?"

I slapped a C-note on the pool table, which was one of those damn kid's pool tables like they used to have outside the Steak n' Shake back when I was growing up.

That old fart just stared at me while I unplugged the box, plugged it back in, shoved a quarter into it, and scrolled through the selection. And, damn it all to hell, there was nothing.

"Hey, Ed, why isn't there anything to listen to in this piece of junk?"

"Look, buddy, you're out of your element."

"Listen to me, old man: I've got no problem ripping your head off and taking a shit in it." Damn, I was high. He stared me down. "Go ahead, Ed, look into my eyes. What do you see?" He kept staring. He studied me hard: my past-shoulder-length hair, my cocaine ZZ Top beard, entirely black-leather garb, two dozen gold chains adorned with large multicolored stones and diamonds.

"Seriously, Ed, you don't want to mess around. KCMF never goes easy. Not on anybody."

I tipped my cowboy hat back, raised my chin, and cocked my head sideways a bit.

Two or three others dispersed, moved away from the pool table. I was really gassed. I tore into the jukebox, slammed it against the wall, chose something by Johnny Cash or somebody like him, drained Ed's beer, walked out into the parking lot and pissed right in the middle under a light.

Some redneck idiot was blind drunk and came charging up at me screaming something like: "That Mercedes is for fags! FAGS!" And all I did was just stand there and when he got up real close he skidded to a stop and fell right on his ass. I spit in his general direction. It was dark and I can't say whether or not I hit him but I know I was damn close.

I burned out of the lot and onto the Interstate. There was a long way to go and not a damn bite of food to keep my brain working. The console of blow kept me distracted from things like food. It kept my nerves on edge and my eyes wired up like the electric chair.

*   *   *

A blizzard moved overland. Snow drifted on the road lightly at first, just powder, then the blast came on hard.

It was a mix of snow and sleet, frozen daggers that slashed across the hood of the Benz like fangs. I had issues with the steering, the rear wheels breaking loose, my eyes focusing between the swipes of the wiper.

I pulled into a gas station, filled up quietly, leaning on the pump and turning my back on an old man rustling through the garbage in the middle of nowhere. I got this sick feeling inside like I was going to become him if I looked at him for too long. I walked over there and stuffed a C-note in his pocket. It might be me one day. Then again, no way; I'd steal a car and drive it off into a tree before I'd search the dumpster for donuts.

The road slid beneath me. I was going through mountains, canyons, whatever the hell it was. There were tons of rocks, ice that caused me to slide across the road and skid toward death. No one else was out there in that snow, not even a cop. Not even a snow plow. Nothing. Just me and a bag of heartless powder to cut through that desolate country.

*   *   *

Day broke and the storm waned. The lunch hour passed without food. I was somewhere about 50 miles out of Billings when the chopper off to my right came and disappeared and came and disappeared. It kept doing that for about half an hour and I was the only damn car on the road, so it made me pretty nervous.

After a while I noticed a vehicle looming up behind me—probably one of those notorious renegade highway patrol officers out for a show-down.

Sure enough, the lights wailed up. Damn. I slapped on the signal, braked too hard, went skidding off onto the side of the highway. I must have imagined that it was worse than it was, because when the cop came up he didn't say anything about me stopping too fast.

"You been exceeding the speed limit, sir?"

"Not that I know of," I said. My hands were steady and my expression was calm. My insides were tight. He went back to his car…

Jail. Prison. Damn it. All things have a way of returning, even this crap. Suddenly, I had a crazy vision: I saw myself reaching for the MAC and spraying the car with a full clip. Hell, I could probably shoot down their chopper if it came to it. I'd have to play lame duck though. I'd sucker the thing in real close, hop out like Charles Bronson, and let the .45s do the rest. Three clips. Maybe I could blow the engine or knock off the tail rotor.

I came back to reality, my hands gripping the wheel of that Benz. These were wild times and the mind seemed to be running on a long leash. Luckily, I retained some sense of control and looked through the glaring sun and into the police officer's eyes.

"You got a license?"

"Yes, sir." I handed him the license, brushing the hair out of my face and running a few fingers through my beard.

Though I appeared calm, it was evident to me that my powers of coherent speech had faded. I was sure he'd notice this and pull his piece on me. If not for my diction, he'd probably blow me away as soon as he ran the I.D. and realized that it was fake. In retrospect it struck me as a terrible idea to have created a fake alias named "Robin Hood," which I had done at some point in Denver while drunk or stoned. It was now, in the face of the law, that I realized how such an absurd title could potentially spell the ultimate roadside tragedy.

The cop stood there staring. Sputtering past was the same old man from the day before, the one that had given me the finger. I hadn't seen a car in three hours, that's how long the 5-0 stood there reading my license on his gut.

Then, as if that wasn't enough, the jackass took it back to his car, ran the numbers on my temp tags, ran the license, played Solitaire, beat some prisoners… whatever they do in those Nazi tanks while you wait.

He came back. "Alrighty," he said, flipping me the Robin Hood I.D.

"Alrighty?" I said, nearly mocking him but catching myself.

"You're good to go. Just keep it slow." Was this Pre-K driving class or did the highway cop just make a rhyme? I didn't have time to ask. He went back there, got into his Panzer tank, clattered off down the road in front of me. The Nazi army and their helicopters and tanks and squad cars and fat old farts had missed me again.

Ride on.

＊　　＊　　＊

Another night had come on the road and I was through Billings and not too far from Spokane. The drive consisted of a bunch of raised bridges flying me over canyons and cliffs. Little creatures moved around down there like bloodsuckers and from the recesses of my head I imagined somebody feeding me to them. It was a horrendous thought but then again so was everything else so why the hell did it matter?

I switched speeds irrationally. Not on purpose, but because I'd often be looking around the interior for more coke or a cigarette or cigar and I'd just forget about driving. With the dome light on it was like it didn't matter about the outside world. A man could just stare at the floor and if it was dark outside he didn't even have to think about which way he was going. That damn Benz just steered itself.

I began to get these headaches. Probably from the coke. Maybe from the lack of food. Maybe because I hadn't had a beer in a few hours. Dehydration? Was that what caused loss of sanity?

I pushed through it, jamming new tapes in the tape deck and jamming the gas pedal into the carpet. I got the feeling someone was watching me. Shit, someone or something was definitely very close. I had the strangest sensation like I was passing into the Twilight Zone.

"Who's back there!" I yelled, swerving, checking the rearview, the side mirrors, slapping my fist on the passenger seat and damn near breaking it off at the top.

"Who is in this damn car!?!" I reached beneath the passenger seat, thrashed around. Bills tumbled out of the satchel in stacks. I pulled out the MAC, held it up silhouetted against the road.

"No one wants to play with—" A vortex of odor engulfed me, so bad that it carried heat along with it. Sweat poured from my brow and I gagged, dropping the gat into my lap. It was everything I could do to keep from hurling. I let all the windows down. The car slowed to half speed. Then I gunned it all the way up to the red line and the frozen air, probably around 23 degrees, tried in vain to clear the interior of the smell.

I closed my nose but the smell coated my throat. It was overpowering, mind bending; it smelled like rotted meat only worse. I knew the smell… from somewhere… or did I? It smelled a lot like the volcano I'd been to in Hawaii: burning rock, brimstone and sulfur from deep in the Earth, disgusting and hard to forget. I had come upon a maggot-infested dead body in the woods once. The goop that came out of that guy was bad. Bad, but not quite like this.

Accompanying the odor was a flicker of light in my periphery. Someone was peering in from the sunroof, then from the mirrors. Some sonuvabitch was crawling on the outside of my car.

I screamed like an animal.

"I'll riddle this thing with shots if you don't get the hell OFF!" How could he hang on at this speed?

The reality of my situation set in. I grabbed my tooter, took a good rip of coke, and the powder from the open container blew throughout the interior.

"Fallie! It's you, isn't it! You sneak in at the last gas station or what?" No answer. "HUH?" I yelled. "You blow my head off and we're both dead. Just remember that. You don't want to die. I know you don't want to die!"

Strong fear overcame me. I was silent. I coughed up vomit into my mouth. I had lost the battle for my nerves and slowly gave in to defeat. My hands trembled against the wheel and tears welled up in my eyes. I swallowed the wad of snot and cocaine and puke.

The car was silent except for the wind. The engine was even silent, but the car kept moving. Faster. The wind. Just the howling and night-marish wind screamed at me like a choir of murderers.

I checked the rearview and sure enough, there it was: a form in the center of the back seat. A head, thin neck, and shoulders. My breath stopped and an unexplainable hotness left me choking, unable to move, unable to respond, just quietly gagging and dying. It was over. The whole damn game. The Big Show, from birth to death. It was all over when I saw it.

I took one more look back there at that scaly, oily, red-eyed bastard. It was something straight from Hell. I knew what needed to happen and it wasn't going to be pretty but it would damn sure beat what would happen if I tried to make a move on him.

I picked a weak spot on the guard rail and gently banked the nose, the giant Mercedes emblem like a bull's eye toward death. The accelerator went through the floorboard and I let out a roar equivalent to the wind. I checked the speedometer: 97 mph.

It was as good a speed as any.

*   *   *

It seemed that his plan was to keep me alive as long as possible. Sure, I'd been ready to take the Benz off the cliff. No doubt about it. The cliff would have been a fine way to go, just as a TV cable in a holding cell or a jet engine at Chicago O'Hare would have done me justice. The problem with this particular attempt was, as soon as I aimed for the guard rail, the thing in the backseat disappeared. I tried to grab it, swatted behind me, but there was nothing.

I stopped at a rest area and checked for evidence as to who it could have been. Spread across the leather was a slight film, an eerie trace that there had been something back there but nothing concrete enough to tell me who it was.

The feeling overcame me, beneath the quiet and barely lit rest area sky, that I'd known who had been in the back seat all along. I thought about it for a few seconds, threw the soiled paper towels into a trashcan and went back to the car for one more inspection. I found a bit more of slime and scrubbed it off, making another trek across the lot to throw away my trash.

"I've been working for that guy," I said, unable to explain what I meant. "I've been working for him my whole life and I never even knew it."

What was I saying?

"It's him, man. It's the guy who's been putting me in harm's way: jail, on the run, selling other people's merchandise. He's the cause of all that."

Did that mean he wasn't real?

"No, man. He's totally real. You saw him. You FELT him."

I had felt him. True enough.

"Listen, man, there's a reason for this. There's a definite reason."

A reason for my criminality or for the slime? Which was it? Both?

"I don't know what it is, but there's a reason."

I checked my map and plotted a course south. I couldn't continue on my present mission. I had a bad feeling about Washington State, like it would be the end of me. All of this felt so strange. It reminded me of when I used to pace the roads at Mansfield View and ask god about the meaning of my life.

"It's similar to that."

To speaking with god?

"To understanding the meaning of life."

I got in the Benz and shut the door. Locked it. The MAC was still loaded and lying on the floorboard beneath my feet. I pulled out of the rest area.

17

THE ROAD TO NOWHERE

1980

HELLS BELLS. I WAS IN A HOTEL ROOM IN RENO, NEVADA. SHERYL WAS beside me. I must have flown her in from Denver. What was I thinking? I had also traded in my Benz for a Volkswagen Rabbit and some cash.

The television was still on from the night before, blaringly loud, me drunker than shit. I stared groggily from my hangover and listened. Something was going horribly wrong. The 8 a.m. newsman was running his mouth full blast. The luck bucket was on the verge of being completely empty.

"Highway 70/80 East and West are blocked in an attempt to catch a known fugitive who has recently arrived in the Reno area. All residents are advised to avoid these routes if at all possible. However, the delay is not quite as bad as…" He kept on. I was pretty sure that 70/80 was the only road in or out of Reno. I went downstairs, and in an anxious frenzy grabbed the map from my car. I patted her roof gently. "Alright, Volks, you're about to get a taste of the action."

I lit a cigarette and walked through the casino without taking my eyes from the map. The casino manager approached me, smiling, trying like a vampire to suck money from my wallet.

"Mr. Behr, Mr. Behr! Are you interested in the 10 a.m. poker tournament?"

"No. I'll be in my room all day. I'm sick. Put me down for another night up there and I'll see you tomorrow."

"Would you like me to call a doctor?" he asked, trying with quick steps to match my speed.

"No. I hate doctors. My dad was a doctor. Get me a case of beer, a bottle of vodka. Extra pillows. I need extra pillows ASAP."

The elevator door shut in his face and I took a big drag on the cigarette and blew it into the map. Reno was under siege. Highway 70/80 was kaput. What a damn curse.

"How about another way out?" I asked. I don't know who I was asking. I was in the elevator alone.

There's another way out.

"What?" I asked, confused as if I heard someone else speaking. I tried to ignore it. "I wonder if I should try to steal an airplane?" I pondered, looking up through the elevator ceiling at the imaginary sky.

Keep looking over the map, Jack, you'll find it.

It was scary. My own mind was playing tricks on me, using my boyhood name like my teachers in elementary school. Something was prodding me toward the correct escape route, but I couldn't understand what it was.

"Alright," I muttered, the cigarette smashed between my teeth. I pointed at the crumpled map. Something materialized in the ink.

"There's a road!" I shouted.

So, there was ONE road on my "comprehensive" Nevada map. ONE road other than 70/80 that led out of Reno. And this road, this tiny white line, stretched all the way up into Oregon somewhere and then faded off into nothing.

"It's our only shot, Sheryl," I said, bursting into the room, the cigarette smoke trailing me like lazy police officers and fading off into the ceiling fan light bulb.

"What do you mean?"

"I mean it's the only chance we have of making it out of here. It won't be long before they figure out where I'm staying. The pigs are probably combing the city as we speak. Hell, they could already be in the hotel."

"Please, Scott, don't say things like that."

"Well, it's the damn truth." I felt the .38, which was in a holster and concealed neatly beneath my sport jacket.

"When do we leave?"

I stood there and raised my arms. "I guess right now."

Room service knocked: Case of beer, vodka, pillows. Perfect.

She packed her things and we took the back exit so that the manager wouldn't notice. I hung a DO NOT DISTURB sign on the handle. I didn't really care who knew we'd left. There were no secrets anymore.

*   *   *

The route had no name, and for the first 20 miles it was a paved two-lane road with no lines. After 20 miles it tapered off to gravel. We passed some homes; some small abandoned sheds that I imagined had been used for horses or livestock.

The Volks carried us between mountains and cliffs, through streams, all the way until the road turned to dirt, all the way until it faded into the buttes. I could tell by the sun which way was north and so kept on traveling.

"You aren't serious, Scott? Are you?"

"What do you wanna do? Turn around and head for Reno? There's no other option here. We've been on this road for nine hours, babe. I can tell which way is north because of where the sun's setting."

"What about after the sun sets?"

"We'll just keep going the same way."

"There's no ROAD, Scott! It's IMPOSSIBLE!"

"It's fine. I got it. Don't worry."

"You're going to get us killed."

"Like hell I am."

"We don't have any water or food." I looked in the back of the car. There was the case of beer and a half-bottle of vodka. I removed the vodka and took a good one.

"If you close your nose this stuff tastes just like Diamond Springs," I said.

She laughed. It was the first moment of relaxation I'd felt in a long time. Women... there were so many of them but they were all so similar that I had a hard time drawing a distinguishing line. I guess it didn't matter. All the girlfriends had blended into one and I could feel that soon I might be alone again in the bottom of some prison. Why? Why the hell would I be in prison? Why hadn't I just done the right thing? I could have stayed at Lacy's, played it straight, told Greg Fenster to kiss my ass.

The car jerked violently over the rocks.

"It was all Greg's fault," I said.

"Greg who, honey?" I looked over at Sheryl. Her face morphed into someone else's. I studied her eyes and hair, transfixed for a moment, and burst into laughter.

"Jane!" I yelled. "What made you decide to come back?"

"You're delirious, Scott. Stop the car." The rocks threatened to roll us and the car flicked from side to side. "Scott, stop the car before it blows up!"

I looked back over and she was Sheryl again. My good mood ended. I swallowed a knot of phlegm and eased my foot down on the brake. I parked the car and we stepped out to survey the land.

"Why did you call me Jane? Who the hell is Jane?" she asked. I could tell she was becoming annoyed with me.

"She's no one. I just made a mistake. I'm sorry." I was deadpan, tired, and once again humorless.

"Are you feeling OK?"

"Day after day, Sheryl, it's the same old shit. I'm just sick of running. Nothing's fun anymore. It's all just food, booze, sex, and prison."

"Stop talking like that, Scott. You're scaring me."

"I say we drive until it's pitch black, sleep until sunrise, and keep going in the morning."

"Whatever you want to do, baby. Just try to take it easy." She took a hit from the vodka and set it on top of the car. Man, it was beautiful out there. I looked around at the sunset, at the rocks, the bushes growing up from out of the dry earth, the cold air carrying wisps of dust across the flat land in the valley, the crests of the hills—my god! There was a silhouette! I saw it! Good god, a MAN was up on the canyon's edge right above us.

"Let's go, babe," I said, sliding into the driver's seat and starting the car. I pulled the .38 from my shirt, checked it one more time to make sure. Yeah, she was ready for action. I cocked the hammer back, uncocked it, looked up at the canyon's edge. We drove down onto the plain, a trail of dust rising behind us the size of a freight train. The man stood there and watched me, his thin skeleton blocking out pieces of the sun.

*   *   *

I drove through the night and into the morning. Somehow I was still headed relatively close to north when the sun came up. We had passed through a dozen Indian reservations and finally, around noon, I became so hungry that we stopped and I paid some natives for food and water.

"Thanks, folks," I said, carrying the bag of food and the two bags of water back to the Volks. I don't think they'd seen many cars before.

"You know how far we are from Oregon?"

The old Indian man stared at me.

"Oregon? You understand?"

He didn't.

I began to speak half-crazed. "You know anything about a lone guy who roams these parts? Stands on top of hills, sneaks into the backs of cars, chases people just for the hell of it?"

He kept staring. Then he said something that I didn't understand. It sounded like, "Taa." But I couldn't be sure.

"Taa?" I looked at him. "I'm talking about a guy that stands on top of the hills, man. He stands up there and just looks... I don't know... he looks down at you..." I felt like I was getting nowhere and Sheryl was looking at me funny. I motioned for her to get into the car.

We drove further north and I kept an eye out for that "Taa" bastard.

*　　*　　*

We made it into Oregon and the car quit somewhere on the highway. It just flat out gave up after all that dirt and deer trails and near misses with cliffs and death.

I pushed it into a ditch, down a hill, and let it roll away into the bushes. It had done the job.

"Just get out there and put your thumb out."

"Why don't YOU do it, Scott?"

"'Cause I'm a 6 foot 4 longhair. Nobody wants to pick me up." I was a sight, carrying all the bags because of Sheryl's aching feet. There was also a chance that would-be rides would discern the unwanted glimmer of the .38 sparkling whenever my jacket caught the wind.

"What if the driver is a serial killer?"

"You watch too many movies. Just get out there and stick your arm out. If he's a serial killer I'll peg him from the woods and we'll forget about it." I slinked behind a tree, took a seat, cracked a beer, and started on the first bit of good sleep I'd felt in—"SCOTT, GET UP! GET—"

I looked up from the daze. The beer was in my lap, overturned, half of it had poured onto the ground and the other half on my crotch.

"Damn it..." I chucked it off into the woods and stood up. There was a tractor trailer on the side of the road and Sheryl was talking to the driver.

"I can take you guys up north a bit further."

"Good," I said, emerging from the woods. The driver wasn't thrilled to see me. "Wherever you can get us is fine. Just get us off the highway."

"No problem." He got out, opened a back door and showed us a spot. "It's not the Holiday Inn, but it'll do you fine." He was running a circus or something and the back of his tractor trailer was loaded with stuffed animals. I took a seat on one and Sheryl took a seat on another. I closed my eyes again, cracked a beer, and before I knew it we were rolling along.

"Who would have thought we'd end up in the back of some carnie truck?" I said, chuckling at all the valueless junk he'd crammed back there. She was sneezing incessantly from the stuffed animals.

"I don't know, but I HATE these damn things." She punched one of the animals and it burst open. All the dust flew into her face and she hacked and coughed and fell down pouting. She looked up wither her bloodshot eyes and noticed that I had been snickering. She shook her head and folded her arms with disgust.

For all the shit I gave it, being on the run afforded me all the laughs.

18

GOOD MONEY

1981

I MOVED TO VIRGINIA BEACH AFTER A BRUSH WITH THE FEDS AT THE Hilton Pool in Southern Oregon. I was damn sick of being on the run all the time, but there was nothing I could do short of turning myself in. I decided to lay low, make an honest living. I picked the name Jeff Andrews out of a phone book and created a new identity. My new character had the same big smile as always, and he got a legitimate job as a software salesman with a company called IPC.

I was up early every morning for work, which naturally weeded out long nights of cocaine and drinking. These weren't the Lacy's days, I couldn't handle sleeplessness without looking terrible the next morning.

Sheryl liked that I was in bed early every night. She said I had lost my mind and needed to get into a normal routine. For a while, it worked. I kept blaming my sobriety on the job and grinding through the paperwork and 8 a.m. sales meetings. Gradually I realized that it wasn't just the job that was keeping me in the house every night. I was getting older. I didn't enjoy drugs as much. They didn't hit me as hard as they used to.

Hell, I'm sure the drugs would have still gotten me high if I did enough. Maybe it was that I didn't want to get high. Maybe that's why I kept away from it. The criminal life didn't excite me anymore so much as it scared me, if such a thing is possible. Not only had being on the run ruined my financial situation several times, it had destroyed my mental health. I had horrible recurring nightmares of being locked in the dungeon sub-basement, shitting in a bucket, drinking contaminated water, hurling onto the floor.

I kept telling myself that things were different now, that if they law caught up to me they wouldn't take me to jail. I had made some new friends at my job, a couple of smart guys that I could count on as character witnesses if the IRS ever wised up to who Jeff Andrews really was.

These normal people, the guys at work, weren't like the men I was used to hanging with. These people cared about things other than money or drugs. They had families, modest cars, modest homes, three beers on the weekend, a mutt rolling on his back in the back yard. At first I was taken aback, disgusted, but I began to enjoy it. I was fascinated by the simple life.

Then again, what was there to be interested in? These people were nobodies. For them, a crazy week meant selling a big software deal or playing golf in South Carolina.

"Your business friends aren't shit," I told myself. "IPC is just like the real world, man. They'll turn on you in a heartbeat once they find out you're a con."

The sun was just barely rising and already I was on the road for work, headed to a local IPC warehouse to meet Ken Banks, one of my newest and closest friends. I thought about skipping the meeting, driving the Cadillac to the dealership, working up a scam, stealing a car and reselling it. Yeah, that's what I'd do. Sheryl had become annoying. The sober life was too much. The axe was teetering like always and it was time to make a run. I just wasn't cut out for this thing. I wasn't a software salesman. I would wait. I couldn't go right now. It wasn't professional. I would give it a week or so, at least until I got my next paycheck. After that, I'd be gone for good.

"It's not always about the money, Jeff." That was the stupidest thing I'd ever said. Of course it was always about the money.

"No, man, sometimes it's about the experience. Where would you be if you hadn't done all that shit? You'd never have a job this good. You're a con artist. People never turn their backs on what they really are."

It was bullshit. I knew I could change. But I also knew that going straight was the toughest decision of my life.

"Just face the facts: In all seriousness, all jokes aside, you'll never stay straight. To stay straight, you'd have to have a clean record. To get clean record, you'd have to do some time in the pen."

I had consulted with my lawyer on my status as a fugitive to see if perhaps facing some of my charges and pleading "no contest" would get the Feds off of my case. His advice was to continue running.

"Well, Jeff, if you get caught it's likely that you'll be going away forever," he said. I didn't think it would be that bad, but you never knew.

Anyway, why turn myself in before it was necessary? I had it good in Virginia Beach, regardless of how hard it was to stay undercover. There were four new Cadillacs sinking into my cobblestone driveway and I had a very respectable house, totally furnished. I was ranked as one of the top 10 salesmen in the state that year. Things were going well. Forget turning myself in. I was going to make it.

"The only way you'll get caught is if the IRS finds a reason to inquire about the Social Security Number," I said, tapping the steering wheel.

Then again, why would the IRS care? I was paying taxes and Social Security, just not to a legitimate account. They were getting their money. Why bother me? Logic was on my side, and I had a hunch that I could keep shape-shifting in ways that would keep them off my back until I died of natural causes.

*   *   *

My Cadillac rolled slowly toward the warehouse. I parked it and, using my company key, unlocked the sliding metal door. I went inside and scoured through the equipment with a flashlight. Another car arrived, crunched to a halt on the half-gravel half-pavement driveway. It was Ken, one of my "normal person" friends.

"Jeff?" he called, poking his head through the warehouse door.

"Hey Ken, you have a good drive?" He'd driven all the way from Richmond to Virginia Beach. It was a two-hour drive, which meant he must have started sometime around 4 a.m.

"Yeah, not bad," Ken said. "You got anything I can use in this place?" He walked in a bit further, stood with his hands on his hips and surveyed the mess. The warehouse was stacked to the ceiling with computer boards, software packages, boxes of informational brochures, you name it. IPC kept everything in one small, disorganized loading dock.

"I think I can find the computer board you need. Here's some new gear that just came in." I dug through the equipment. "Take what you need from here and I'll just order another one. It's not a big deal." I felt like a loser. This was the closest I ever came to doing something under the table. I missed the thrill of being the bad guy. There was something very satisfying about ripping people off.

"I appreciate it, Jeff. I'd never be able to pull off a trade show without you."

"Yeah, no problem." I searched for a product list. Finally, after about 15 minutes, I found the piece of hardware that he needed. I handed him the box and he placed it in the passenger seat of his car.

Ken had opened an IPC office in Richmond and was going rogue from Chip Chapstein, the CEO of the corporation. Chapstein had required that Ken pay 10 percent of his profits to the IPC Virginia Beach corporate account. 10 percent was ruining Ken's business, nearly forcing him under. It had been my idea, several months prior, for Ken to abandon Chapstein and take the Richmond market on his own.

Speaking of Chapstein, he had already begun nagging me on the car phone. I was the only person I knew who had a phone in his car and I regretted it every second. It was horribly loud, ineffective, and obnoxious. I often went as far as saying that a car phone was the most annoying piece of equipment ever invented.

I answered the call while following Ken to a local breakfast spot. I told Chapstein that I'd be a few minutes early that morning. He jabbed me about preparing for the sales meeting and I hung up, a victim of poor signal reception.

I looked out over the ocean, at all those people on the Interstate, at all the warehouses and docks and boats sitting there waiting for someone to use them. Next week I would probably steal a new car and drive to Tucson.

*　　*　　*

"So, Jeff," Ken began, taking a glass of water from the waitress. "You ever think about coming to Richmond and working for me?"

"It's a possibility," I said.

"I'd give you a good position. You'd be my head sales rep."

"I'll consider it."

"There's also something I wanted to talk to you about…" he looked down at the table, avoiding eye contact with me. I felt like he was about to say something important. He looked me right in the face. "I don't know, Jeff…" He averted his eyes to his glass of water. "I get the feeling that you're not really who you say you are."

"What do you mean?"

"I mean I get the feeling that you're not really Jeff Andrews. That that's not you're real name."

"No, that's my real name. What gives you that feeling?"

"I don't know, man. I saw the signature on your driver's license and it looked a lot different from the one I've seen you use recently. And that one day when I called you Jeff and it took you about 30 seconds to turn around."

"Ken, relax, man." I looked around the diner. It reminded me of my first conversation with Greg Fenster in that old bar down the street from Imporium. "You're right, Ken. Jeff's not my real name. I'm in witness protection. My real name is Pat Reynolds—well, it used to be Pat Reynolds."

"What? Pat Reynolds?"

"Yeah."

"Your parents run out of names or something?"

"What do you mean?"

"When we first met you told me you had a brother named Pat who lived in L.A."

"Damn…" I said, pressing my lips together tightly. I'd tripped up for the first time in years. No coke and no booze meant no fuel for the fire. I was a mental sloth. How did I expect to make it through a bank draft scam? How did I expect to steal a new car next week? I was off my game.

I sized up my situation: Ken was a good guy and I knew I could trust him. He was interested in helping me, not turning me in. He'd give me a job if I needed one, he'd lend me money, he'd support me because, after all, it had been my idea for him to create his own branch of IPC in Richmond. The way I saw it, I was a pretty big figure in Ken's financial success.

"How about you come back up this weekend and we'll have a few beers. I'll fill you in on the whole story. I hope you don't think I'm a bad guy."

"I don't think you're a bad guy, Jeff." He cleared his throat after saying my name. I couldn't tell if he was being sarcastic about it. "I just want to know who my friends are. And, plus, if you're going to come work for me in Richmond I'm going to need to know the whole story."

The mist blew in from the ocean, speckling the window of the diner with fine dots of salt.

"It's just strange, Jeff. You're recorded as one of the highest-paid salesmen in the state after working at IPC for less than a year and no one has any idea who you are or where you came from. Tom Burford told me you were from Atlanta. Chapstein told me you were from Florida. Dave Hughes said he thought you were an orphan from New York who had been adopted by some banker."

"Those are all somewhat true," I said, chuckling and taking the first bite of my food. "Beers this weekend? Your place or mine?"

"How about yours?" Ken said. "I like coming down here."

"Yeah, sure, we'll go out to the beach or something."

* * *

Sheryl was constantly going back and forth from Colorado to see her daughter. She didn't like Virginia, hardly seemed to like me anymore except for the cash. Sheryl was a criminal's girl, and now that I was playing it straight she had decided to put herself back on the market when I wasn't looking.

A girl like Sheryl lived for the Reno days. To her, normal life was the bum's thumb, an easy way out, a pathetic and spineless comparison to the run.

She stood in the kitchen one morning at 8 a.m. preparing to leave on some errands. I had provided a really nice house, a lot of money, a good job, everything a woman could ask. This wasn't enough. Sheryl demanded more.

"I need 50 grand, Scott."

"Why can't you women ever get it right? Huh? What's the damn problem?"

"Alright, sorry, JEFF. That doesn't change that I need 50 grand. NOW."

"What do you need that for? There's no way you NEED that much cash." I was understandably shocked. Sheryl, the gym bimbo, always along for the ride, had grown hair on her chest overnight. She was big-boying me, pushing me into a corner because she knew I'd have to back down.

"I just need it. You have it. I'm your girlfriend. Don't argue with me or I'll really get pissed."

"I can't give you 50 grand. Sorry." Someone had put her up to this. The money wasn't just for her.

"You don't give me 50 grand by the time I'm home this afternoon and I'm going to call the Feds."

"Oh yeah?" I laughed at her. The look on her face told me that she was somewhat serious. Her eyes cut through me like blades. She poured another glass of orange juice and swallowed it in one gulp. She slammed the glass on the counter top and walked out to her car. The old time bomb went off in my head, a million bells chimed, I hung my head and breathed. I grabbed my briefcase, loaded it with all my cash, and got on a plane to Kansas City.

I had lost Ken Banks, my one good friend in the world. He would probably never want to speak to me again. The flight attendant greeted me kindly, "Hello Mr. Andrews, how does it feel to be back at square one?"

* * *

Shug was living in Lawrence, Kansas, and I had called him from the Richmond airport to see about staying at his place for a while. No one knew me in Kansas and I figured that maybe he'd be able to give me the lay of the land. So much for the straight life. It was always the women that ruined me. No one could deny that.

I took a taxi to his place. I stepped out onto the curb, a very nice neighborhood, and Shug came walking down the driveway to meet me.

"Long time, no see," he said. "I guess we haven't really hung out since Boston, huh? Since I was playing for the Athletics?"

"I guess not, man. How was Golden State?"

"It was a trip, Jay."

I looked at him for a few seconds. He had just called me Jay. A car rolled slowly up the street.

"Who told you my name was Jay?" My hands gripped the inside of my pockets. I felt a twinge of shivers rattle through my shoulders.

"You told me one day while we were watching football, don't you remember? I said I knew your name wasn't Scott Anderson and you said, 'Yeah, I know, it's Jay Carver.'"

"Sorry, I forgot. I haven't used that name since I was living in Hawaii."

"It's alright." Few people can understand how I felt as that car rolled past. It's a strange feeling to be standing in place, still, your posture as casual as the breeze, wondering when the end is going to come. The sun beat down on my suit jacket like an inferno. The sweat poured and I breathed deep, holding the air in my chest and bracing just in case the barrels were honed in on my spine. I turned and looked at the street, at the passing car, a Dodge Monaco. It rolled close to the curb, keeping steady speed, tinted glass, chrome, and a little boy held his hand out the back window, playing in the wind.

I set my briefcase in the foyer and lost the jacket. I could hear Barb and one of her friends laughing on the back porch.

"Barb's cooking up barbeque, you want some?"

"Yeah, definitely. I didn't get anything at the airport."

"I don't blame you."

"How's Barb these days?" I asked.

"Go see for yourself. She's out back." He looked up from a bottle of wine that he was opening. "Don't piss your pants when you get out there."

"What?" I asked.

"I mean, don't freak out or anything."

"What are you talking about?"

"Nothing. You'll see."

I walked through the kitchen, past the gigantic refrigerator and two-range stove and oven. I ran my fingers down the unfinished marble countertops and the wood grain cabinets. Shug's kitchen was about the nicest I'd ever seen. The guy had class. Real class.

I straightened my tie when I heard the sound of the girls' voices. My sock feet padded across the thick carpet of the living room like the first astronaut on the moon. The television played quietly. Basketball scores.

I slid the back door open and there was Barb.

"Well damn!" she said, excited. She came over and gave me a hug. Her friend sat in a chair, her back to me, long brunette hair hanging beyond her shoulders like a cloak.

"How've you been, Barb?" I asked.

"Really good. You?"

"Alright."

The girl in the chair stood up. I knew her hips, those slender arms, the way she let her hair dangle when she reached down to brush a gnat from her ankle. She turned around and we faced each other for the first time in three years.

"I'm sorry," I said, my mouth gaping with disbelief.

She cocked her head sideways, pursed her lips and shrugged as if to ask me what I wanted to do about it. "It's OK. You told me you'd leave me if I cheated on you and I did. You don't need to be sorry."

"I shouldn't have left you there alone. That was stupid."

"It wasn't stupid. Besides, the Feds showed up a few days later anyway. You did the right thing."

"You get in any trouble?"

"No. They wanted you... like always."

We stood there awkwardly and Barb left the grill and went in through the sliding door.

"I still love you, Jay. I never lost that painting of you. I still have it on the wall in my room."

"Where are you staying?"

"Here. I've been living with them for a little while. I just got to Lawrence a few months ago." She looked inside at Barb. "They helped me after you left Boston. I thought you'd come back for me some day but..."

"I've been busy."

"I bet you have," she mocked me.

She came over and I embraced her like we'd never missed a day since 1977. No, I embraced her for every day between 1977 right then. For every damn woman who hadn't meant anything and for every stepped-on bag of coke I'd snorted since Hawaii. I lifted her off the ground, held her up as high as I could and we were frozen, her hair flying sideways in the wind, transfixed, just like we were on the back porch in Kailua, just like an old and familiar photograph that one day turns up in a dark drawer and never goes away.

＊　　＊　　＊

Jen and I moved into a place right across the street from Shug. It was a nice house, way too big for just the two of us, but that was the way things worked in a neighborhood like that.

One morning around 9 a.m., when I knew Ken Banks would be in his office, I gave him a call to check on things in Richmond.

"It's Jeff Andrews, man. How's it going?"

"Alright," he said warily.

"Good, good. Sorry I had to leave town so fast."

"I heard you burnt Chapstein for a bunch of merchandise."

"He's lying. I sold everything before I left. I didn't hang him out to dry." It was true, I'd never stolen anything from that company.

"Where are you?" he asked.

"I'm out of town right now. I can't talk about it. I just wanted to see how things were going back East."

"So, you're out West?"

"No, I'm up North. That's not the point. I just wanted to see how IPC was coming along."

"Pretty slow. You ever give any thought to coming and working for me like we talked about?"

"I got a crazy woman riding my ass, Ken. You remember my girl-friend from Virginia Beach? Sheryl?"

"Yeah?"

"Well, I left town was because she demanded 50 grand from me or she'd turn me over to the police."

"So you ARE a criminal?"

"Slightly," I said.

"What do you mean?"

"I mean I've gotten myself into some shit once or twice but it's no big deal."

"If you come to work for me I'll stick by you, man. I think you've got a real future in sales. Maybe you should take a job with me and turn yourself in." Why was this guy so nice to me? There was no real reason for it. We had shared a few beers together, walked around the board-walk, talked about business, nothing too serious. Maybe it had to do with my role in his business in Richmond. After all, the venture had been half my idea and I had demanded nothing from him.

"Hmm…" I thought about turning myself in. "I'll call you in a few months once I get my life figured out."

"Where are you?"

"Austin. Don't tell anybody."

"I won't."

"Good."

So I took another slug of the vodka and stared out the window at the 9 a.m. neighborhood commotion as the housewives checked the mail with toweled hair and cups of coffee and the lawn care boys hopped out of dead pickup trucks and threw shovels at the work. I saw Barb across the street watering her flowers and Shug in the driveway beside his Benz.

How long until I made it back to Richmond? Would I make it back? I gazed over all the furniture I'd bought for the house. Thousands and thousands on furniture for that damn place. I was burning a hole in my bank account but it was alright. I could always get more money; it was the years that a guy could never buy back.

I really slugged the vodka.

Maybe I should listen to Ken and head back to Virginia for good. I could take the job, turn myself in, pay the restitutions and the fines, maybe serve some time. No one wants to lock up a guy who's gone straight. The judge will take pity on me, right?

I lit a smoke and blew it into the sunlight. The yellow rays angled through the blinds and into the dim living room, decorating the floor with perfectly parallel stripes.

"Do you want some eggs, Jeff?" Even Jen was calling me Jeff Andrews.

"Yeah," I said. I killed the vodka and closed my eyes in the chair.

"I'm going to run to the store really fast. Do you need anything?" she asked.

"We need beer. Get a case of beer."

"Anything ELSE?" Was this an attempted jab at my need for booze? Did the woman not understand my stress level?

"No, that's IT. That's ALL I need!" I laughed and grabbed the fifth from the coffee table to refill my glass. She had pushed me over the edge and I knew that the morning would definitely require alcohol if I wanted to make it through sane and alive. I poured a tall one and the door slammed. Good old Jen... what would she do if she couldn't give me a hard time?

I mulled over several ideas in my head, tried to piece my plan together. There were sounds as though someone was coming down the stairs from my bedroom. I rolled my eyes toward a creak in the wall.

"Jen?"

There was no one. At least, no one answered.

"Who's up there?" The paces came down the hallway and across the living room. They paced in front of me but there was no body, no visible form, just footsteps.

"Calm down, man." I said to myself. "You're imagining this shit. What have you turned into? Are you a lunatic or something?" I stood up and walked to the center of the room. It felt like liquid was shifting around in my brain, like a piece of my head was being twisted or cranked. I sat back in the chair and took a hit of the drink. Something in the kitchen fell and I jumped up again. I was drunk as hell and braced myself on the mantle above the fireplace. It was all I could do to hold my eyes open and curse under my breath.

I was so used to being jacked on cocaine while drinking that I hadn't really remembered what it felt like to be good and drunk. I opened the drawer beside the sofa and poured a strong mound on the coffee table. The television was off and I watched the dim reflection of the living room in the glass table as I straightened the pile and prepared to rail a line. Standing behind me was some creature, some strange and illusory shadow figure. I disregarded it and put my face to the white. It was high time I got the hell out of Kansas. I was seriously about to lose my mind.

I called Ken Banks and told him that I'd be in Richmond in a few months. I told him I wanted to work for his company and that I'd consider turning myself in if it meant a permanent position. He agreed that no matter what happened he'd stick by me. I guess the guy had faith that we could be a good team together. He was the only person I'd ever known who had trusted me. Hell, I don't think Jen fully trusted me and we'd been talking for the past week about getting married.

The vodka came on harder and the shadows from the trees in my front yard rippled across the windows. I took another sniff of coke and, very gradually, very excitedly, I began to wake up. One of the cats rounded the corner from the kitchen, hopped into my lap, and the day moved by very slowly after that.

*   *   *

Some months later I returned to Richmond with Jen. I had all my furniture shipped to my new apartment in the Bowers Coffee building. Ken Banks hired me to work for IPC and I thought that I'd never leave the company.

Jen and I got married in Shockoe Slip. Shug flew in as my best man and Ken was an usher. It was strangely pleasant to be back with Jen. At the altar I found myself remembering our first night together in the Yacht Harbor Towers in Waikiki. I remembered thinking that I would love her forever, and look at us now, after all these years.

I smiled while the priest spoke, recalling the sound of Carlos and Norberto in the middle of the night. I shook Norberto's hand stark naked in his own bedroom with his girlfriend wrapped in a sheet. Strange days.

*   *   *

Business at IPC was difficult at first, but it picked up the longer we worked at it. After about two years things leveled out and I was offered a job in Miami working for a similar company. The job in Miami had unlimited potential and Ken said he wouldn't blame me if I took it. I think he'd grown content with his position and wanted to sit back for a little while and take a break from the 12-hour days.

Jen and I moved to Miami and I worked selling software just the same as I had for IPC. Things down there were great, but I never settled down the way I envisioned. One morning I received a phone call from the IRS questioning my Social Security Number. I put my head flat on the desk for an hour.

We hadn't been on the run in almost five years. I didn't know if I could handle it anymore. What was the next step? Did I need to split from the office right then, grab my briefcase, cash out my bank account, buy a .38, steal another car? What the hell was I supposed to do?

My desk phone rang.

"Jeff Andrews," I said.

"It's Ken Banks."

"Hey, what's happening?"

"Some guys showed up at the office looking for you today. I gather since you answered the phone that you're still in Miami?" Fear shot through me.

"Om... did you tell them that I was in Miami?"

"I told them I didn't know where you were."

"Good..."

"They were Feds, Jeff."

"I know. It's fine. I gotta go."

"Where are you going?"

"This is part of my life man, sorry. I can't tell you. I'll never see you again." I gathered a few personal items from my desk, tossed them into my briefcase.

"Wait a second, you can't be serious?"

I was dead serious. I had been pretty lucky for 15 years and I damn sure wasn't about to give it up over a fake Social. I'd head down south, maybe out of the country, maybe to South America. I could cash out some serious money from my bank account, enough to live on for a decade in a foreign country.

Ken asked me what I thought about coming back to Richmond and turning myself in. He explained that he needed help at his IPC office and that he'd stick by me if, after I was released, I promised to come back to work for him until I retired.

I thought about it for a solid minute.

"I hate it down here," I said. "I'm not much of a Miami guy."

"If you come back here and work for me I'll put up money for your bail when you get locked up. We'll fight each case together."

"Why would you do all this for me?"

"Because you're a good guy. You get the job done, Jeff. Not many people can do that."

"Even if I turn myself in I'll be arrested all the time. Probably every other day for six months."

"That's fine. I'll do it. I'll be there for whatever you need, man. Just trust me."

It could have been the dumbest decision of my life, but I trusted him. I had been in the con artist game for so long that I could tell when a person was lying to me. Ken wasn't a liar. I drove all the way back to Virginia on the instinct that I could make a career out of it.

Ken had all the papers ready when I arrived and I signed them, instating myself as an employee for Information Processing Consultants, Richmond, Virginia.

*   *   *

As I had predicted, I was arrested every other day for six months. It got to be somewhat hilarious: The same cops would show up each afternoon at around 5 p.m. to my office and I'd walk out the door with an arrogant swagger, a look on my face like the charges didn't mean anything.

It was true that no one could get me down... at first. I had good money behind me, a stable job, the prettiest wife they'd seen, and fast ways of getting the judge or grand jury on my side.

It was a startling incident at a courthouse in Virginia Beach that brought my shield of supposed invincibility crashing to the floor. I was sentenced, by a fat and angry judge of 80 years—a man who was virtually dead on his feet, pissed off and drunk on power—who looked me right in the face and said, "You're going to prison."

No matter what anyone else said, I would get hard time. That was that.

"You've been let off the hook all over the place, Andrews. You lied on your financial statements, lied to the state tax committee, to the IRS, the federal government. Damn it, Andrews, you even lied to ME and told me that you DIDN'T lie to any of those people. You need to be locked up. I'm sick of this record."

The bailiff cuffed me and led me toward that heavy door. I walked past Ken Banks and Jennifer. She reached out for my arm but we were too far away. Damn it, I was separated from her again. One last glance at the real world and I could feel the familiar knot welling up in my throat. The door slammed behind us.

The guard tapped my feet further apart, leaned my head against the wall and undid my handcuffs. The door to my right creaked open and the other guard asked me to please enter. I went inside the old dungeon birdcage and lay down, binding my fingers behind my head and feeling the cold cement leak through into my muscles. A man down the hallway cried softly and somewhere there was violin music playing. Maybe all this was in my head. Maybe it was not.

19

THE WRONG REASONS

1987

I HAD BEEN BEHIND THE DOUBLE RAZOR WIRE AT DANBURY FOR 21 months, working as a parts order clerk in the prison's Unicor cable factory. Us boys at Unicor had been responsible for making the wire harnesses for our nation's F-16 fighter jets. (Nothing but pure quality.) Unicor had been a crummy job, but it beat the mailbox factory, which is where they had recently transferred me.

There was a loud-mouthed Egyptian guy who used to work with me at Unicor. I had always avoided him, and I cursed my luck the day they transferred him to the mailbox division. Here, along the sweaty assembly line, the Egyptian filled an empty position next to yours truly. He was an annoying man, always trying to coax me into conversation about weights, spirituality, life lessons, anything useless he could think of. I guess he needed a friend or someone to vent to. Didn't we all?

The mailbox factory, although significantly less exciting than Unicor, was an improvement as far as housing was concerned. It was located in the "Work Camp" facility at Danbury, not in the main prison complex. There was no longer the sparkling sheen of razor wire guarding my every move. In Work Camp there was freedom. A man could take a piss without asking, he could watch TV after work, and lift weights whenever he wanted.

The Work Camp was chock full of familiar faces. Everyone had, at one point or another, been housed in the central facility. In some ways it was like a jolly class reunion of long-timers as we edged nearer to the outside. Some of the guys I'd known from inside were working on the fire squad. They told me they needed a replacement for a man who had just been released.

The men were good teachers and very quickly taught me everything they knew about fighting fires. I took a bunk in their room and was sworn in as a member. There were six of us firefighters living in that tiny hole and I never heard a damn person complain about it. By that point, everyone was used to the bullshit.

I wrote a few letters to Ken and Jennifer to tell them how things were progressing.

Jennifer was very slow to respond to these letters and I felt bad bothering Ken because I knew he was busy. Several times I would send Jen letters and get nothing in return. My own wife didn't have the patience to put up with my prison sentence. How quickly the times do change.

These long months gave me plenty of time to think about what I would do once I was released. I couldn't make up my mind. Would it be safe to stay with Ken? Would some new warrant surface and put me away for good? I began to have second thoughts about going straight.

＊　　＊　　＊

Disinterest with day-to-day activities overtook me. The world stitched itself together with obscurity and all hope became irrelevant. There was no good, no evil; no prison, no freedom. There was just... this.

Nights we spent indoors playing cards, lifting weights, arm wrestling, sharing stories. Same old, same old. It was 1987 and I was 40 years old, doing time for the shit I'd pulled in my 20s and 30s. It was stupid. All of it.

I had wanted to change my life for years, but this wasn't how I envisioned it. Prison wasn't changing anything. The only thing I learned behind bars was how to take care of myself physically. Every day was like living in the prehistoric jungle. I needed something more than this. I needed a real change, a way to guard myself from getting out and buying a bag of cocaine and a fifth.

Words from the outside always helped, and after a long time Jen wrote me back. I opened the envelope immediately. She had included some pictures of herself, several where she was entirely nude. I thumbed through the pictures happily, imagining what I'd do when I finally made it out of the can. I read the letter, which was nothing out of the ordinary, and put the pictures in my pocket.

Later that evening, just after dinner, I removed the pictures for another viewing. Damn, she was still just as beautiful as the day I'd met her. Hardly a thing had changed. I stared very closely, soaking it in, imagining it, wondering what she would say if she were here with me. The railing on our staircase came alive and I felt it: the cold brass on my hand and the wood beneath me. Her robe fell across my face, floated as she descended. I looked into the mirror beside her, where the flash from the camera had inadvertently bounced back at itself. Wait... there was something wrong. There were legs in that mirror. Hairy, long, pale white legs. The legs of a man. The underwear of a man. The upper body of a... man. And it damn sure wasn't me.

Son of a bitch. SON OF A—I hurled the pictures at the wall and stormed out of the TV room. No one seemed to notice or care.

Then there was a small fire in one of the ovens in the main prison complex and we were called down there in the rain. We had to run a three-hour procedure checking the electrical spaces for fires or damage while the guards pointed machine guns at us and spit tobacco juice. I did all this work as best I could, my emotions spoiling all concentration.

All things considered, it was probably one of the worst days of my life. Well, aside from the time I hanged myself with the TV cable in '75. Or the time the feds busted my apartment in San Diego when I was on the couch with that Russian girl. Or, I guess, the time Jen and I had to leave millions of dollars in our basement in Denver. That money, by the way, was snatched up by the feds 12 hours after our departure. Norberto mailed me a picture from the newspaper of a mountain of cash with a bunch of handguns on top of it. I assume it was Norberto that mailed me the clipping, but there was no return address so I never really knew for sure. It was enough just to know that it was gone. I didn't care any further than that.

I sighed that night and watched the darkness through the thick cell window. With Jennifer gone, I had literally NOTHING to show for myself except a gigantic debt to the government and one guy on the outside who promised he'd stick with me.

I began to feel increasingly discontented with my life. Would I ever get out of prison? How would I function in the real world after my release? I couldn't live without all the usual vices. Jennifer, my main addiction, was gone. Booze and drugs would have to remain out of the picture if I wanted to make a legitimate living.

Who was I kidding? I'd never make it as a company man. The past five years at IPC had been a joke. Visions of that newspaper clipping, the guns and cash, haunted me every moment of the day.

It was simple: I was destined for the run.

"Just do it," I said.

Do what?

"Just put yourself up there and end it. It's too much. You're either dead or you're back to the same bullshit that got you here in the first place."

I looked up at the ceiling. There was a bar we used for pull-ups that stretched the length of the cell. No one killed themselves in work camp, so the bulls didn't worry about the architecture nearly as much.

"Just rip the bed sheet, tie it up, and do it. You'll never fit in with the suits. Jen's gone. She's got another man. The whole thing's over. There's no point in living. You don't want to end up working five days a week for bare bones. You can't function that way."

I pulled the sheet off the bed and studied it, held it in front of me and pulled gently, wondering if it would tear.

No, that's not the way. Why kill myself? I had always been the type of guy who loved challenges. I was a risk taker, a rogue, a badass. I could apply the same concepts to a legal business. It would be a challenge.

"Jen's gone, buddy. You've failed. You're a dead man."

A cellmate rolled out of his bunk. I hadn't seen him there.

"What the hell's going on, Jeff?" He studied me, the sheet, my sweaty forehead.

I snapped out of it. "The damn bedbugs are making a move on us again."

"Eddy killed about 200 the other day. I thought they were all gone?"

"Yeah, so did I" I said, indicating an unrelated red bump on my arm and setting the sheet on my bunk. "Say, Lou, you got an extra square?"

"Extra square, huh?" He got out his pack, took a look inside and chuckled. "Extra square? Well, let me see..." He looked around the inside of the pack like it was a cavern. "I don't see any extra cigarette," he chuckled again, preparing his line. "How about this: the day I find a pack with 21 cigarettes, I'll give you the 'extra' one."

He laughed, muttered something, and turned away from me.

I wanted to kill him. He was the only jerk in the whole squad, the only tick that had burrowed under my skin. I almost chased him, but I had to let it go.

"What do you mean?" I asked myself.

What did I mean what did I mean?

"I mean why didn't you kick his ass?"

I needed to relax. At last, after all these years, I was finally losing my mind. The walls were closing in, the rats were gnawing at the wires, and the prison seemed to scream at me like I was a parasite living in its throat.

As a way to get out my frustrations, to avoid hanging myself, to avoid beating someone into a coma, I began writing the business plan for a company I would call IPC Technologies. It was a strange way to kill the aggravations, but the prospect of money was more invigorating than a few days in solitary for thrashing some greaser.

*   *   *

A buddy and I were lifting weights across the hall from the TV room. It was a normal evening and I had no idea what day of the week it was, nor did I really know what season. Sure, if I thought hard enough I could figure all that stuff out, but why think about it? It hardly mattered.

"Grab those for me," Eddy said. He pointed to a set of dumbbells on the bench. I removed them, put them back on the rack, and picked another set.

The Egyptian guy from the Unicor assembly line, the one who used to annoy me, came sauntering past. He was walking with a group of people—not a gang, either. What were they?

"It's the Bible study class," Eddy told me. I watched them head toward their study room.

Someone bumped into the Egyptian and knocked him into the wall. It had been a total accident, but the Egyptian immediately copped an attitude.

"You think I'm just some nut you can push around?" he asked with a thick accent. "You wanna just push me around, buddy? Well I'm not going to stand for this shit. NO, I'M NOT!" I guess he was used to people picking on him. He was small, appeared outwardly peaceful, but he had a voice like crackling thunder—as though the lightning strike were only 100 yards away.

"Whoa, man, it was an accident," someone interjected.

"No accident. This guy's given me a hard time before, back in the yard. All I'm trying to do is move along through this shit hole and all you idiots keep on harassing me!"

"Just relax, buddy. Let's let it slide this time."

The Egyptian finally gave up. One of the other Bible scholars put a hand on his shoulder. I gave them a long stare and wondered what a person could possibly find in a palm-sized book that was worth spending an hour each night talking about. Where did they think they were going? The Promised Land? Heaven? What a pipe dream. It was a load of shit.

I finished my reps and set the dumbbells on the floor. Eddy and I walked over to the pull-up bars.

"Check it out," Eddy said, snickering and pointing at Buck Wolkner. Wolkner, shoulder-length blonde hair and tattoos, had removed a chair from one of the cafeteria tables and was preparing to use it as a weapon. Action like this wasn't too common in Work Camp. Most guys played it relatively cool.

Wolkner checked over his shoulders for witnesses. Nobody was paying any attention. The guards were telling jokes and tall tales about fishing trips, exaggerating with their hands how they'd caught "the biggest damn fish anyone's pulled from that lake in…"

Wolkner hurled the chair at the Bible study group. They were five brave souls out of 200, and now had a flying chair to deal with. The chair smashed into one of their backs, nearly taking the poor guy to the floor. Wolkner laughed, screamed something obscene, and the men continued walking toward their makeshift study hall.

"Wolkner's a funny old jerk, ain't he?" somebody said.

"I don't think that's funny," I said. "That dickhead needs to pick on somebody his own size."

Eddy looked over at me and put his hands up on the bars.

"He's about a foot taller than you, Jeff. Why don't you go say that to his face and see what happens?"

The Egyptian from the Bible study group turned. His divisive stare froze me, my arms stuck to the pull up bar above my head. The Bible in the Egyptian's hand gleamed like a pistol and, for a second, I didn't know what to do. I was hanging there, waiting to begin my pull-ups, and found myself transfixed.

*　　*　　*

My frustrations boiled over onto the stove. The boiling water of my soul hissed and popped and evaporated on the burner. I was mad, genuinely mad, and I was damn close to snapping on someone. I didn't care who it was, nor did I care why. My lady had left me and someone was going to get their ass kicked.

It was the following day when I approached the Egyptian at his usual spot in the cafeteria.

"Mind if I join you?" I asked.

"Sure, Jeff. How are you doing?" He must have remembered my name from the assembly line. I was surprised. We had barley spoken other than him running his mouth to me about his opinions on life and weight lifting etiquette.

"I'm doing pretty lousy," I said, not giving him time to interject before I continued. "Look, it was Buck Wolkner who threw that chair at you guys last night, huh?"

"I think so. Why?"

"How about I get him back for you?" This was my chance, my last resort for a legitimate confrontation. If this failed, I'd just find the biggest guy in the room, preferably someone covered in tattoos, and spit in his face. I felt like a fool for not seizing my original opportunity several days before when my cellmate had tricked me with his "extra cigarette" line.

"It's fine, Jeff. Don't worry about Buck Wolkner. I can take care of it."

"No, that guy's a jackass. I'm sick of the way he messes with people."

"It's not the spirit of our group to consciously take revenge. It would not look so good for the Bible Study class to hire a loaded gun, if you know what I'm saying." He looked at my arms, somewhat insinuating that all I was good for was physical brutality.

"You yell at people all the time!" I said, remembering countless times when I'd heard his voice booming through the weight room. "I saw you push a guy once. You're not blameless!"

"I said that it is not in the spirit of our group to take revenge. I won't allow it."

"Well, I'm not in your group. See? That's the beauty of it."

"I don't think it's necessary. Thank you, though. We do appreciate your help. It's hard being so few among so many."

"Yeah... well, I'm still coming tonight."

"That's fine with me. I would love to have you."

"Good. See you later."

"I assume that you're not coming solely for a fight? That you'll stay and study the Bible with us?"

"Eh, maybe."

"If you come, please stay and read with us."

"I'll stay. I can't promise the reading thing."

He nodded and continued with his food.

I got up from the table and looked around the place. I walked along slowly, thinking about how pathetic it was that I hadn't kicked the Egyptian's ass for being smart with me. I moved like a slug, speaking angrily to my tray of rapidly cooling food. I contemptuously surveyed the crowded tables of stickup artists, mob shooters, heroin runners, wife beaters, scammers, embezzlers, auto thieves, crack peddlers, illegal immigrants, gang bangers, mobsters, racists, hell raisers, serial home burglars, violent anarchists, dope fiends, sex offenders… you name it, we got it.

I saw Wolkner over there drinking from a milk carton. I bet he hadn't changed a lick since elementary school. Seeing him at the cafeteria table drinking milk only confirmed it. What a piece of shit. I couldn't wait for Bible Study.

*　　*　　*

I walked right behind the Egyptian the whole way. We went through the TV room and I kept my eyes forward, made no attempt to look for Buck Wolkner. I figured that if he was going to pull some shit he'd be more likely to try it if he didn't know that I was with them.

We kept on moving. I could feel the energy. At any second he was going to spit at somebody or holler something derogatory from across the tables. At any second the whole TV room was going to feel the blow. I had my plan worked out: I had done it a few times before where, by surprise, I would kneel down and pretend to be hurt halfway through the fight. As soon as the other guy looked away I would bring my right fist up all the way from the floor. It was an uppercut from hell, and the best thing was that no one ever saw it coming.

We made it to the study room without incident. The Egyptian smiled; he knew that I was now committed to listening to his sermon.

The Bible study room was ridiculously cramped. There was cardboard on the windows from where the students had attempted to section it off from the TV room. I wondered if Buck would get the crazy idea to light it on fire while all six of us were inside. This wouldn't have been a bad move for him, considering it was the only shot in hell he had of getting one over on me before I could step out there and put him through a wall.

The Egyptian spoke and spoke and spoke about God. He never got sick of it. I had this little orange book in my hands, several useless papers on my desk, and a horrible headache.

"Jeff, would you like to read first?" The Egyptian studied my face. I hadn't been paying attention. It was just like grade school.

"Om…" I stuttered. I felt a rush of adrenaline, which I hadn't felt in years. I was scared and nervous, afraid of confronting something that I'd never understood. "No, I can't read very well right now… my eyes are… hurting."

"Your eyes are hurting? Are you alright?"

"Yeah. I'm fine. It happens once in a while. No big deal."

"I see…"

It was a grueling hour of blabbering crap. I sat there trying not to nod off, biding my time by imagining what would happen if Wolkner came bursting through the cardboard door with a machine gun. I imagined springing into action like Rambo, tearing his head off with my bare hands or blowing him away with his own weapon.

Class ended on a somber note, something about what it would feel like if YOU were nailed to a cross.

"How do you think it would feel, Jeff?"

"Eh," I stuttered again. "Pretty bad I guess."

"Have you ever been nailed to a cross?" He looked around the room. "Any of you?"

Several men nodded.

"Jeff, haven't YOU been nailed to a cross?"

I didn't know. No. What did he mean? A cross? Nails? No. Never had. I shook my head.

"You're in prison, Jeff. Is this not a cross for you to bear?"

I had no idea what the hell he was talking about. "Yeah, sure. I guess…"

"Remember, it is because He has been tested and has suffered, that He may help those who have been tested as well."

Sure… whatever that meant.

We exited the study room and quietly reassembled into our respective groups. Buck Wolkner was out there lifting weights and griping about the meals. He never noticed us that day and all I could do was just keep on walking and imagine what I'd have done if he had.

*   *   *

It was night, lights out, and I was lying in my bunk listening to the snores and strange sounds of a six-man fire squad sharing the same bedroom. I would sometimes read books after lights out. The light from my window, if it was clear outside and the moon was showing, was just enough to see by. I turned my head and looked up through the glass.

It was a good moon that night. Funny how the simplest things could make or break a guy's day. I pulled one of my Clive Cussler novels from the mattress, removed my bookmark, and continued.

I'd read the book a week before and couldn't stay focused. I knew what happened in the end and for some reason I just wasn't interested in reliving it. I stared at the ceiling. Three more months of this shit and I'd be out. I would have the debt to pay, possibly another warrant or two, but all in all I'd be able to breathe for a while and get my head straight.

"Breathe... what are you talking about? You're a dead man."

I had no idea what I was saying to myself. A dead man? How?

"You'll never make it. Your only chance is to make a big play, snag a load of cash. You know where you can find it. You're dead if you take the job with Ken. You might as well just kill yourself now."

It made no sense. It wasn't me talking. I felt like someone was holding me down, fencing me in, cramming thoughts into my head. I liked Ken. I knew we could work together. I knew that IPC was where I wanted to end up.

"Ah, that's horse shit. You want to end up in Miami just like the rest of the retired crooks. That's your crowd. We'll change the name to Jaco or maybe even back to Jay. I liked that name, what was it? Oh yeah, 'Jay Carver.'"

No. I wouldn't do any of that. It was all talk. It kept my mind from eating itself over Jen's absence. What would I do without her? I couldn't bear the thought that she would be out there living it up on some coke dealer's yacht while I slaved in the office for 50 hours a week.

I stretched out in the bed and counted the dots in the reinforced tile ceiling. It was time to think of something else. I closed my eyes. A hard object was stuck at my feet, way down under the blankets. I reached down and removed it. It was the small orange Bible the Egyptian had given me. I studied the cover for a moment, then set it aside.

I kept on watching the ceiling, wondering if maybe it would open up and let me fly away. The tile was only two feet from my face. It was sad how so many guys had stared at that ceiling and were probably dead by now or staring at another one just like it.

"What kind of world is this?" I moaned, turning onto my side.

It was an alright world, I just had to make some better decisions from now on. I couldn't let my addictions run my life.

"Nothing can change our instincts. You're a fighter. You're born the way you're born and that's that. Some people aren't cut out for the suit and tie jobs. It's just not in you."

I guess I was right. You can sit on the couch drinking cold beer until the nightmare dies but it still won't change the fact that at 6 a.m. some whistle's going to blow, some guy's going to check his watch, and it's going to be your ass on the wire.

That little orange book, so small, what did people find inside that thing? I flipped it open to a random page, just like a person will do with a book they know they will read over and over again, and studied the words. It was written differently than Cussler. It was a bunch of poems with two columns per page and small print. I decided on a random passage and read:

If I speak the languages of men
and of angels, but do not have love,
I am a sounding gong
or a clanging cymbal.
If I have the gift of prophecy,
and understand all mysteries
and all knowledge,
and I have faith,
so that I can move mountains,
but do not have love, I am nothing.
And if I donate all my goods to feed
the poor,
and if I give my body to be burned,
but do not have love, I gain nothing.
Love is patient; love is kind.
Love does not envy;
is not boastful; is not conceited;
does not act improperly; is not selfish;
is not provoked; does not keep a record
of wrongs;
finds no joy in unrighteousness,
but rejoices in the truth;

Something captivated me, kept me going through the words even though the tiny print was difficult to read. I felt there was wisdom in the words, that if I listened I would be able to change myself.

Just then I felt something shift inside my head. The shadow of a guard floated past the cell door and I shuddered in my bed. A cleansing tide was washing over me, tearing out my fears like a disease.

I knew that something was wrong with me. I felt that the words I'd just read, if I could understand and follow them, might save me from all of this. The book was good for me. It was a book about love. I needed to learn about love, didn't I? What the hell was love? What the hell was anything except jobs, money, and consequences?

I liked this book right off because it wasn't about my world. It was about something different, a place I had never gone, a concept I had always hated but never understood.

Maybe this book could teach me how to deal with my new life. Maybe I would learn how to keep myself away from anger. Perhaps I could even grow to love someone. But who would I love other than Jen? She was gone now. It was all lost. I continued reading, hopelessly lost in the fresh grief of her photographs.

When I was a child, I spoke like a child,
I thought like a child,
I reasoned like a child.
When I became a man, I put aside
childish things.

"A man... what the hell does this book know about men?" I scoffed. Alright, it was over. I was done with the book. Who were these people to tell me whether or not I was a man? Who the hell were they? A man was a person who could keep dull nerves in order to weather the gauntlet. The knives and guns of our world would penetrate flesh, but it was the absence of pain that kept a MAN strong and ahead of the pack.

But wait... where had the guns and knives gone? I couldn't see them anymore. I didn't care to see them. In fact, I wouldn't see them again.

What was the purpose of feeling pain? Who gave a shit about Jen? About money or drugs and booze? Who gave a shit about anything as long I wasn't in prison? Anything beat rotting in the cell.

I stopped reading and searched the room. Something was missing. I could see more clearly, as though I had emerged from a tunnel. It was difficult to grasp, to explain, but a dull film of anger and resentment had been lifted from my eyes. My anger and anxiety was being peeled back.

I noticed small and beautiful things I had never noticed before. The cinderblocks, the lines on the wall, the faces of men in the bunks; everything was so peaceful and I didn't want to disturb it.

"You're losing it, Jack." I heard myself whisper. Something overtook me. I was no longer in my bunk...

The Mercedes was back and I was driving, searching the rearview mirror for a man in the back seat. It wasn't me this time, though. It was someone else behind the wheel but I was looking through his eyes. I checked the speedometer, lit a cigarette, tapped my thumb on the wheel. I was headed to Reno again.

Something from the back seat gripped my neck. I breathed in deep and remained focused. I didn't give the bastard any attention. I wasn't going to cave in this time. I was going to stay on the road, keep the car moving at a steady pace.

"You're going to miss me, baby." It was Jen's voice in the back seat. I smelled her breath blowing through the cabin like deadly perfume. I grinded my teeth violently and kept my eyes away from the mirrors. I knew that it was not Jennifer in my back seat. If I looked, I was as good as dead.

"Alright, Jeff, suit yourself. But remember, you can never have me back."

I heard the rear door open and her living body slapped the pavement, skipping like a stone along the frozen Montana highway. The door slammed shut and I was alone, back in my cell, staring at the full moon.

I felt ill as soon as I realized what had happened. It was the sickening sensation men get when giving up a habit. The old me was dying, dying, withering. It was a good thing, and I knew it had to be done, but the process was painful. I continued to read the book, knowing that it would help me.

Now I know in part, but then
I will know fully, as I am fully known.
Now these three remain:
faith, hope, and love.
But the greatest of these is love.

If I did not have love, I had nothing.

Sure, I'd moved some mountains: mountains of dope, jewelry, cash and stolen cars. Yeah, I'd run my mouth a lot to big-time suits and stolen their money or walked off with their girlfriends. So what? All that work but nothing to show for it!

I had been there, seen that, stolen this, scammed this organization, made off with this much money, screwed this person, beat that guy up... I had done it all.

"I've never done a thing."

I had seen the world.

"I've never seen the world."

I had known women.

"I have never known love."

I had carried money.

"I have never know joy. I've never really been happy."

Was the old Cadillac driver from Stinson Beach right about my good times being a bargain with the Devil? I guess so. If joy wasn't found through truth, it was found through evil. I remembered the driver slugging on port wine and me in the back seat high on speed and shots of vodka. I remembered the NFL player's girlfriend, the bars, the dancing, the sex, the endlessness of the run.

I reread:

Now I know in part, but then
I will know fully, as I am fully known.
Now these three remain:
faith, hope, and love.
But the greatest of these is love.

It made sense. The greatest was love. Sure. Right. Of course: without love there was nothing. Without truth there was nothing. I had been doped by the world into becoming a loud-mouthed idiot; a Godless moron without any conception of compassion.   A feeling came over me as though I had been tossed into water. My body remained still but moved and undulated with the waves. The Earth turned and the cell remained motionless. Far off a dog barked, a phone rang, someone robbed a bank, a guy went to the store to buy cigarettes and never came back, songs played, humanity continued to move forward and the moon stared down at me like a painting on the wall.

A voice manifested itself in the cell:

Pick up your cross and
follow me.
You will not return to who you were.

And then it said something I really liked:

Do this
and all of your dreams
will come true.

Tears jumped out of my eyes. I hadn't cried since I was maybe eight or nine. I hadn't really felt anything since then. Right then, I felt it. All of it. I knew what these words meant. I realized that this must have been God, Jesus, something like that. It was the book. It was helping me. Perhaps this meant that I had a chance.

20

SHADOWS AND LIGHTS

1987

THE EGYPTIAN SAT CLOSE TO THE TABLE, HIS WRISTS RESTING ON THE EDGE and his eyes closed in silent prayer. The Bible study was in session, each man at rest with his head down. For me, there was no rest; every section of the room seemed to teeter from side to side as though it were in flight. A noiseless breeze was blowing tiles like leaves, rippling the floor like water, and I could see right through the walls and as far off as the horizon.

To my left I could feel a shadow at the door. The dark silhouette crossed the plane and broke the light. It was the creature from the Mercedes, there was no doubt about it. His fence around me had been severed and I wasn't his slave anymore. I felt good about choosing the straight path, reading the bible, believing in God, but all this stuff didn't mean that I was totally out of the woods.

There was a hint of odor as if a dead animal were close by. The scent faded and the room continued to glow and radiate all sorts of new and indescribable energy. Is this what the world looked like to the normal person? Probably not. To honest and upright men? Perhaps. I didn't know what I was experiencing, just that it was different and better than before and I felt better about leaving prison and staying straight.

We were supposed to be in silent prayer, but my eyes wouldn't remain shut. I had never prayed before. I had a lot to learn about how to converse with God.

I had spoken with myself and knew how to change my life in accordance with this new belief. The problem was that it was difficult to remain focused. I was still very scared of all of this stuff. It reminded me of high school, back when the kids called me Snowman because I froze around women. Why was I always afraid to make commitments? I'd always left the girls after only ONE goodnight kiss.

I sighed at the table, folding my hands over the orange book. For me, crime had been another goodnight kiss with no happy ending. I'd never taken any of my careers farther than the doorstep before throwing them into the trashcan.

Now, even when I knew how to change my life, I was scared of fully committing. I was frozen to the floor, glued in place, immobilized. I knew the truth now, I knew the path to follow, but my feet were unsure on even the most solid ground. Logic, I thought, can sometimes be the flaw of man. Especially when it trumps instinct.

I picked up the Bible, looked it over. What kind of man had I become? What would I do without a warrant to run from? Without a plane to catch or a car to steal? I guess I wouldn't run at all. There was no need to run anymore. The run had become an addiction, a means of identifying my personal character as a badass or superhero. There was no need to identify myself as anything other than Jeff Andrews. To parade around under hundreds of aliases, fake personalities, on irrefutably evil missions, was nothing short of immature and embarrassing. Yes, embarrassing! There was nothing redeeming about it. The money made no difference because, no matter how hard I tried, stolen wealth was not permanent and never amounted to true success or happiness. Such is the result of all progress sprung from treachery.

"When I get out of prison I'm going to work for Ken," I muttered. I needed the sound of my voice to assure myself. Luckily, no one in the Bible Study heard me.

But there was something nagging at me. A man came to the door of the classroom and peered in. It was Buck Wolkner. Or, wait, was I just imagining him? I opened my eyes. Had they been closed? Either way, I had been imagining him.

The walls and desks continued to radiate. It wasn't like sparkles of glitter, and it wasn't that it was any brighter than before, just that it was... different. There had been something removed from my vision. A new perspective had taken hold. It was love and conviction. For the first time in my life I was taking myself to the next level: I believed in something that wasn't cool because it worked for me and helped me succeed. I didn't need to be seen as "cool" in the eyes of my friends anymore. My kingdom was no longer of their kingdom. It was as simple as that.

Everything had taken on a new beauty. I studied the walls with deep enchantment, as though the cinderblocks were a gorge or mountain range. With my new understanding of compassion, love, and inherent human accountability, I was not only capable of feeling empathy for the entire world, but also feeling the need to make myself available to it. I knew that I needed to tell my friends what had happened to me. But what if they didn't understand? What if they didn't believe me?

The shadow crossed the open doorway and a wretched scent wafted throughout. The horrible bastard was on the cusp of returning. My immediate thought was to stand and attack him. Sure, I'll run and grab that demonic son of a bitch and tear him to shreds.

The smell grew, pushed me back into my seat, made me sick. The room ceased to glow and I was left alone.

Silence.

All of the times on the run, those near-suicide nights, the months of intense longing—nothing compared to this moment on the edge of the world. I could feel that I was resting in some middle ground, a gray area between love and hate that was occupied by no one but me. Without the Bible, without Evil, what kind of flag did a man fly? I begged that my new strength would stay with me, but it was not an item that could be bought or begged for. It had to be believed. But, then, it was harder for me to believe than I'd imagined.

The silhouette at the doorway paced back and forth, panting like a wild beast, as though waiting for me to leave the "safe zone" of the Bible classroom. I heard a shriek from the door. Maybe it came from the weight room, maybe the TV room, or maybe it was the Demon himself. I dismissed it as nothing. Then it came again. The hair on my neck stood up. I could NOT go back to my old ways. I couldn't go back to working for evil.

"I won't go back," I said. "I won't go back. I'm not going back. I'm here now. I'm safe. I'm not going back to that. I'm over it. I've changed."

I felt him enter the room. He was huge, a lumbering and scaly beast. He trudged across the tile floor and the knot in my throat rose to my mouth.

"Please..." I said, asking for help from anyone who would listen. "Please, someone stop this. Stop him! I have changed! I gave it up. I'm a good guy! Please! Someone!" The men in the classroom paid no attention. Time was frozen. I was no longer existing on human terms. I was the only animate object in a room that had now become an ancient black-and-white photograph.

Dark shadows swirled on the wall with the same grace and power as the light had exhibited only minutes before. In a way, the darkness was almost equal in its magnificence. I surmised that these were the methods of the Demon: to resemble God in all ways possible and therefore undermine His plans through the weakness of the human mind.

The room was definitely more dark than light now. It had become more dark than gray. What was scary was how easily I recognized and accepted this. I had seen the world this way for a long time. I hadn't remembered it being this bad, but at times it had been much worse. A minute passed and the thick darkness moved in like a slow-rolling storm. I was shocked by heat, and the creature ran his scaly hands across the back of my neck. He begged for me to let him back in. My instinct was to stand and punch, but I knew that a fight was just what he wanted.

He extended his hand: a thick and hellish-looking claw. A pack of cigarettes rested there. He didn't say anything, but I knew that he wanted me to take them. I removed them from his hand, opened the back, and studied the contents.

"Yeah, it's a pack of cigarettes. What's the point?"

"Take one," he said.

I pulled at one, pulled harder, tugged it. I needed a cigarette. I needed one bad. I pulled at it, yanked the pack into a million pieces. It was fake! There weren't any cigarettes at all! Bastard! I stood up, pinned him against the wall, We were close, really close, and the sweat and breath mixed in front of both of our faces and I was scared, really scared, and he was laughing, and I knew that I was outmatched but I also knew that I was a hell of a fighter. Something struck me as odd, something really hit home, and I felt very unsettled by how calmly he grinned. His skin was as hot as a screaming tea kettle and dripped slime and sweat and he smiled—damn, how he smiled at me! Damn that horrible bastard!

"21," he said, chuckling, flipping a cigarette between us. "Without me, you'll never get the extra cigarette. Stop trying to push me away."

"Push you away? I'll push you in front of a damn train."

All of this was very strange, as though I would have dreamt it. He suddenly disappeared and the cigarette was in my hand and I was standing there, braced against the wall. I studied that cigarette for a long time before tossing it onto the floor. I wiped my palm on the leg of my chair and sat back down.

I took a very deep breath and tried to collect myself.

It became obvious that this thing, this Demon or whatever he was, was not present in the sense that I imagined he was. To those in Bible study, the room was lit just as usual and the walls were motionless. To have seen me throw punches at the cinderblock... it would have only raised questions about my sanity. Luckily, no one had noticed this most recent outburst.

But, then, hadn't time ceased? Wasn't this just a photograph and I a character inside it? Wait... a man coughed, another scratched his head. The photograph had come back to life. Fear overcame me. Fast music was playing in my head; screeching violins squealed and moaned at me. The world was REAL and this was REALLY happening. My breathing intensified and my mind began to race.

A pack of cigarettes, slightly misshapen to accommodate 21, rested on the table beside my Bible. I looked and the cigarette was no longer on the floor. This slimy bastard was a trickster. He was a part of me. He was my con-artist brain, the entity that I had worked for all my life.

I took another deep breath. Damn, the air stunk of death and decay. I tried to focus on something other than evil. The shadow disappeared. The cigarettes were gone again. What was there other than evil? I was in prison! My wife had cheated on me! SHIT! My debt was enormous and I had no easy way to pay it off! My only friend on the outside was the owner of his own company and even HE didn't have all the answers! My brother, Fenster, Leslie, Carlos, Norberto, Jen, Sheryl... all these people... where were they? Where was John Payne? That poor sap! I'd stolen his life for a few days and what had he gotten out of it? Nothing! Probably a bad reputation or a letter from the IRS! How about Bill Fallie? That SUCKER! Probably rotting in the can just like me! HA! Awful jackass!

I became hysterical, at times laughing to myself and at times on the verge of tears. When I opened my eyes—well, I tried to open them but there was nothing. Darkness remained the sole element. I needed a drink, a glass of vodka or beer. I struggled to see through this darkness and failed. I... wait... blackness... nothing... dizziness overwhelmed me. I gripped the desk and found it to be pliable, bendable, like Jell-O or hardened water, if there was such a thing.

"No," I said. "Please, don't. I have nothing..."

The problem was that I did have something, I just hadn't thought of it. I had the love from that book. I understood how to save myself. I knew the methods to defeat evil; I just couldn't commit to abandoning my lifestyle. I had learned how to become a good person after just a few moments of reading the Bible, but I had so quickly forsaken it.

Luckily, the Lord understood my problems. He heard my plea. He understood that a man's mind was not always his own, especially while behind bars. Using His infinite power He pulled me back, stripped the smoldering residue from my neck, and explained His plan so that I could make my choice.

I listened very carefully this time and followed Him.

The Egyptian sat up straight from the table and engaged me. I swallowed hard and remained focused on his eyes. They were not his eyes and when he spoke I knew it was not his voice but someone else's.

"You've seen both sides of the coin, Jeff. Pick up your cross and follow Me. You will be unable to return to who you were. Do this, and follow My Word, follow and believe in all of its ways, inwardly and outwardly, in life and also in death, and all of your dreams and aspirations will come true."

I stared across the table and tears formed at the edges of my eyes. The Egyptian remained stoic, the most expressionless face I have seen on a man.

"You have a place for guys like me in Heaven?" I asked, knowing very little about the afterlife. "Is there a place for guys who've screwed up the first half of their lives and try to turn it around?"

I was scared and shedding tears in torrents. I was still the Snowman. I didn't know if I would fit in up there.

"Jeff..." he sighed and smiled empathetically. "If I didn't have a place for you, I would have told you."

And then it was over, and the hum of the air conditioning was the only sound above the whispers of men's prayers and the clanging of metal plates in the weight room.

21

JENNIFER

1988

I OWED SOMEWHERE IN THE NEIGHBORHOOD OF $500,000 TO THE government and various businesses. I was out of prison, had stayed off the booze, was doing alright, but restitution was going to kill me. It would be difficult to pay it off in the time demanded by the judge. Ken loaned me some money, let me borrow a Cadillac that I'd sold him several years ago, but even with all this there was no way to make the payments.

I was alone in my apartment one evening going over my case files, trying to find a mistake, something that would relieve me of a few debts. As usual, there was nothing. I didn't have my cigarettes, my cigars, my booze… any of it. I slammed my fist on the counter. It wasn't anger that got me down, it was frustration. I couldn't move on from my old self. Either I needed a half-million dollars or I needed a drink. There was no way to get 500k within a reasonable timeframe and still make the payments on my apartment, my lawyers, my living expenses, etc.

The Bible looked very small sitting on the desk beside all of my folders and financial documents. I removed another folder from the drawer, pushed it onto the desk. The Bible fell to the floor and I reached for it, pulled it back and set it on the table in the center of the room. I returned to the desk and continued working. It was impossible to see through these numbers. It was hopeless and depressing. The debt was too great to bear.

A bottle of vodka would put me to sleep. It would ease the pain, settle me down, facilitate a mood change. I paced the thick-carpeted floors and searched the windows for signs of life, anything to take my mind off my problems. A knock came at my front door. Adrenaline shocked my system. I knew it wasn't the police. If the police came this late, they broke down the door.

Cautiously, with the greatest care given to each step, I glided across the room and eyed the peephole. A finger was plastered over the glass. I backed away and stood in silence, my fast breaths echoing loudly down the hallway. Who had a reason to kill me? Who had I screwed over? Was this the end?

"Jay," I heard a voice from outside. "Let me in, Jay, it's me. I was just kidding with the peephole," she said.

I opened the door cautiously, wary that perhaps she was in cahoots with one of my enemies. She came inside, removed her coat, settled down on my couch. I stood and watched her, unable to move beyond the tiny foyer.

"What's the matter? You're frozen stiff."

"Call me Jeff." I loosened up, felt years of tension washing away from my neck.

"You'll always be Jay to me, baby."

"We're divorced, Jen. You slept around. You couldn't wait for me." We stared at one another in silence. "You need to leave." I felt strong, sure, and the old Snowman melted away, exposing my reborn soul beneath it.

"Why'd you let me in?"

I went into the kitchen, poured a glass of water from the sink. I offered her something to drink and she asked for a vodka. I explained that I didn't drink anymore and she patronized me with laughter. I brought her a glass of water and we tapped them in a sarcastic toast.

The traffic outside my window rolled by and I focused on the lights of the cars. The years had weathered themselves on her beautiful face. She didn't look quite the same as she used to. I understood that no one aged perfectly, but it's easier to notice the cracks in polished marble.

"I'm with someone else now," I said.

"That doesn't mean we can't work together."

"Yes it does."

She reached into her bag, removed a small flask of liquor. She took a hit, capped it, tossed it to me. I wafted it beneath my nose and grimaced.

"Stop acting like such a baby."

I set the flask on the table beside me. She reached into her purse again. This time she exposed a brick of cash. I stared disinterestedly, unimpressed, bored.

"That's not good enough?" she asked.

"It'll take more than that to get me back."

She removed a large bag of cocaine, probably a kilo brick. It was good stuff, still hard like ice, probably straight from Central America. If I knew one thing about Jen, she never settled for anything other than the purest.

"I got a friend in Hawaii. He can get this stuff all day. I got money, a car on the island, an apartment, customers, everything."

"Sounds like you've got it made," I said.

"I'm here to help you, Jay."

"It's Jeff."

"Whatever, call yourself whatever you want. I'm here to help you get your head out of the gutter." She nodded at the Bible on my coffee table. It looked awful small next to the stack of hundreds.

"It's a good book," I said.

"I bet."

"It helped me forget about people like you."

"You haven't forgotten me," she smiled.

A shadow moved in the doorway and across the wall. I recognized the silhouette all too well. My body shuddered.

"You come alone?" I asked.

"Of course. You know I always work alone."

"Unless it's me, huh?"

"You're the exception to my rule."

"You didn't come alone."

"I DID," she slapped her hand on the arm of the chair. "Now sit down before you have a heart attack. You're seeing things again."

"Maybe so…" I said, my eyes focused on the door like a junkyard dog. After a few moments I settled down.

She stared at me expectantly. I looked at the rock, the cash, her body. I grabbed the bag, walked over to the lamp, and the old pro began a routine inspection.

Jen stood up, glided across the room, and pressed herself against my chest.

"A flight leaves for Chicago at 11 p.m. From there it goes to the island. We can make it if we hurry. My car is out front," she said.

I stood there, white bag in hand, and Jen's hair fell over her shoulders like a waterfall. We were momentarily trapped together, each one holding the other tightly and deciding what to do, anticipating the next move.

I pushed her away and hurried to the bedroom where I packed my things. I felt excited, overcome by giddiness, and I smiled widely as I worked. I didn't have much, so packing meant grabbing the toothbrush, razor, an extra suit, and shoving them into my work briefcase.

I left everything in the room, even the Bible, and we exited quickly, her heels clacking down the cement steps like I'd heard so many times. She tossed me the keys and I drove. She'd always admitted to being a terrible driver, and with time running out on the flight I knew I had to make the best of her little V6 rental.

"So, did you have a price set on that Bible all along?" she asked.

I shrugged.

"I knew you couldn't stick with it. It's not in your nature." She rolled down the window for a cigarette. She passed me one and I waved it away. She laughed at me. She took a rip of cocaine from her tooter and passed it to me. I looked down at it, put it up to my nose, and without hesitating I ripped the longest rail of my career. The only thing about my hit was that I hadn't pressed the button to shovel over the next chamber of coke. Instead of getting a nose-full of powder, I got a nose-full of air. I couldn't afford to be high at a time like this. After three years of sobriety I'd have turned into a wild animal after just one sniff.

"It's good to have you back, baby." She leaned her head back on the headrest and flicked cigarette ashes into the wind. Twisted memories washed over me like knives. I glanced in the rearview and there he was: the same face from prison, the same face I'd seen in the back of my Benz all those years ago. I took a deep breath and steadied my nerves.

"You've never thought about giving it up?" I asked Jen.

"Giving what up?" she eyed her cigarette questionably.

"The whole thing. Drugs, booze, cash..."

"Sounds like a stupid thing to give up."

There was no sense arguing with her.

We arrived at the airport and I parked the car in the drop-off zone. I grabbed my bag, hustled inside, and purchased tickets to Chicago. We rushed up the escalator toward the security check-in, the cash and cocaine wrapped in aluminum foil deep within her purse. She had grown reckless in her latter years but she was talented, smooth, ice cold, and I knew she would never get caught.

We had a half hour to kill until boarding. The flight was late. I stood there impatiently, deciding the best way to execute my plan.

We entered the airport bar and Jen ordered a martini. I took a water. Jen immediately buried her nose in a magazine. She was content with the idea that we were back together. She hardly noticed a word I said, just sat there reading and sipping on the drink. She was at ease now, finally, after all of those "hard" years while I was away.

"I love you so much, baby," she said, still flipping through the ads.

I grimaced and shook my head. Her speech was rhetorical. She expected no words in return. She assumed that I loved her the same way.

"I've met another woman, Jen." She nodded, kept reading. "I corresponded with a woman while I was in prison. I recently met her on the outside. I never thought I'd be with a woman again, but I've found someone who fits me." Jen wasn't paying attention. She thought I wasn't being serious, that nothing could spoil her plans. She was high, drunk, contented with life, immersed in a lackadaisical state of dopamine bliss.

"That's not possible, baby. You'll never find anyone better than me."

I flexed my fist on the table and slugged the water.

"I can't do this, Jen. I never intended on doing this. I was afraid at first. That's how you trapped me. I've always been afraid of leaving this shit behind. I've thought, for some childish reason, that this SHIT was all I had." I gestured at her briefcase. "I don't feel that way anymore. I'm done with it. I'm done being scared."

"What does that mean? Scared of what?" She was still slightly disinterested, despite my vehemence.

"I guess I've been scared all my life, right up until now."

"You're always so cool. You're never scared."

"I was. I just tricked everybody. I was scared as shit." I nodded my head up and down, reaffirming what I was saying, pounding it into my own skull. "I am not scared anymore. You're on your own. I'm done here."

"Why?" she asked.

"I told you, I met another woman. You cheated on me while I was in prison, remember? Besides, my new girlfriend is a better person. She's not a backstabber like you."

She looked up from the magazine and pinched her lips together repulsed.

"You're an asshole, Jay. This isn't funny. I'm sorry I cheated on you, but you don't need to treat me this way."

It was more than that. Much more. There was no way she could have known. If a person hasn't seen the dark side meet the light, if they haven't tasted blood and booze, if they haven't felt the heavy trunk thumping down the long spine of the highway, there would be no way to comprehend my loathing for those things.

I pushed myself away from the table.

"I'm sorry, Jay, what are you doing?"

"Nothing," I said, staring at the floor. "Forget it. Forget everything." I stood up. "I've got to go, Jen. You're a terrible person. I can't do it anymore."

"Jay!" She rose sloppily from the table. Several of the waitresses turned their attention toward us. "Where are you going?" she pleaded.

"To the bathroom," I said, defusing the situation. "I'll be back in a minute." She sat back down, watching complacently as I walked down the tile. She had no idea that I was serious, that I had come unfrozen and was leaving her for good. Jennifer was concerned solely with herself.

I felt great as I walked, each step taking me further into the light. I was no longer bound by the criminal marriage. I could make my own decisions now, chose my own women, my own way of life. Jen did not understand this because she could not do it herself.

When I looked back at her, sitting all alone at that airport table, all I could feel was pity. I had matured and she had not. It was despondency, not anger, that plagued me as I moved forward.

I navigated quickly and deliberately through the labyrinth of road-sized airport corridors and outside into the orange streetlight nightmare of honking horns and yelling travelers. A police officer was in front of Jen's rental talking into his radio.

"Sergeant Barton here... Yeah, I got a rental vehicle stuck in the terminal lane, lights on, engine off, one occupant in the back seat who is not responding to..."

I stepped quickly past him, threw my hand out, and flagged a cab.

"The Gables apartment complex, on Broad Street," I said, sliding into the cab. I looked back at the rental car, that dark silhouette in the back seat, and the cop standing there with his radio and ticket book. The silhouette remained motionless, the eerie shell of my past life, stuck in time like a faded tombstone.

I turned forward and listened as the airliners exploded the sky above us. There was a force outside of the human race, a higher power than mankind, and I was beginning to understand it now. I gazed nostalgically through the windows and down the Interstates and city streets where the buildings swayed like palm trees and the cement rippled like water.

Somewhere, on some distant and lonesome road, the old Benz engine still rumbled like a freight train against the blacktop. It would never stop going, whether I was there to drive it or not. It would continue moving forward, propelling those lost souls to the far and strangest corners of this world; to places where men should never travel but did, and places I would never see again.

ACKNOWLEDGEMENTS

From Jeff Andrews

Many thanks to Jesse Stretch for his personal efforts above and beyond the call of duty while writing this book. And to Cheryl Cooper and Steve O'Brien for their unbelievable support and effort in editing and designing the book. Thanks as well to First Baptist Church, Needle's Eye Ministries, Prison Fellowship and all my friends and fellow supporters of this book, many of whom are listed in the appendices.

From Jesse Stretch

Thanks to Jeff Andrews for choosing me to write his story. It has been an honor as well as a pleasure, and it has opened many doors, both mental and physical, that will decisively and positively impact my writing career.

Thanks to Marshall, Ellen, Jake, my entire family, and all of my friends, especially Charles, who were so supportive and critical when helping me bring this project to completion.

Appendix

*A Few Helpful Words for the Incarcerated Men
and Women of this Fallen World...*

You have 25 bucks cash to your name. It's raining, 4:50 p.m. on a Thursday in February. Cold air is moving in, probably snow. You're standing there with a pair of prison-issue pants, an Oxford blue button up, soiled tennis shoes, no wallet, one DMV issue ID card, no telephone, and nobody to give a damn.

Your mind is in a million places, but your body... your body is in one very particular place: on the "free" side of the prison gate. A few guards stare down at you from the tower. One gives you a nod. You walk off into the parking lot, toward the payphone. You were going to call a cab, but that would cost too much. Maybe you can hang around and snag a ride with someone else? A buddy of yours was getting out today... well, not really a buddy, a guy you knew from the yard. Maybe not, though. He might not get out today. You don't remember.

The cab shows up after a half hour and already you're hungry and catching a cold from standing in the wind. The driver is angry because he knows there won't be a good tip from an ex-prisoner. He drives fast, pushing through the hills and into the city. You get to the city and he demands 15 bucks. That's more than half your roll. What do you do? You have to give him the cash.

You walk into the grocery store and damn, prices have gone up since you went away. People are looking at you funny. One of the managers seems to be following you. You have 10 bucks and nowhere to stay, no food, no friends. You pick up a 12-pack and a whole rotisserie chicken, still hot from the cooker. When no one's looking, you dart out the door and around the side of the building. You're into another parking lot and eating the chicken so fast that no one bothers to notice.

That air is getting colder. You need a jacket. Maybe you could steal one from the sporting goods store? Maybe you could steal a sleeping bag too. Who would have thought you'd end up homeless? This is no way to go. Why didn't you pay attention when they told you it would be hard to fit in when you got out? Damn, those people really knew what they were talking about.

You vowed never to do crime again, but there's no other way. You have to make just one quick push in order to survive. You head into the sporting goods store and don a ski jacket, grab a sleeping bag, shove a pair of gloves down your pants, a pair of wool socks in your pockets, a cap on your head. The feeling of nervousness has been there ever since you walked through the main gate, but now it's multiplied. You're crazed, unhappy, tired, hungry again, angry, misunderstood. All you need is to stay warm and all you've got is 10 bucks.

"10 bucks isn't shit these days," you tell yourself. "They're leaving me no choice."

You walk right out the door and the sensors go off. A manager follows you for a moment but breaks off, afraid of what you'll do if he catches you. You walk briskly across the parking lot and hop a few fences. You're clear.

You climb a roof and find a nice spot beneath an overhang. Another guy has his spot there but he doesn't mind if you join him. He needed a new friend anyway.

"In the morning," he tells you, "Ww can go down to 18th street. I got a guy there who can set us up with work."

"What kind of work?" you ask.

"Corner work."

"Slinging?"

"What else we gonna do?" he asks.

You never thought it would come to this. If the pigs see you near 18th they're going to know what you're up to. It's how you got locked up the first and second times. Besides, there are other people who don't want you around right now. There are other guys out there who would have no problem putting a bullet in you for showing your face on the wrong side of town.

"Alright... just for tomorrow, though. I can't keep on doing this shit," you say.

"That's fine," the guys says. "Nobody's asking for a contract. All I'm trying to do is help." And the sad thing is, it's the truth. It's the only way he knows.

Tomorrow you go down to 18th street and B.J. fronts you a hundred bucks worth of work (crack rock.) B.J. used to be your buddy and he likes you, which is why he gives you such a good front. With 100 bucks crack at cost, you can make some serious dough.

You make it three blocks and bingo: the blue lights go up. They've been watching B.J.'s house. He told you so, but you didn't think it could happen to you. The cops must have recognized you when you came out. You're done for. It's over. You start running because, shit, what else can you do?

You make it two bocks with the heat right on your ass but that ski jacket snags on the fencepost and you go flying to the ground. A bag of work ejects from your pocket and lands right at the cop's feet. You won't get out of the pen again for at least 10 years, maybe more.

All because you didn't plan ahead.

＊　＊　＊

PLANNING AHEAD
A Note from Jeff Andrews

Many inmates leave prison with the intention of continuing a life of crime. There are many others, however, who understand that crime only leads to longer incarceration for the repeat offender and not much else.

To these people, the ones who want to make a productive life for themselves, there are organizations that can help. They are called churches, like my church, First Baptist Church, 800 Thompson Street, Ashland, Virginia 23005. There are also hundreds of para-church ministries, such as Prison Fellowship, Needle's Eye and Desperate Highway Ministries..

An old friend of mine once said this: "If you want to act like an animal, they have lots of cages they can put you in. But if you want to CHANGE YOUR LIFE, there are thousands of people who are ready, willing and able to help you." Jimmy Massie, Jr.

He went on to tell me about Evangelical Christians, people who fear only God Himself and know that their assignment is to serve Jesus Christ first. The question then becomes: "Why would Jesus want to help me?" He wants to help you because Jesus unconditionally loves sinners, even before they accept Him as Lord and Savior. Jesus went to the Cross and was crucified, on purpose, for every one of us. He is the Son of God, but came here to be a flesh-and - blood man just like each of us. He died so that everyone on Earth could be free from the bondage that ensnares us.

PLAN A: Stepping Forward with the Lord. Get to know Jesus...It's the only option!

In order to get your life straightened out, you have to take responsibility for your actions; you must admit to yourself and to God that you have been wrong. Saying the Sinner's Prayer is a way to confirm to the Lord that you want to be one of His, that you respect the Bible and have made a conscious decision to turn your life around. Read this prayer aloud.

THE SINNER'S PRAYER

Lord I confess that I am a sinner.
Father, forgive me for my sins.
I believe that Jesus Christ died on the cross for my sins.
I believe that He was raised from the dead for my justification.
I now receive and confess Him as my personal Savior.
In Jesus name I pray, Amen.

You have now made a commitment of submission to Jesus' power and authority over life and death, whereby He freely gives that same power and authority back to you in exchange for your faith and your willingness to follow His every assignment in your life, as long as you never forget Jesus blood was painfully given in exchange for your sin.

He has known you and you were in His mind 20 billion years ago...Today, He has a plan for you for the next 20 billion years. His success is absolute and final...He has already planned it all and seen it all from start to finish...and it is perfect.

PLAN B: Stepping Forward with Your Fellow Man – Not Recommended

The link below will take you to the Department of Justice Reentry Locator Map. Once it is opened, there are services listed that are available for specific areas of Reentry. This is a relatively new Web site, and there is not a lot available for you at this time. There are, however, programs that promote awareness, employ people, etc. This is a good start, but it will do little to help you in your time of need.

http://www.reentryresources.ncjrs.gov/
index.cfm?event=StateResource##top

There is very little that your fellow man will do to aid you in your time of need. More than likely you are sitting behind bars right this second, reading this text, hearing the howls and groans of the prison. You are probably wondering how your friends would react if they saw you carrying a Bible. How would they feel if you denounced your gang and held yourself up to the Lord's standards? How would everyone react if you changed your life for the better?

The truth is, they would probably be very jealous. They would probably dislike and shun you for it. They would call you ignorant or weak or afraid. Their anger comes from their inability to break the mold, their inability to cast aside crime and deviant behavior for a much more ful-filling existence.

You can take strides forward with your fellow man. Sure, that's fine. You can look for jobs while still incarcerated. You can write letters to people asking for help, asking for money, asking for anything. These efforts will often bear little fruit... I've tried almost all of them.

Plan A is, in my opinion, the ONLY option that makes any sense for a convicted felon. For any human being, for that matter.

I have limited space to discuss this matter with you, and so will rec-ommend a few pieces of reading material. Once you have decided to find the Lord (and by the way, He already knows you, but you must choose Him) and change your life I would suggest buying a good study Bible and some study aids. I have found these to be very helpful:

a. *The Message, Remix* by Eugene H. Peterson
b. *The Quest NIV Study Bible*
c. *Holman Christian Standard Bible*
d. *Holman Bible Handbook*
e. *Holman Illustrated Bible Dictionary*
f. *My Utmost For His Highest* by Oswald Chambers
g. Any good Bible dictionary
h. *Believers Bible Commentary* by William MacDonald
i. *23 Minutes in Hell* by Bill Weise
j. *90 Minutes in Heaven* by Don Piper
k. *The Greatest Salesman in the World* by Og Mandino
l. *When Heaven Invades Earth* by Bill Johnson
m. *The Reason for God* by Timothy Keller
n. *The Power of Faith* by Smith Wigglesworth
o. *Total Forgiveness* by R.T. Kendall
p. *Angels* by Billy Graham
q. *The Captivity Series*, Katie Souza
r. iPod Casts from Bethel Church, www.ibethel.org
s. Get Baptized!

I hope that my story, my testimonies, my errors and successes, have been sufficient to show you that the Lord is capable of turning pure evil into good. I pray that your salvation will come, that your life will change for the better, and that if you already are a believer, that your faith will multiply with the compassion necessary to help those in need.

Jesus said, "I tell you most solemnly that anyone who chooses a life of sin is trapped in a dead-end life and is, in fact, a slave." The Message - John 8:34.

"It cost God plenty to get you out of that dead-end, empty-headed life you grew up in. He paid with Christ's sacred blood, you know. The Message - 1 Peter 1:18.

"Now that you've cleaned up your lives by following the truth, love one another as if your lives depended on it." The Message - 1 Peter 1:22.

"Yes, I'm on my way! I'll be there soon! I'm bringing my payroll with me. I'll pay all people in full for their life's work. I'm A to Z, the First and the Final, Beginning and Conclusion." The Message - Revelation 22: 12-13.

Blessings and Godspeed,

Jeff Andrews

Appendix, part II

Jeff Andrews went on to leave Danbury Federal Corrections Institute via a transfer to Morgantown FCI in 1988 and upon his release became the V.P. of Sales and Marketing, then Executive Vice President of IPC Technologies, Inc. Yes, it was the new name and business plan that he and Ken Banks had dreamed up while Jeff was in prison. In fact, the business plan was part of the presentation at the parole hearing that afforded a cut of three months off the mandatory 33-month sentence.

Jeff has since served in various capacities for a multitude of organizations including Prison Fellowship, The House of New Beginnings, Needle's Eye Ministries, The Gideons International, Justice Fellowship, and Desperate Highway Ministries. He is a former president of the Ashland Kiwanis Club, and currently a deacon teaching adult Sunday School at First Baptist Church in Ashland near his home.

He spends much of his time spreading the word of Jesus Christ to those who are willing to listen and receive him. He is available anywhere there are people who need help. Not only does Jeff offer the word of God, he offers people his skills by aiding them in their search for employment. He is currently serving as a mentor for an inmate who is awaiting release.

Following his in-prison divorce in 1987, Jeff was re-married in 1989. He and his wife have owned a home in the Richmond area since the early '90s.

Jeff has retained his position as Executive Vice President of IPC Technologies. He and Ken, with the help of a skilled team of professionals, have turned the company into a rapidly expanding success.

Jeff went from being a lone wolf, a self-focused sociopath, to having hundreds of friends, acquaintances and people he learned to care about more than himself. Pivotal moments of his life and a few of the people he came to know through Christ are included below:

1. His best friend and soul mate, his wife. For almost 20 years they and her family have celebrated holidays and vacations together...his wife and her family were clearly a gift from God.

2. After being separated from his family for more than 15 years, Jeff visits them regularly around holidays and special occasions. His Dad died at 80 years of age in 2001, and after a terrible relationship during Jeff's youth, all differences were reconciled and his Dad asked him to lead at his funeral. They were very close at the end and his father accepted Jesus and went Home to wait for his family.

3. Ken Banks, CEO of IPC Technologies, Inc. became Jeff's best friend, best man, and business partner over the course of 28 years. Jeff was also best man at Ken's wedding five years ago when he re-married. The couple has six awesome children.

4. Jack Kelly, Jeff's tax attorney introduced Jeff to Needle's Eye Ministries and Rev. Buddy Childress, Executive Director, and Marcia DeVereaux, Executive Assistant at one of their monthly luncheons. Jeff served as board chair for two of the seven years he was on the Executive Board, then the Directors Council and the Advisory Board where he met hundreds of people he maintains contact with, Including: David Mathews, Sonny Haynes, David Fairchild, Chad Seay, Annhorner Truitt, Chris Meyer, Rev. John Hershman, Renee Cobb, Russ McDowell, David Barrett, Bob Barton, Blair Massey, Bill Bosher, Rev. Bob Carlton, Dan Carrell, Jim DePasquale, Rev. Larry Frakes, Caren Fields, Bob Fitch, Tom Gallagher, Frank Goare, Lee Hilbert, Jim Hunter, Bradley Nott, Raymond Parker, Edward Parker, Gordon Prior, Lowell Qualls, Grahame Rees, Andy Redford, Elizabeth Shaffer, Emerson Shelton, Christine Slate, Hon. Neal Steverson, Litt Thompson, Buddy Tolleson, Ted Tussey, Jeff Williams, Chris Withers, Mark Zell

5. During his first speaking opportunity at the Needle's Eye Luncheon series, Jeff met Edward (Ned) Parker who introduced him to Justice Fellowship and then Prison Fellowship, where Jeff met Jimmie Massie, Jr., Mac Pitt, Dick Harris, Titus Bender, and a great group of prison reform advocates like Chuck Colson, Mark Early, Joyce Minor, Wayne Watkins and Paul Stock.

6. At his second speaking at the Needle's Eye Luncheon series, Jeff met the late Bill Miller who introduced him to The Gideons Ministry where he was a statewide speaker for many of their banquets where he met hundreds of pastors and Gideons.

7. Steve Isaac, Needle's Eye Luncheon speaker and president of Stenrich/Martin Direct, his wife's boss before she retired 12 years ago, introduced him to the Ashland Kiwanis Club, where Jeff made many new friends and was at one time president and founding member of the Ashland Aktion Club for disabled adults. While there, Jeff met Linwwood Attkisson, Todd Attkisson, Frank Bentley, Tim Boschen, Don Bowers, Linda Budi, Mike Carter, Steve Chidsey, Judy & Bobby Chiles, Ed Cooper, John Cox, John Davis, Al Dickerson, Phil Doty, Delores Dunn, Tom Eggleston, Andy Ellis Jr., Dink Engleby, Tim Ernst, Lou Flannagan, Nelson & Carter Flippo, Pettus Gilman, Bill Glave, John Glazebrook, Larry Ham, Bill Hamner, Frank Hargrove, Sr & Jr, Hon. Overton Harris, Snapper Harris, Charles Hartgrove, Bill Helfele, Kyle Hendricks, Tom Herbert, Fred Hodnett Jr, J. Jones, Jr, Jody Korman,

John Longmire, Jack Luck, Mike Martin, Upton Martin, Art McKinney, Dwayne Murphy, Andy Newchock, PK Perrin, Charlie Peterson, Jim Pollard Jr, Ranny Robertson, Richard Saunders, Rick Santackas, Van Shamburger, Jay Small, George Smith, Jim Smith III, Jim Smith Jr., Jack Stanley, Ben Steele, Eddie Stiles, Joe Stiles, Jeff Stoneman, Tom Varner, Eddie Vaughan, Tripp Vaughan, Walton Vaughan, Rob Wait, Mark Walker, Melvin Watkins, Arthur Whittaker, Ed Wickham, Berry Wright.

8.   Kiwanian A.D. Whittaker invited Jeff to his Sunday School class to meet Billy Flowers, the teacher. Jeff learned much from Billy and after Billy passed in June 2005, Jeff became the teacher. He had joined the church in 2002, and was baptized in 2003 with A.D. and Jean Whittaker standing up for him. Now he serves as a deacon working with his pastor Robert Thompson. The guys and gals he is closest too and counts on are Bill Ager, Linwood Attkisson, Jessie Axselle, Millie Axselle, Margaret Baker, Jerry Barnett, Johnny Beck, Gwen Bennett, Irene Bishop, Rick & Gay Blankenship, LeeRoy Boschen, Kenny Boschen, Freddy Brown, Rev. Stuart Carlton, Frank & Marrie Cassell, Chris Christiansen, Paul Coburn, Gary & Lydia Collins, Troy Collison, John & Dotty Cox, Gail Dail, George & Doris Davis, Mildred Davis, Alex Durham, Tom Eggleston, Lennie Ellis, Tom Ficklin, Don Fields, Aubrey & Ellen Fletcher, Stan Funk, Jeff Gerhart, Beth Gibson, Buddy Gilbert, Larry Gilman, Brent Lingenfelter, Lynn Long, Robert Glisson, Britt & Susan Glisson, Parke Goodall, Argyle & Margaret Haley, CJ Haley, Max Haley, Argie Haley, Roy Haley, Watson Hall, Carolyn Hardy, Col.Clarence Hargrave, Ben Henderson, Barbara Hollowell, Fred Horn, Dave & Betty Hutchins, Dick Ivey, Ralph Johnson, Randy Jones, Ann Keller, Watts & Ollie Kyle, Sid Lane, Frank & Nan Lawson, Dorothy Lee, Jim & Judy Lowry, Hill Mallory, Jeff Marsh, Cal & Jane McAlexander, Cynthia McCreary, Mary McLean, Bill & Ruth Metcalf, Larry Mitchell, Don Morgan, Kay Morrell, Dwayne & Janice Murphy, Curtis Necessary, Liz Owen, Catherine Painter, Kevin Parsley, P.K. Perrin, Ashley & Judy Pierce, Fred Powell, Venetia Redd, Johnny Robinson, Fran Sadler, Roy & Hope Saettel, Graham Sherrod, Bill Sherrod, Maxey & Fran Slater, Jim & Eleanor Smith, Gary & Betty Stadnick, Frank & Sally Stone, Durwood Stone, Gerry Teravest, Bill Thomasson, Jay & Elsa Gray Thompson, Kathy Thompson, Nelda Thompkins, Andy Tilton, Jim Townsend, Ed Turnage, Greer Utley, Henry & Tammy Vangils, Rob & Jane Wait, Ellen Wakefield, Don Welch, A.D. & Jean Whittaker, Ed & Hilda Wickham, Billy Wood, Doris Yowell.

9.   Jeff participates in Bible Study and Prayer Groups almost every day of the week.

Business associates in and out of the office are a big part of his life now as well, such as: Eric Bowling, Rev. Jeff Fehn, Kurt Wright, Bill Southers, Stormy Hamlin, Jeff Barnes, Doug DeFranco, Bruce DeLeon, Linda Dorsey, Lorelei Gregory, Marcia Hudson, Jim Krieger, Christina Rivera, Steve Sarkees, Mac Smith, Doug Woods, Ryan Kahn, Jan Danielson, Steven Banks, Larry Woodall, Mike Weidig, Chris Viverette, Bob Rideout, Ann James, Steve Cates, Grant Grayson, Aubrey Ford, Hon. Dennis Dohnal, Tom Bowden, Jerry Nichols, Rocky Marrin, Tim McCreary, Raymond Parker, Karen Lankford, John Rudin, Dan Pharr, Del Mugford, Tom Kilby, Clinton Norris, Patty Kimbal, Eileen Kitces, George Boatright, Rajiv Perera, Tom Smith, Raouf Wakilpoor, Joe James, Dexter Gilliam, Chuck Krogman, Jim Bonello, Greg Braswell, John Skaggs, Harry Garmon, Wayne Nystrom, Neal Lappe, Paul Hunt, John Rockenbrod, Linda Ruth, Donnie Harper, Tony Wilson, Bill Shepherd, Bob Andrews, John Kinghorn, David Crittenden, Michael Daily, Bill Farmer, Bill Clyborne, Brad Nott, Dave Norton, Rudy Burgess, Randy Peeler, Otis Smith, Harold Sheffield, Woody Fisher, Mark Fero, Buddy Palmore, Jack Kotvas, Feldman Lane, Don Quinby.

Further acknowledgments

The writing of a book goes way beyond the thinking of the author. Mentors and influential friends have everything to do with a book like this one. The biggest change in my life was to be married to someone with not only a strong faith, but someone who truly loves and cares about me. My wife has been a strong supporter of who she saw deep inside when she first met me and she has paid a heavy price in supporting me through all of this past 20 years and this book actually shocked her as she helped me edit it. She said, after reading the first draft, "Who are you?" "Who did I marry?" She obviously saw someone very different, after my conversion in prison; when we first met, which was two weeks after I was released.

My wife for keeping me focused on the truth and Jesus Christ. It is because I wanted to be a good husband that my real focus on Christ became critical to our marriage. I knew I could not be a good husband without Jesus.

Ken Banks for believing in me way back when nobody did, I didn't believe anything. He took a lot of risk in hiring me and even when others, like probation officers told him he was a fool, he stood with me and allowed me to grow into a productive citizen.

Sugar & Dix Riley stood by me during periods of turmoil in my life. When I met Shug he was going through some difficult times in his career, so we just held each other up through the whole journey. Shug and Dix were like my family when I was a fugitive. They didn't really pay any attention to what I was doing, they just cared for me from their hearts when I had no place else to go, the kind of love one would typically get only from Jesus; unconditional.

Others that believed in me and stood by me:
Robyn & Sandy Nenninger were supportive and kind to me when I was in trouble.

Jean Diehls gave me a place to stay in her home when I was released in 1988.
Hon. Dennis Dohnal went above and beyond the call of duty as part of my legal defense team...I was represented by Murray Janus and Denny.

Jack Kelly was my tax attorney back when I had massive tax problems, like not filing a return while I was a fugitive for 10 years. He introduced me to Buddy Childress and Needle's Eye Ministries.

Buddy Childress was my first Spiritual Leader in Christ, I called him my pastor. He said that he wasn't...but put up with me anyway.

Edward Parker had a big heart and gave me a lot of encouragement when I needed it. He introduced me to Justice Fellowship and Jimmie Massie and Mac Pitt.

Jimmie Massie, Jr. was the first man that I ever saw that I saw Jesus fully present in his life when I came out to his house once for a Justice Fellowship retreat. Right after I first arrived and we settled in for a long retreat weekend, I saw Jesus fully in his eyes...I remember it blew me away...I also learned then what submission to Jesus looked like.

Steve Isaac for standing by me and introducing me to the Ashland Kiwanis Club.

He was a strong Christ filled mentor as well.

A.D. Whittaker for his efforts in getting me to Church when I had little interest. He has also been a strong supporter and mentor.

Billy Flowers who has now gone on to be with the Lord was a good mentor and teacher. He was always there for me when I first joined church.

Robert Thompson has been an awesome pastor and one of my biggest advocates in Christ. He has been an encourager in my walk and this book.

Tom & Irene Bishop & Catherine Painter who were the first to come forward when I made an appeal for financial support to write this book. Since then Tom went on to be with the Lord. It was amazing how Jesus filled them with the love and desire to finance this book. I was immediately encouraged and reminded that the Lords hand was in this project.

LeeRoy Boschen who also at about the same time came to me and said he wanted to help me write the book with his financial support.

As of 3/12/09 here's the support that has been given without reservation. And I am sure there are many others not listed here that are praying...

Prayer and Capital Warriors:

William Ager
Jeff & Nancy Andrews
Ken & Trish Banks
David Barrett
Robert Barton
Irene Bishop
Lee Roy Boschen
Robert Carden
Rev. Buddy Childress
   & Needle's Eye Ministry
Rick Collins
Cheryl Cooper
John & Dottie Cox
FBC Deacon Board
Lennie & Cindy Ellis
Billy Flowers Bible Study
Friday Morning Bible Study
Jeff & Susan Gearhart
Hon. Larry Gilman
Andrew Glomb
Argie Haley
Argyle & Margaret Haley
C.J. Haley
Donnie Harper
Ken Hein
Paul Hunt
Ann Keller
Jody Korman
Neal Lappe & WSI
Elaine Mallory
Ruth Marks
Jeff & Bernie Marsh
W. Blair Massey

Russ McDowell
Mary McLean
Bill & Ruth Metcalf
Joyce Minor
Dwayne & Janice Murphey
Bradley & Jane Nott
Steve O'Brien
Catherine Painter
Rajiv Perera
P.K. Perrin
Jim Pollard
Fred Powell
Gordon & Vera Prior
Donald Quinby
Robert Rideout
Fran Sadler
Maxey & Fran Slater
James & Eleanor Smith, Jr.
Hon. Neal Steverson
Paul Stock
Frank & Sally Stone
Cynthia Sullivan
Tuesday Morning Prayer Group
Rev. Robert Thompson & First
   Baptist Ch.
William Thomasson
Joe Vasko
Robert & Jane Wait
Wayne Watkins
Wednesday Morning Bible Study
Don Welch
A.D. & Jean Whittaker

STOPS

Cali

    San Diego County Jail (Snake Pitts)
    San Mateo County Jail
    San Jose County Jail
    Marin County Jail
    San Francisco County Jail
    San Quentin
    Salinas Valley (Soledad)
    California Medical Facility (Vacaville)
    Orange County Jail (Glass House)

Colorado

    Adams County Jail
    Arapahoe County Jail
    Boulder County Jail

New York (The City)

    Manhattan Detention District South (Tombs)
    Riker's Island Correctional Center

Massachusetts

    Charles Street Jail
    New Bedford House of Correction

Florida

    Dade County Jail,
    Broward County Jail

Virginia

    Henrico County Jail,
    Norfolk City Jail

Illinois

    Cook County Jail

Louisiana

    Parrish Prison, Orleans

Connecticut

    Danbury Federal
    Correctional Institute

West Virginia

    Morgantown Federal Correctional Institute

All songs credits go to the original authors of these tracks. The word "by" merely insinuates that the version song mentioned was heard by Jeff Andrews when performed by the listed artists. All dates are approximate.

1966 *Devil With A Blue Dress On* by Mitch Ryder and The Detroit Wheels
1966 *Good Lovin'* by The Rascals
1968 *Born to be Wild* by Steppenwolf
1970 *All Right Now* by Free
1970 *Layla* by Derek and the Dominoes
1970 *Traveling Band* by Credence Clearwater Revival
1970 *Venus* by Shocking Blue
1971 *Midnight Rider* by The Allman Brothers' Band
1973 *My Maria* by B. W. Stevenson
1974 *We're an American Band* by Grand Funk Railroad
1975 *Get Down Tonight* by KC and the Sunshine Band
1975 *Lady Marmalade* by Patty Labelle
1976 *Carry On Wayward Son* by Kansas
1976 *Hotel California* by The Eagles
1976 *More Than a Feeling* by Boston
1977 *Staying Alive* by The Bee Gees
1978 *Straight On* by Heart
1978 *Hot Blooded* by Foreigner
1978 *Last Dance* by Donna Summer
1978 *Lonesome Loser* by The Little River Band
1978 *Everyone's a Winner* by Hot Chocolate
1978 *Love Will Find A Way* by Pablo Cruise
1978 *Running with the Devil* by Van Halen
1978 *Hold the Line* by Toto
1978 *Shame* by Evelyn Champagne King
1979 *Jane* by Jefferson Starship
1980 *Hit Me With Your Best Shot* by Pat Benatar
1980 *Flirting With Disaster* by Molly Hatchet
1980 *Hold on Loosely* by .38 Special
1980 *Pour Some Sugar on Me* by Def Leopard
1980 *Any Way You Want It* by Journey
1980 *Highway to Hell & Hell's Bells* by AC/DC
1981 *Ride Like the Wind* by Christopher Cross
1982 *Sexual Healing* by Marvin Gaye
1982 *Hurt so Good* by John Cougar Mellencamp
1982 *Eye of the Tiger* by Survivor
1982 *Beat It* by Michael Jackson
1983 *Sharp Dressed Man* by ZZ Top
1983 *Jump* by The Pointer Sisters
1984 *Rock You Like a Hurricane* by Scorpions
1985 *Summer of '69* by Bryan Adams
1985 *Caribbean Queen* by Billy Ocean
1986 *Higher Love* by Steve Winwood

1986 *Wanted, Dead or Alive* by Bon Jovi
1987 *I'm No Angel* by Gregg Allman
1987 *Paradise City* by Guns N' Roses
1987 *Here I Go Again* by White Snake
1988 *Devil Inside* by INXS
1989 *Forget Her Name* by Black Velvet
1989 *I Can't Explain* by Scorpions
1991 *Steel Bars* by Michael Bolton

AUTHOR BIO:

JESSE STRETCH, the author of Desperate Highway, is a writer from Richmond, Virginia. He is an avid seeker of new and exciting fiction and non-fiction projects. He is currently working on a novel and has partnered with the President of Virginia Blood Services to write a non-fiction book, the title of which is still in the works. He looks forward to continuing a diversified career that will span all genres of writing. For more information about his works, or to contact Jesse Stretch, visit one of these websites:
www.JesseStretch.com
www.DesperateHighway.com

CONTACT:

Wayne Watkins
Executive Director
Desperate Highway Ministries, Inc.
P.O. Box 861
Dillwyn, Virginia 23936
www.DesperateHighwayMinistries.org